for Susie
with lots of love from ~~~~ xxx
my first trip to Africa

Kate Eshe   Gloucester Nov 2014

From the Cam
to the Zambezi

From the Cam to the Zambezi

Colonial Service and the Path to the New Zambia

Edited by Tony Schur
With a Foreword by Baroness Chalker of Wallasey

THE RADCLIFFE PRESS
LONDON • NEW YORK

An imprint of I.B.Tauris

Published in 2015 by The Radcliffe Press
An imprint of I.B.Tauris & Co Ltd
6 Salem Road, London W2 4BU
175 Fifth Avenue, New York NY 10010
www.ibtauris.com

Distributed in the United States and Canada
Exclusively by Palgrave Macmillan
175 Fifth Avenue, New York NY 10010

ISBN: 978 1 78453 004 4
eISBN: 978 0 85773 728 1

A full CIP record for this book is available from the British Library
A full CIP record is available from the Library of Congress

Library of Congress Catalog Card Number: available

Printed and bound by CPI Group (UK) Ltd, Croydon, CR0 4YY

MIX
Paper from
responsible sources
FSC
www.fsc.org   FSC® C013604

CONTENTS

CONTENTS

CONTENTS

LIST OF ILLUSTRATIONS

The photographs in this book have been supplied by the following contributors:

Mick Bond   4b, 11b, 13b, 14a, 14b, 15a;

Max Keyzar   2b, 3a, 4a, 5b, 6a, 6b, 7a, 7b, 8b, 9a, 9b, 10a, 12b, 13a, 15b, 16a, 16b;

Tony Schur   2a, 3b, 5a, 8a, 10b, 11a, 12a.

The photograph of the members of the Cambridge Course is reproduced by kind permission of Lafayette Photography.

GLOSSARY

African   The term used in this book to refer to the indigenous people of Northern Rhodesia/Zambia. It was in common usage at the time the events described took place. See also 'European', below.

Boma   The building housing the headquarters of a district. Also used to refer to the township in which the headquarters was situated.

Cadet   See 'District Officer', below.

Chief Secretary   The most senior member of the colonial administration after the Governor (below).

CiBemba   The language of the Bemba people. The 'ci' prefix, or a variation of it, is used in many Bantu languages. For example, ci-Ila is the language spoken by the Ila tribe.

Dambo   An area of grassland through which one or more small streams flow and which floods during the rainy season. A dambo will typically be surrounded by woodland.

District Assistant (DA)   A rank below District Officer (below). Many districts had District Assistants as well as DOs. A DA could be selected to attend the Cambridge Course and then be promoted to DO. Some DAs were recruited as school leavers, when they were known initially as Learner District Assistants (LDAs).

District Commissioner (DC)   See 'District Officer', below.

District Messenger (DM)   District Messengers were recruited in each district from the local population to assist the District Commissioner. Provided with distinctive blue uniforms, they had the same powers as police constables and performed a wide range of duties. Many had previous military experience.

District Officer (DO)   A senior administrative officer in the Provincial Administration (below), usually a graduate and having attended the Cambridge Overseas Civil Service Course. Named a District Commissioner when in charge of a district, and called a Cadet when first appointed and on probation. Each district would normally have one or more DOs in addition to the DC.

European   In accordance with the practice at the time, white people are described as 'European' irrespective of whether they regarded their home country as being in Africa or in Europe.

Federation   The Federation of Rhodesia and Nyasaland (also known as the Central African Federation) was in existence from 1953 to 1963. The three countries involved are now called Zambia, Zimbabwe and Malawi. More information about the Federation is included in Appendix 2.

Governor   The senior representative in Northern Rhodesia of the British Government during the period of colonial rule, with overall responsibility for the administration of the country.

Governor-General   The British Government's senior representative in the Federation (above).

Indirect Rule   Instead of imposing its will directly, as other European nations did, Britain governed its African territories by working through indigenous institutions such as the Chiefs and their councils. See also 'Native Authorities', below.

Kapasu   Similar to District Messengers (above), but with a smaller range of powers, *Kapasus* were employed by Native Authorities (below) and wore khaki uniforms.

Learner District Assistant (LDA)   See 'District Assistant', above.

Native Authority   Initially the Native Authorities comprised the Chiefs and their councils. Later, younger, more educated people were brought in as councillors, with some being given full-time responsibilities for such matters as the authority's schools and roads. Eventually the Native Authorities became elected local government authorities.

Native Court   Native Courts, which took their authority from the Chief, dispensed both civil and criminal justice according to tribal custom, provided that this did not contravene Government regulations or go against the principles of natural justice.

Provincial Administration (PA)   The organisation which during the colonial era was responsible for the overall administration of the provinces and districts into which Northern Rhodesia was divided. In charge of each of the seven provinces was a Provincial Commissioner answerable to the Minister of Native Affairs in Lusaka. Each province was sub-divided into a number of districts, each of which was under the control of a District Commissioner.

Provincial Commissioner (PC)   See 'Provincial Administration', above.

Tour   Used both in the sense of a tour of duty, which lasted two or three years, after which an expatriate officer would be entitled to several weeks' home leave, and in the sense of going on tour, which typically involved spending two or more weeks visiting local communities and sleeping under canvas.

ACKNOWLEDGEMENTS

My thanks must go first of all to each one of the contributors to this book, not only for the time and effort they have devoted to preparing their chapters, but also for responding so patiently to the editors' suggestions and queries. A particular debt of gratitude is due to Wendy Bond and John Theakstone, who have provided much good advice and encouragement as well as valued help with the editing process. I should also like to thank Lester Crook and Joanna Godfrey of The Radcliffe Press for the skilful, informed and sensitive way in which they brought our book to publication.

I am very grateful to Kapumpe-Valentine Musakanya, who owns the copyright to the writings of his late father, Valentine Musakanya, for permission to include extracts from the writings in this book, and to Dr Miles Larmer, Fellow of St Antony's College, Oxford, for providing me with access to the papers and allowing me to make use of material in his book *The Musakanya Papers*, which provides more information about a remarkable man.

A debt of gratitude is also due to Tony Goddard, who has allowed me to draw on his book *My African Stories* for his chapter, and to John Hudson, a former District Commissioner in Northern Rhodesia, for permission to quote from his book *A Time to Mourn*. The extract from a paper David Alexander presented to a conference in 1982 is included with the kind permission of SCUTREA (The Standing Conference on University Teaching and Research in the Education of Adults) and with their appreciation and thanks to David for his work.

The map, showing the location of the different places mentioned in the chapters which follow, was prepared by Ruth and Mick Bond. My thanks are due to them for their skill in producing such a helpful addition to the book.

Finally I am especially grateful to Baroness Chalker of Wallasey for writing the Foreword, as she has a great knowledge of Africa from her time as Minister for Overseas Development and through her current role as Chairman of Africa Matters Limited.

FOREWORD

I am delighted to write this short Foreword, having had great fun reading the contributors' memories, some of which even predate my active involvement in Zambia!

Whilst my memories are much more recent, from 1980 onwards, I am glad to say that Tusker beer is still available in east Africa now in 2014. I still hear 'Twingi' ('many little things' in ciBemba), which Neil Morris refers to, mentioned outside Lusaka.

The most memorable of my many visits to Zambia in the last thirty-four years was in 1990, when a number of Ministers of International Development from European countries had gathered with those of the Commonwealth African countries to discuss future European Union support for the many needs of the growing populations on the continent. The unforgettable evening at that conference was when F. W. de Klerk announced that Nelson Mandela would be freed from prison and the ANC unbanned. I shall never forget the joy and the celebration through most of the night that followed, and the joy of meeting Madiba for the first time in Johannesburg some months later. Lusaka has always been a favourite African city as a result.

But the contributors have memories of wonderful places that I have only heard of, but never visited during my Zambia time. The tales of running elections, preparing a meal for Kenneth Kaunda before he was elected President, the illuminating extracts from Valentine Musakanya's writings and all the detail of individual experiences have made me get a more detailed map of Zambia, so that on second reading I can trace all the places where these experiences took place. Then I shall take a copy to read to the past President on my next visit to him when I am in Lusaka.

There are so many memorable stories. Perhaps as a statistician, one that sticks in my memory for amusement is about the vehicle statistics in Mongu, where the 'vehicles' were horses, and Government auditors wished to establish from the District Secretary why their check revealed the district to be 'deficient in one vehicle', and why it had been disposed of without the authority of a 'Board of Survey'? (The oldest horse had died.) The District Secretary's response was classic: 'How would the Board account for an unauthorised increase in the transport fleet?' – the imminent birth of a foal.

But it is not for me to repeat more of these fascinating memories – each of you must read this stimulating collection of memories for yourselves. We owe a big thank you to all the contributors.

Baroness Chalker of Wallasey

INTRODUCTION

In October 1961 a group of young men assembled in Cambridge. We were about to join the 1961/2 Overseas Services Course before going on to work in the Provincial Administration of the Northern Rhodesia Government. Two of the twenty-two who came together at that time were African graduates from Northern Rhodesia, twelve were graduates newly recruited in the UK and eight were non-graduates who had been recruited under a different scheme and had already worked in Northern Rhodesia for a few years. When the course ended each of us was posted to a different district in the territory, mostly in rural areas. The opportunities for meeting other members of the course during our service in Africa were few, but each of us has remained in regular contact with at least two or three of the others ever since we first met over fifty years ago. Two reunion dinners have been held to mark the twenty-fifth and fiftieth anniversaries of our meeting one another for the first time. It was following the second of these dinners that the idea of producing a book of our experiences in Northern Rhodesia was proposed.

The chapters have been contributed by fifteen of the original course members and three wives. They cover the last few years of colonial rule in Northern Rhodesia and, in some cases, the early years of the new nation of Zambia after it gained its independence in 1964. Some of the stories are light-hearted anecdotes; some are more straightforward descriptions of the kinds of life British overseas civil servants and their wives led during those years; and some contain firsthand accounts of important historic events. One is made up of extracts from the writings of Valentine Musakanya, who died in 1994. Having held a number of senior posts in Zambia in the years after Independence, he was arrested in 1980 and sentenced to death, before being acquitted on the grounds that the only evidence against him was a confession which had been obtained by torture. Each of the stories is written in the author's own words.

The world in which these events took place was very different from the one we now live in. It was a time of tension in the Cold War between the Western powers led by the USA and members of the Eastern Bloc under the leadership of the Soviet Union. In October 1962, for example, just as we were settling into our new postings in Northern Rhodesia, there were real anxieties about what might happen as the two leading powers confronted each other over the siting of Soviet nuclear missiles in Cuba. And in the UK the death penalty was still in force for murder; abortion was illegal; and it was a criminal offence for men to engage in homosexual activity, even in private.

It was also a time when racial discrimination was more widespread than it is now. In the UK the first Race Relations Act, which did no more than outlaw discrimination in public places, did not come into force until 1965, and Valentine Musakanya describes his experience of discrimination when looking for somewhere to live in Cambridge in 1961. There was discrimination in Northern Rhodesia, too, particularly in the urban areas of the Copperbelt, where the influence of apartheid-era South Africa was strong. It was not until 1960 that such practices as the exclusion of Africans from European restaurants, hotels and cinemas were banned by law. It may seem strange, looking back, but the descriptions 'Native Authorities' and 'Native Courts' continued to be used until the last few months before Independence. These terms were not intended to be derogatory, but had been in use since the early days of British involvement in Africa to describe the institutions through which Chiefs and their advisers managed the affairs of their peoples. It was through these authorities that the British-governed Northern Rhodesia and other African territories under a system known as Indirect Rule. Later, as they evolved, these bodies became known as local authorities and courts.

There are also references in three of the stories to hunting elephants. Today, knowing that the very survival of African elephants is under threat from ivory poachers, it is difficult to understand how anyone could choose to shoot one. But in the early 1960s there were large numbers of elephants in Northern Rhodesia. They frequently caused problems for the inhabitants of rural areas by destroying the crops on which they depended for their food, and so individual elephants were shot to encourage the herds to keep away from villages. In addition, a restricted number of licences were also available for trophy hunters to buy. It is perhaps also worth remembering that attitudes towards wild animals were generally different during those years. David Attenborough, for instance, was still collecting animals for London Zoo in the BBC series *Zoo Quest*.

A glossary of some of the terms used most commonly in the text is included before this Introduction. Additional information about Zambia, about the period of colonial rule and events after Independence, and about the Cambridge Course can be found in the appendices. Biographical notes on the different authors are provided at the end of the book.

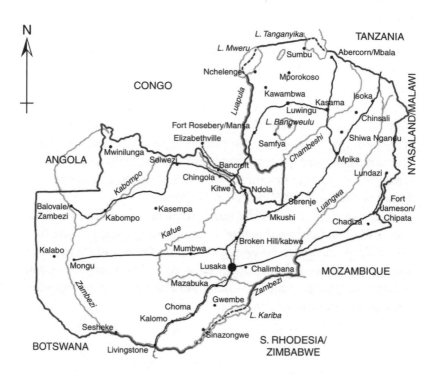

Northern Rhodesia/Zambia around 1964

1

MWINILUNGA

David Taylor

'Looking at Africa.'

The three Central African countries were joined in a Federation. It was thought that the countries complemented one another – Southern Rhodesia with its agriculture, Northern Rhodesia with its minerals and Nyasaland with its abundant labour looking for a job. It should perhaps have worked but it never really did. Maybe it was done too late or maybe it was badly managed, or maybe the stresses and the differences were more powerful than the neatness of the idea.

Whatever the verdict, it is a simple fact that we had a Governor-General as the Queen's top representative. The Lord Dalhousie's ancestor had held the identical post in India, almost exactly a hundred years before, and is the one widely charged with blame for the Indian Mutiny. He wasn't there when it happened, but then, to be absent when the balloon goes up is the secret of dynastic as well as political greatness. Dalhousie worked his socks off, so it is said, in the office and had not the faintest idea what was brewing in the backstreets of Delhi, never mind in the faraway cantonments of his enormous fiefdom. By the time that murder and mayhem engulfed the subcontinent, and was visited with barbarous revenge, His Lordship was comfortably back home.

The rhythms of history ensured, with rhyming injustice, that it was left to Canning to carry the can.[1]

It may have been to demonstrate that the family lesson had been well and truly learned that our Governor-General declared that he intended to see for himself the remotest corners of his Federation. You couldn't get further into one of the corners than our patch, and thus it was that the Lord appeared to us from out of a Land Rover and in time for a late lunch.

Made flesh by a generous hand, Dalhousie was moist and out of sorts after the long and dusty journey. The Countess glowed with discomfort and the ADC, who had crouched amid a couple of hundredweights of toppling baggage, was bruised, unloved and plain wet. The poor young man was doing his utmost to please and a little encouragement would have gone a long way. He was stabbed to the heart, and all of ours came out in sympathy, when His Lordship confided to Robin in an aside which rent the air like a bugle at dawn: 'Really! One learns not to expect too much in the way of brains, but this one is incredible.'

Later, much refreshed and according to the agreed diary of events, Her Ladyship was taken to try and catch a fish. 'Jacko' was to be her boatman, and her gillie, and had been drafted by Robin. Jacko was the public works buildings foreman and we never knew his other name. Mr Jackson had always been Jacko and that was that. His plan was to enchant the Countess by treating her with a throwaway and earthy familiarity. Robin's nerves were on edge because there were signs that Jacko had fortified himself for his assignment and his earthiness was all too easily stimulated. She called him Jack, which was as far as condescension could be taken. It was inspired; it threw Jacko completely and, in the nick of time, deflected his bonhomie on to an altogether more compliant, less dangerous target. By simple elimination, the ADC who went along to run a soldier's eye over the boat and to squander his miserable life if necessary, had to be 'Jack'. 'You all right, Jack?' our boatman kept asking, and then doubled up because the ADC looked blank and had clearly not latched on to the subtlety of it all. The boat was Jacko's own, was his pride and joy and had been polished and painted for a week. It passed muster, started up 'first pop', and they were off.

When they came back, all three were ecstatic. She was able to point at the bottom of the boat and three very handsome tiger fish which had given her, as tiger fish did, a good run for her money. She was deliciously fatigued, but Jacko's adrenalin was on the run because he had leaned across to support the angler's forearm and, without the ADC noticing, so he swore, she had stiffened girlishly at his touch. The ADC, and it was good to see, was beaming; something of which he had been a part had gone so right for a change. And then Dalhousie had to spoil it all by pointing in a common fashion at his wife's bottom, which had picked up a smudge of paint. The ADC got the blame and the military shoulders sagged all over again.

We, Robin's three juniors, had walk-on parts and we were not called upon again until the sun was down. Neither Robin nor his poised, diminutive and beautiful wife Veronica was cut out for this; nor were they looking forward to it, but by about seven we were at their house in evening dress for a dinner over which Veronica had taken immense trouble. Jacko had not been invited, which was cruel but understandable on several grounds. As it had turned out, his part had been admirably played, his ambitions dangerously excited and, if he possessed an evening suit at all, his shirt would probably have been pink and frothy. After desultory polite conversation, we moved into a dining-room, which, in a DC's house built in a remote bush station, was never designed for entertainment of the vice-regal. The meal was excellent and, thanks to Robin and Veronica's grace and good wine, passed off reasonably well. Then the ladies, all two of them, delicately 'withdrew' and the brute males tore back gratefully, like swine, down the cliff of farce.

Thrusting the port enthusiastically to his left, His Excellency opened fire with one of the feeblest and oldest dirty jokes that any of us had not actually forgotten. The ADC laughed away with a will and Robin's grimace was covered by the fact that his teeth were clamped onto his pipe, which was beginning to draw like a furnace. Vaughan, a New Zealander, who was sitting next to me, was moved to shift things up a gear with the opening gambit of a joke of real and abiding quality which he had, almost certainly, picked up in the All Blacks changing-room and which I had heard before. I kicked him under the table because I doubted that the Dalhousie heart was in good enough nick. The joke petered out leaving everybody, even the obliging staff, waiting for the punch-line and looking sideways to see if anybody else had got it. And then, at last, music to our ears, our Governor-General sank his port at a gulp and said 'Shall we go and look at Africa?'

This delicate euphemism concealed the intention not to waste precious water on flushing the lav. And so we hearty lads, easing our shirt collars in the heat, trooped outside and walked off across Robin's lawn into the refreshing obscurity which the tilley lamps of the house could not reach.

Africa was worth looking at from that garden. A wide sky of brilliant stars down to a low and dim horizon, with scarcely a light, a sound or sign of rude humanity below it, and the dark curve of the river making its way peacefully to the bridge and the faintest streaks of white water. And so we stood on the edge where the ground began to drop away and we stood in the strictest order of seniority. On the left of the line the portly Lord, dangerously shadowed by an edgy young soldier festooned about the shoulder in gilt aiguillettes and entrapped in tight cavalry trousers and spurs; Robin, infantryman that he had been, placidly sucking on his pipe and hands on hips; Vaughan, who, for all the difference that it would have made to him, could have been stark naked; and then, where we belonged, Jim and me, both so tense with the onset of sneezing laughter that we nearly missed our chances altogether.

But, in the end, the visit was all well worth it. Neither the province nor the territory exploded in violence as they might otherwise have done.

Note

1 Charles Canning succeeded Dalhousie in 1855 as Governor-General and as first Viceroy of India, and had to deal with the Indian Rebellion in 1857 and its aftermath. His father, George Canning, had been Foreign Secretary and, briefly, Prime Minister.

2

ABERCORN, KASAMA, MPOROKOSO, ISOKA, LIVINGSTONE, GWEMBE, KABOMPO

D'Arcy Payne

'A project I had to develop from scratch.'

On my eighteenth birthday in May 1957 I sailed from Southampton en route to Northern Rhodesia via Cape Town. I was employed by the Northern Rhodesia Government (NRG) as a Learner District Assistant in the Provincial Administration. This position was 'the lowest of the low', and I was at this time the most junior and lowest-paid member of the Administration, at the princely annual salary of £480, from which NRG made deductions at source for house rent, pension contributions and anything else that was remotely justifiable. Up to then I had been working for the family business and not enjoying it. As my father, grandfather and great-grandfather had all spent time in the service of the crown in various parts of the British Empire, I jumped at the idea of getting out of Great Britain – a naive romantic, I suppose, but then, Britain in the 1950s didn't seem to have a lot to offer. I was, in a word, green.

I was very fortunate in my first posting, which was to Abercorn (now Mbala) in the Northern Province. Abercorn lies at around 5,400 feet above sea level, and therefore, although in the tropics, enjoys a climate that is very agreeable to northern Europeans. There was also at that time a fairly sizeable expatriate community (around a hundred, including wives and children) comprising members of the Provincial Administration and other Government departments, staff at the headquarters of the International Red Locust Control Service and Roman Catholic (White Fathers) and Protestant (London Missionary Society) missionaries, together with a few very colourful characters who had settled in the district as farmers or traders.

Although the Northern Province was populated predominantly by the Bemba people, Abercorn District was occupied by two tribes, the Lungu and the Mambwe. The latter only occupied the high plateau country, but the Lungu also lived on the shores of Lake Tanganyika, some 30 miles north of, and 3,000 feet lower than, Abercorn. Both these tribes had their own language, although ciBemba was widely understood, except on the lakeshore, where Swahili was the predominant language. This presented something of a problem as I was expected to learn ciBemba. The solution was to send me out into the bush entrusted to the care of a District Messenger who spoke no English (he did actually, but had been instructed not to by the DC).

And so the early months of my service were spent miles from anywhere with no European company, only a copy of Longland's *Field Engineering* to guide me on road construction and bridge building and a gang of labourers who were good company when enjoying the local *pombe* (beer), but thanks to my lack of knowledge of their language and their total lack of English not really able to provide much of an intellectual stimulus. As I gained more experience I accompanied the senior District Officer on tour, learning to collect taxes, to listen to the concerns of the local population and to introduce and monitor the progress of development initiatives. Whenever we arrived in a village the entire female population would greet us, as they would a Chief, ululating loudly, which they were able to keep up for a considerable time. A bicycle was an essential part of the job, and the Government in its generosity paid us 10 shillings a month bicycle allowance, although the allowance rarely covered the cost of replacement, as the cycles had a hard life.

I also learned that we were expected to be able to act as doctors, or at least as nurses, dealing with local health complaints. In most of the rural areas there were no roads and no 'Western' medical facilities. If someone was ill or hurt in an accident, they had to walk, cycle or be carried considerable distances to the nearest town or mission where there was a dispensary – or wait for the District Officer to visit. Thus we carried with us a range of wound dressings, lotions and pills and used the knowledge we had gained in the Boy Scouts to guide us in dispensing them.

The other half of my somewhat schizophrenic existence was spent amongst the expatriate community. The Europeans enjoyed the facilities of the Abercorn Club which had a nine-hole golf-course (with sand greens) and tennis-courts. They also put on various entertainments in the form of dances and amateur dramatics and found any excuse for a party. It was here that I learned to play golf, or at least the local version where ball boys could be hired for a tickey (a silver three-pence coin) a round, and everyone carried two extra items in their golf bag: a sand scraper to smooth a path for one's putt on the 'green' and a stick to break the back of any gaboon vipers found sunning themselves on the greens or in the bunkers. I was never much good at golf – my handicap stayed resolutely at twenty-four – but I did manage to carry away the cup as the winner of the longest-drive competition. This event was staged at sun-up on New Year's Day, when you could use a driver only if judged to be 'well over the eight', otherwise you had to use a putter.

As the most junior officer in the boma, I got some interesting jobs. At Christmas I had to write and produce the children's nativity play which, surprisingly to me, was a great success. Another was to unload the steamer which visited the port of Mpulungu on Lake Tanganyika every three weeks bringing vital supplies such as cement and which towed a barge of petrol and diesel in 44-gallon drums. (It was a much more reliable route than the road from the Copperbelt, which was often impassable during the rainy season.) This job was seen as a real chore; it was hot work, the temperature at 2,400 feet in that part of the world, even in the cold season, is very high and air-conditioning was unknown (not that we had electricity to power it, anyway). I enjoyed it, though, as one of the privileges of being 'harbour master' was free food on board the steamer (SS *Liemba*, operated by East African Railways and Harbours) and during my time they had a superb Goan cook on board. It also provided an opportunity to drink the East African beer 'Tusker', which many of us regarded as being vastly superior to 'Castle' or 'Lion', and to meet new people in the shape of the ship's officers or the occasional passenger who was touring the lake.

It was during one of these 'stints' that I received a message from the District Commissioner asking me to get hold of some yellow-bellied bream (*Serranochromis robustus*) from the lake and drop them off on my way back to Abercorn at the farm run by the Gamwell sisters. Marion and Hope Gamwell had arrived in Abercorn in 1928. They had driven south from Dar es Salaam intending to travel on to Southern Rhodesia (now Zimbabwe) to buy a farm and grow coffee. Instead, they were so taken with the area, that they bought land from the British South Africa Company and began farming it. At first they had tried coffee, but this was not a commercial success, so they then grew Nindi (*Aelocanthus graneolens*), whose oil is used in perfume-making and is thus a very valuable cash crop. The elder sister, Marion, had been unwell, and had asked the DC if someone could obtain some yellow-bellied bream, which, certainly to European palates, was by far the most succulent of all the many species of fish to be found in Lake Tanganyika. I duly delivered the fish and was treated to one of the best traditional English teas I have ever had, with savoury muffins, cucumber sandwiches and a fantastic chocolate cake thousands of miles from England in the middle of nowhere.

The sisters were very well connected and District Commissioners at Abercorn stood in awe of them. The Governor of Northern Rhodesia at that time was Sir Arthur Benson, who was reputed to be either their godson or nephew. Amongst other things the Gamwells were the moving spirit behind the

Tanganyika Victoria Memorial Institute, which, with a small museum, library and other facilities, was a type of cultural centre markedly different from the Abercorn Club. One of its activities was to show films. The films came via South Africa and were subject to South African Government censorship. This was the era of apartheid, so the censorship was somewhat puritanical in nature, reflecting the thinking of the Dutch Reformed Church. On one occasion someone who had recently returned from overseas leave complained bitterly that the film they had just seen had been completely ruined by the censor as they had seen the original version in the West End. This prompted Marion to declare that she would 'have a word with Arthur' and that would solve the problem. The expatriate community was much bemused by this, wondering how the Governor was going to fix the South African censor. The next film that was shown was just as the British Board of Film Censors had passed it. Marion had sent a message to her old friend J. Arthur Rank, and in future all our films came direct from the UK via East Africa.

This most enjoyable introduction to life in the Provincial Administration was unfortunately not to last. After about a year I was transferred to Kasama, the headquarters of Northern Province, where I was assigned to work in the Provincial Commissioner's office. This was a most instructive experience, as one got a 'helicopter' view of the work of the Provincial Administration. One of my jobs, as the most junior official, was to act as cipher clerk. The longest coded message we received was one from the Governor's office in Lusaka encrypted in the cipher that was only used for 'top secret' classification. I spent about four hours deciphering it and was disappointed to discover that it listed the drinks to be provided for the Governor's next visit to the province. Also located in Kasama at this time was the office of the Development Commissioner for the Northern Province, whose purpose was to stimulate economic growth. The Deputy Development Commissioner was Derek Goodfellow, a long-serving officer in the Provincial Administration, who on first acquaintance appeared to be a very gruff and somewhat intimidating figure. On my first encounter with him he drove me in a Land Rover at considerable speed, with frequent demonstrations of his unique skill in steering with his knees as he lit his pipe with a box of matches and his one (right) arm – not to mention changing gear with his arm through the steering wheel. Needless to say, I was absolutely terrified both of him and his driving. I was later to learn that beneath the forbidding exterior was a very competent, kind and perceptive man. After the heady heights of the PC's office my next posting was to Mporokoso – a district largely infested with tsetse fly and with a relatively small indigenous population and a handful of expatriates.

Returning from leave in 1959, I was promoted to District Assistant and posted to Isoka, again in the Northern Province, where I spent most of my time out on tour. During this period the new Governor, Sir Evelyn Hone, visited the district to talk to the Chiefs about the forthcoming Monckton Commission, which had just been established to consider the future of the Central African Federation. For this meeting the Governor wore his full dress uniform including his plumed hat. The Monckton Commission duly arrived a few weeks later, unaware of the drama immediately preceding their visit, when the ceiling in the District Commissioner's dining-room had completely collapsed under the weight of a termite (white ant) nest.

After about eighteen months I received a letter from the Provincial Commissioner telling me that I was to be seconded on a temporary basis to the Department of Rural (later Community) Development. The Government was concerned about high levels of unemployment amongst school leavers, and was proposing to run Community Service Camps for all school leavers, but it first needed to train leaders for these camps. The idea was to train such leaders on Outward Bound-type courses. To my great delight a site in Abercorn was selected for the experiment on the grounds that the district was remote and endowed with hills and access to Lake Tanganyika, both of which could be used for the necessary activities. Participants in the pilot courses came from all over the country. Results were encouraging and the trial was judged to be a success. This very satisfying interlude was followed by another short spell in Kasama, where I helped the Provincial Operations team during a period of political unrest, prior to travelling to the UK for the Cambridge Course.

In Cambridge I was fortunate in being able to spend two terms living in St Catherine's College, rather than in lodgings. This provided me with a wider experience of university life than was normally available to members of the Overseas Services Course. No longer needing to learn basic ciBemba, I was able to spend more time studying anthropology, which I enjoyed and was later to prove most useful. At the suggestion of John Keigwin, the Northern Rhodesia Commissioner for Community Development, I spent my spare time during the vacations volunteering as an Outward Bound instructor.

Returning from the course, and now a District Officer, I found myself working for a few months in the Provincial Commissioner's office in Livingstone, where I had to organise a visit to the province by Lord Dalhousie, the Governor-General of the Federation. This was followed by a posting to Gwembe, also in Southern Province, where I had responsibility for the central part of the district.

In the middle of 1963 I was transferred, at the instigation of John Keigwin, to Kabompo in North Western Province to take charge of the Development Area Training Centre (DATC) there, and to become Acting Provincial Community Development Officer. The previous officer in charge of the DATC, Bill Jackett, who had been running the centre with his wife, Vi, had already departed on leave, with the result that I had to assume responsibility without the benefit of a face-to-face handover. The task of the DATC was to pass skills on to both men and women by running courses at the centre and through extension work out in the villages. For men the training was mainly in simple construction techniques to equip them for building schools and dispensaries in rural areas. Courses for women covered child care, basic hygiene and clothes-making. We also worked with the Agriculture Department on a scheme for small-scale farmers and on some veterinary initiatives. The women's courses were led by Grace Matoka, whose husband, Peter, became a member of President Kaunda's first cabinet and, later, Zambia's High Commissioner to the UK.

Frequent changes seemed to have become an established part of my career in Northern Rhodesia, and after nine months in Kabompo I moved back to Abercorn District to set up a national base for Outward Bound courses. Following the earlier successes of the Community Venture courses, both the Government and the mining companies were keen to provide opportunities for young people, who would soon find themselves in positions of authority in the new Zambia, to increase their self-confidence and to experience challenging situations in the company of others from different tribal and ethnic backgrounds. This was a project which I had to develop from scratch, with a target of running the first course three months later, and which involved raising finance, buying and converting a hotel and recruiting staff and students. In the middle of this I was seconded to Lusaka to help with the management of the national ceremony to mark the granting of independence in October 1964. The DC, who was in charge of the arrangements, was Jack Fairhurst, whom I knew from the Northern Province and from Cambridge, where he had been attending the senior 'B' Course. Among other duties I was made responsible for organising the tribal dancers, an interesting task because the various groups came from different parts of the country and spoke ten different languages. Whilst the main celebrations were taking place in Lusaka, members of the staff of the Outward Bound Lake School in Abercorn climbed Mount Sunzu, at 6,782 feet the highest point in Zambia, and placed the new Zambian flag on its summit.

The courses duly started with the agreement of the Outward Bound organisation in the UK, and with a Chief Instructor recruited from the UK. The other instructors came from a variety of backgrounds, including the police, the mining companies, other commercial concerns, Government departments and British school leavers under the auspices of Voluntary Service Overseas. On the standard courses participants came from mining and other companies, from the Zambian Police, Army and Air Force and from various Government ministries. The junior courses were filled by students who came from schools in different parts of the country. One of the benefits of the courses was that Africans and Europeans had to mix and work together, as did people from different tribes. President Kaunda, who was our patron, visited the school on a number of occasions. Once the scheme was up and running my job included marketing the courses, raising money for equipment and ensuring a steady supply of students.

I had enjoyed the challenge of setting up the project, but did not want to make a career out of this type of work. And so after ten years I resigned in September 1967 to start a new life in the UK. Those years in Zambia were immensely rewarding and I still have many fond memories of my time there.

3

LUWINGU, SAMFYA, BROKEN HILL

Neil Morris

*'I shook the Chief's hand, dispensed with the need to dip his
finger in the dye, then took him to collect his ballot-paper before
directing him to the booth. Then we waited ...'*

At the end of the Cambridge Course there were exams and an
order of merit was established. I don't recall that more than
three or four were interested in such competitive gestures; certainly, there had never been any suggestion that we wouldn't all
pass out successfully. When our postings were read out, mine,
to Luwingu in Northern Province, drew concerned whistles
from the two or three old Northern Rhodesia hands present.
'I wouldn't take a young family up there; remember what happened in 1959.' They then regaled us all with the story of a visit
to Chilubi Island in the middle of Lake Bangweulu in March
1959, when a group attending a political meeting took exception to the presence of the then District Commissioner and
surrounded his party. Efforts to calm the crowd had no effect
and at one point someone threw a spear which hit the District
Assistant in the shoulder, causing a large wound with much
blood. There was an armed confrontation, shots were fired, four
locals were killed and some twenty injured. The official party
then had to retreat back to their boat and put out into the lake.

Luwingu, then, was my posting with a wife and a nine-month-old daughter.

After the usual few days of home leave, we embarked with others going to Central Africa on a Union Castle mail ship to Cape Town in early July. We enjoyed fourteen days of very civilised cruising, then disembarked on Thursday afternoon, 19 July 1962, at Cape Town and transferred directly to the railway station for the 66-hour, 1,600-mile train journey to Northern Rhodesia.

At Lusaka, the capital, the group finally broke up as we dispersed to take up our postings. A Land Rover had been sent down from Luwingu to collect me and my family; before it came we had several nights in the capital. During this time we were invited to cocktails at Government House, where HE Sir Evelyn Hone, the Governor, and senior officials did their best to assure us that all was well in the territory, that there was no serious unrest anywhere and that we had, if not a full career, at least ten good years ahead of us before self-governing status or independence would occur.

At Luwingu the house allocated to us was, like all the others, a bungalow; it had been built many years before and was due for replacement by a smaller, modern house. Ours had a veranda on three sides, with mosquito screens of dubious efficiency: we were strongly advised to use nets on all beds all the time. The floors were red cement, polished by generations of house-servants' feet pushing cloth pads impregnated with polish over them. The kitchen was rudimentary but adequate, with a wood-burning stove; hot water came from a 'Rhodesian boiler' outside in the yard. This consisted of two 44-gallon drums interconnected and placed high enough on brick pillars for the hot water to feed by gravity into the house. The fire underneath was tended by prisoners, one of whose principal tasks it was to go into the bush in the boma's 5-ton lorry often enough to keep all the senior administrative officers' houses supplied with firewood. These trips didn't represent a security risk: in jail the prisoners received two meals every day, the accommodation was certainly no more spartan than in most of the villages and the company often more stimulating! The overflow pipe from the drums sometimes shot boiling water into the air if the prisoners had been too enthusiastic, so children and dogs were discouraged from playing in that area.

When we had been barely two months in Africa, we learned that the Governor-General of the Central African Federation, Lord Dalhousie, was to pay a flying visit to Luwingu during a whistle-stop tour of the northern outstations: cocktails for all at the senior DO's house, a dinner for a select few (not us!) at the DC's house and an overnight stay. It was doubtless during this unusual series of visits to the outstations that we were told of the imminent demise of the Central African Federation (which occurred at the end of the year) and, as a result, a speeding-up of the timetable for Northern Rhodesia's move towards independence. Again, the official line was to try to reassure the members of the Provincial Administration out in the field: there would be a continuing need for expatriates' skills for several years to come.

'Good morning, sir. I come to talk to you about the situation.' He's young, but perhaps he's a valuable informer...Into the office next door; the DC looks up, irritated at being disturbed from reading a file and reasonably asks me to find out more before bothering him with 'probably a job seeker'. And so it proves; the lad in question is a relative of one of the admin clerks, who manages to slip him in to see me, the new bwana in his first week at his first posting, still wet behind the ears. A word with Reuben Sinyangwe, head clerk, son of a local village headman and source of much useful information, enables me to avoid this kind of situation in future.

Joseph Chituta, nearing retirement and looking it, is a very senior District Assistant. While we are still being assured that our career prospects are excellent, rumours of localisation of DC posts go the rounds and, some two years after Prime Minister Harold Macmillan's 'wind of change' speech, the call comes to Joseph to prepare for a move from our backwoods station to become the territory's first African DC – at Feira, an equally off-the-map boma in the Southern Province and notorious for being down in the Luangwa valley, with the hottest temperatures in the country during the pre-rains summer months.

We had all learned ciBemba with Bwana Quick in Cambridge, but as the country has four main languages and over seventy minor languages/dialects, only a few of us ended up in areas where ciBemba is predominant. So I am lucky, in that I don't have to learn another variety of ciBemba or any other language, as do many of the others. We are in the heart of the Bemba ancestral lands and I have responsibility for three Bemba Chiefs' areas.

The district, and indeed the whole Northern Province, is the poorest and most backward in the country, with subsistence farming, no industry and no cash economy to speak of. In the villages one finds only women, children and old men; the young men migrate to the Line of Rail to look for work as soon as they are old enough. They send back part of their earnings, but in their absence the village gardens aren't properly tended and malnutrition is often the result

To get to know his district, the DO was required to go on tour throughout his area. Traditionally, this had been done on foot and took about six weeks in each Chief's area. Since it had become common for wives and families to accompany DOs even to outstations, the practice of touring by bicycle – in two weeks rather than six – had been, albeit grudgingly, accepted. In my thirteen months in Luwingu I toured two Chiefs' areas in the traditional way (but on bicycle). For the Chief's tour I had to take with me everything I would need for two weeks' absence: tent, camp furniture, food and drink (stream water was boiled for use each day but I took whisky!), bedding, spare clothing; but also a tin bath, a lavatory seat and a paraffin lamp plus fuel.

On tour, the routine was simple: breakfast, a quick shave then pack everything so that the porters could load up and depart direct to the site of the next night's camp. The porters were accompanied by most of the Messengers and the next camp was generally pitched and ready by midday: DO's tent up, latrine dug and wooden seat solidly installed, grass fence constructed all round it and the bath area, firewood collected for the kitchen and housing arrangements sorted out for everyone else – in two large tents or in the village, according to tastes and opportunity. Felix, the house-servant who accompanied me on tour, prepared inside my tent: camp-bed up with mosquito netting in place, table and chair erected with hanging arrangement for the tilley lamp, tin trunk with clothing inside the tent.

The main party consisted of myself with Chief Clerk Reuben and the local authority Treasurer, Fidelis; the Head Messenger and one or two others; and the local Chief if he was travelling with us. If absent, the Chief was represented by several of his tribal elders, to keep up with all the local doings and gossip, but also to ensure that tribal custom was properly observed when the Treasurer and I read and assessed the records of the native courts.

The local authority had its own equivalent of the District Messengers, called *Kapasus*. They were in effect local policemen, although they had very brief training and very limited powers. Two of them came on tour with me, in the train of the Chief, to bolster his prestige.

A day's work on tour consists of a ride through the scrubby bush along well-defined tracks with a stop in each village. A *Kapasu* has gone ahead a day or two beforehand to warn the headman that we are coming and to ensure a good turnout. The meeting-place is usually under a tree or, if it is raining, in the village school (if there is one). A few chairs and a locally made wooden table indicate our place: I am seated in the middle with the Chief next to me and any remaining chairs occupied in an order of precedence fixed by the Chief. I start the proceedings by introducing myself very briefly and then inviting the Chief to speak. My ciBemba is certainly not yet good enough to do this, so I use Head Clerk Reuben as interpreter. Neither Reuben nor I has any experience of consecutive translation so I have to keep my phrases both simple and short. The first morning I forget, and go on a bit; poor Reuben doesn't dare ask me to repeat so is reduced to: '*mwaumfwa* ...' 'You hear what he says ...', which produces a gale of laughter all round, and helps those at the table, for whom the experience is novel and somewhat unnerving, to relax. By the end of the first day, when this performance has been enacted in half a dozen villages over 20 miles' cycling, the Chief, Reuben and I are like practised troupers in a touring repertory company: I could almost have given Reuben three key words and left him to enlarge for two or three minutes. It certainly does wonders for my ciBemba vocabulary, so that by the end of the tour I occasionally rein him in if he starts to embroider too much on the simple ideas I have given him to start from.

The news I brought to these villagers was of considerable importance. First, the tribal structure (of autocratic if benevolent day-to-day rule by a Chief and a group of village elders), which had endured for centuries with little modification by the colonial administration, was to be replaced by elections to a rural council on the basis of universal adult suffrage. Then, this alien concept of voting was to be introduced at a national level as well, in elections to a Parliament in Lusaka; that in turn necessitated the registration of all adults as voters in the new 'one man, one vote' system.[1]

In the bush villages our presentations were received with little reaction; the ideas were so far from the realities of daily existence that they must have taken a long time to sink in. At that time, as mentioned above, one found only the very old and women and children in the villages because, most of the time, the able-bodied men were away on the Copperbelt, 'on the Line of Rail', working or looking for work in order to send money back to the village. For the DO, who had to check that the local author-ity staff maintained the large books of census records and from that try to collect the annual 10 shillings poll tax due from every male over the age of eighteen, the result was that this population record was full of large gaps. However, we had two elements in our favour: the first was the fact that the DO issued ammuni-tion permits to those holding a valid firearms licence; naturally, he first required to see a current year's poll-tax receipt in the name of the person seeking the coveted permit. The second was a ploy which profited from the wish of the young men to reg-ister as voters for the upcoming general election in order to be seen to support the newly created United National Independence Party (UNIP), led, since he came out of gaol, by Kenneth Kaunda

– universally known as KK. To be eligible to vote an individual had to be over twenty-one, which in turn implied that he had paid three years' poll tax; but many young men (especially if they had no shot-gun) avoided being around when the DO came on tour and so were faced with a dilemma when they tried to register as voters: without three poll-tax receipts they were either under twenty-one or in arrears with the tax.

One of the most popular signs of progress in this remote area was the construction of a primary school. We were always asked by the villagers when they would get one and I always passed the question over to the Chief for answer, on the grounds that he and his elders should make the recommendations as to where this scarce resource was to be allocated once the Provincial Education Department had obtained the provision of funds in the local authority's next annual budget. Approval implied that the Education Department would supply (and thereafter pay for) two teachers. The capital funds would be £2,500, which would buy all the materials needed for constructing a two-class school building and two teachers' houses on the basis of £1,500 for the school and 2 × £500 for the accommodation: cement and aggregate for the concrete slabs, roof timbers and *malata* (corrugated iron) for the roofs, and also (I think) desks and benches. Transport of the materials from the nearest provincial centre (often a considerable distance over rudimentary roads or tracks) was the responsibility of the local authority, which had to include this item in its own annual budget.

The villagers for their part agreed: to make the bricks from locally available clay and fire them; to dig the foundations; and to construct the three buildings, all free of charge. In principle, the work was done under the supervision of the Education Department but in reality this meant the villagers alone, with occasional visits, if possible, from the DO.

After little more than a year in Luwingu, I was called in one day to the DC's office to be told that I was to be transferred at short notice to Samfya, the boma on the other side of Lake Bangweulu, where there was a personnel shortage. In the run-up to Independence a number of senior expatriates had decided to leave Government service, taking advantage of favourable 'loss-of-prospects' terms for early retirement, which looked very generous when seen from the bottom of the salary scales, where I was. After fifteen years' service an expatriate admin officer could hope to leave with the maximum: a tax-free gratuity of £15,000 – enough to buy a large house in most English towns. A new DO leaving after one three-year tour could expect about £400. Enough to buy a second-hand Mini, as I was to find out.

Samfya was an attractive station, set on a hill looking out over Lake Bangweulu, with Chilubi Island 30 miles away to the east (but not visible) and beyond it the huge area of swamps which filtered most effectively the waters which then became the Luapula River, a confluent of the Congo. In the middle of the lake the water was very clear and reputedly drinkable; certainly it was put into accumulator batteries on occasion. There was a large population of fishermen, who dried their catch and either brought it to Samfya, where traders bought it to sell in the Copperbelt towns, or went to the far side, to Mpika on the Great North road, whence traders took the fish direct to Lusaka. Local folklore had it that the lake dwellers were web-footed because they spent all their time in waterlogged conditions.

When the campaign to register voters for the general election began, two of us camped for a fortnight in a village beyond the Lubwe mission called Twingi, in the middle of the swamps of the deep south of Samfya District. *Twingi* is ciBemba for 'many little things' – in this case, mosquitoes. We camped in the local school – it was the school holidays – with our trunk of tinned food and drink, our bedding with the essential mosquito nets – and Felix to cook. We stayed put for the duration and the villagers came in from some 30 miles around to be registered. We were open each day and all day; many adult men returned from the Copperbelt, on instruction from the activists of UNIP, whose strong-arm tactics were challenging the supremacy of the older African National Congress under Harry Nkumbula. The workers from the mines all had their receipts for the poll tax (automatically deducted from their pay-packets at the beginning of each tax year), but the local authority clerk did steady business issuing between one and three receipts to other young men: it was clear that the aversion to paying the tax was less strong than the pressure to register as a voter. By the end of the first week we began to recognise certain men who brought groups in, village by village: UNIP was very efficiently building a grass-roots organisation, even in this remote part of the country.

After voter registration came the election, at the end of January 1964. Polling districts were large: some voters had to travel 30 miles to reach their polling-station. With no local public transport and no private car ownership to speak of other than on the Line of Rail, this meant long journeys on foot or by cycle to fulfil one's civic duty. To man the twelve or so polling-stations in Samfya District all the senior Government officers of every department except the police were mobilised and the District Messenger force was dispersed as never before, to give a presence at each polling centre.

I was appointed polling officer for the Lubwe area, where I had spent a fortnight for voter registration. The polling-station was in the local school in the depths of the swamps, on a small island near Twingi, a two-hour journey by jet boat from Samfya through channels which had to be cleared regularly to keep them open for navigation. Because of the incident on nearby Chilubi Island four years before, I was given six Messengers, each with a .303 Lee Enfield rifle, probably dating from well before World War II, and in my strongbox I stowed ten clips of ammunition. Chief Clerk Reuben Sinyangwe was to be my chief assistant and interpreter, and I put Felix on the muster list hoping there would be space for him!

On the island three *Kapasus* awaited us. They assured us that all was quiet and that we would have a good, docile turnout the next morning. Nonetheless I told the senior Messenger to give firm instructions to his men not to let their rifles out of their hands even for a moment, and to remain alert and sober for as long as we were on the island. Leaving Felix to unpack my affairs, Reuben and I headed straight up to the centre of the village to see the schoolhouse which would be the polling-station next day. There we found everything as near ready as could be expected: wooden frames for two booths awaiting only the curtaining fabric which was part of my 'election kit', the classroom furniture cleared to one side. As I was about to congratulate the *Kapasus* on their initiative, they introduced me to a neatly dressed man with a nervous manner: 'This is UNIP *capitao* for island, Bwana. He has paper for making all ready for you.' Intrigued by this introduction, I set Reuben to finding out what he could about this *capitao*. (There are a number of Portuguese words in ciBemba because of that country's long presence in Mozambique, just to the east of Northern Rhodesia.) Reuben soon reported back that he was indeed the local branch leader for the party and that he had received written instructions from party HQ to do all he could to ensure that polling passed off without hitch or incident. This was good news, and the Messengers, especially, looked relieved. Reuben said that he would find out all he could about him, as we both realised that he would become a leading figure in local politics once the system for elected councillors was introduced – as it certainly would be in the first session of Parliament after these elections.

Next morning at the polling-station I find not only Reuben, all six Messengers (with their rifles) and three *Kapasus* waiting for me, but what appears to be the whole adult population of the island (and a fair percentage of the children, too) lined up in an orderly queue marshalled by the local party leader and several minders. The Senior Messenger, delighted at this opportunity to display his skills, calls his uniformed squad to attention as I approach and salutes smartly. This is standard daily practice at the boma: the DC and each DO get the same routine on arrival for work, but it seems most incongruous in our present circumstances. However, sensing an opportunity to add a sense of occasion to what is in fact a historic day for the country, I put down the ballot-box, voting-papers and curtain material for the booths, return the salute and proceed to inspect the parade. When I thank the Messenger in three simple phrases for his good work there is a buzz of conversation from the queue. Next, we go inside and finish setting up the station. It is now 8 o'clock, opening time. The court clerk is at the first table with the census record, which will have to serve as the electoral roll; then Reuben and I with the ballot-papers; finally the Senior Messenger with the bottles of purple dye and some leftover curtaining material, to prevent double voting. (Every voter has his left thumb dipped in the dye, which supposedly cannot be washed off for forty-eight hours.) The queue has moved up near the schoolhouse doorway and those at its head can see in through the open windows and thus observe what will be expected of them, before getting inside.

Before starting the proceedings I call in the Chief and his elders (the local party man has added himself to the group uninvited) and explain through Reuben what should happen. (The candidates' names were on the voting paper, but more importantly there was also a party symbol against each name. I think that UNIP had chosen an elephant, the ANC a hoe. There were several other parties, but I cannot recall their names.) I warn Reuben not to give any indication in favour of one party or another; we must at all costs be completely impartial. But he is to explain clearly, with repetition, that voting consists of putting a cross on the paper – and one cross only – in the box beside the candidate of one's choice. Also, the ballot-paper has to be filled in inside the booth; the pencil has to be left for the next voter; and the ballot-paper has to be put in the box on the desk in front of me and not taken away.

All this was said loudly in full view of those queuing outside the windows, and the message duly began to be passed along.

As soon as Reuben had finished, the UNIP branch leader disappeared and could be heard speaking to the crowd, presumably also passing on all that had been said. I told the *Kapasus* to let the voters in one at a time; the first to enter was the Chief. He was dressed in much-worn trousers and shirt, with equally worn sandals, but had on a leopard skin hat and a brightly coloured blanket over his shoulder, in honour of the occasion.

Reuben greeted him respectfully with a frequently used formula: '*Mwashibukeni mukwai, mwalileni?*' This translates as: 'Good morning sir, have you eaten?' but the last word literally means: 'Are you eating?' with overtones of: 'Were the rains good and the last harvest abundant; do you have enough food to last you through to the next harvest?' The precariousness of life in much of the Third World was encapsulated in the nuances of this standard greeting.

I shook the Chief's hand, dispensed with the need to dip his finger in the dye, then took him to collect his ballot-paper before directing him into the booth. Then we waited ... and waited ... After at least three long minutes the Chief's face appeared around the curtain and he gestured urgently to Reuben, who looked at me doubtfully. 'You'd better go,' I said. He disappeared into the booth and a long conversation took place after which Reuben came and reported *sotto voce* that the Chief had asked him, 'Where is Kaunda's name?' 'I explain that the UNIP leader is not in this district but in Lusaka; he does not want to believe until I tell him all about constituencies' (a word that Reuben had learned from me only a week before). The Chief dropped his paper in the box and went outside. 'Now you see he is asking the UNIP man if he can believe me.' As indeed he was. He seemed to be reassured, and soon afterwards he left us to continue the work without him, while the minders moved among the waiting voters, showing them drawings of the UNIP symbol that had been hastily sketched on sheets of paper provided by Reuben.

By 10 a.m. everyone in the queue had voted, with a turnout of already well over 80 per cent. During the rest of the morning a few stragglers came through but by midday I felt confident enough to leave Reuben in charge and return to the rest-house for a sandwich lunch. Afterwards, on unlocking my tin trunk to pack my affairs into it ready for a quick departure after closing time, I found the ten clips of ammunition, stored there for safety. I thanked my lucky stars they hadn't been needed – but put a couple of clips into my pocket, just in case.

Polling closed at 4 p.m. We had had almost no custom since midday but obviously we had to observe the correct hours. We made a quick departure, crossed the lake before nightfall and by 7 p.m. were back in Samfya harbour, where a Land Rover was parked for the last stretch up to the boma and our quarters. The ballot-boxes from all over the district were locked in the DC's office overnight with a Messenger guard outside before being sent to Provincial HQ in the morning for the count, and the Messengers' rifles were checked back into the police armoury.

'Everything went off all right then, Neil?'

'Yes sir, no problems. The ballot-box is in your office with the others, and here are the keys of your Land Rover. Oh, and here are the clips of ammo, didn't need them, of course.'

Independence Day was fixed for 24 October 1964, nine months after the general election had given KK a resounding mandate. During the first half of the year three administrative officers were posted away from Samfya: Callum Christie and John Woodmansey (who had been with us on the Cambridge Course) and Paul Bourne, DC.

The imminence of Independence and the introduction of favourable 'loss of career' early retirement terms for expatriate officers had led to a rash of applications, especially from those with ten to fifteen years' experience: exactly those whom the country could least afford to lose at that moment. In Samfya the effect was that half of the boma's establishment of DC plus three DOs was not filled from Paul Bourne's departure onwards; this pattern was repeated throughout the rural areas. With Paul's transfer to the Southern Province I was left, a junior DO still in his first tour, in nominal charge of the district, a state of affairs unthinkable when we arrived in the country less than two years before. I was on my own for one week, then a new DC, John Hart, arrived. In due course the *Government Gazette* published John's appointment, while the same edition recorded my acting as DC for a week – and, to my surprise, my bank account two months later showed a £5 credit, for Acting Allowance!

Life in the African bush suited me far better than it did Fiona. Bringing up two very small children occupied but didn't satisfy her; she felt we were even more cut off from civilisation in Samfya than in Luwingu. She also began to have unidentified stomach pains, to the point where she was sent off to a doctor in Kitwe on the Copperbelt for a check-up. His diagnosis was gall-bladder inflammation and possible stones, tempered with a strong dislike of bush living. Thus it was that, soon after Independence, I was told that I was to be transferred to Broken Hill (now called

Kabwe), the capital of Central Province and on the Line of Rail. There I was styled a Local Government Officer and very soon a Senior Local Government Officer (Acting), working with all the local authorities in Central Province. This was a significant promotion which also raised my annual salary from £1,400 to nearly £1,900. I visited all the half-dozen local authorities in the province; most agreeable was Mumbwa to the west, where a contemporary, John Theakstone, was DO (Chapter 19). We had decided quite soon after Independence that I would not stay on beyond the end of my three-year tour. I was now twenty-eight, and 'I'll never be able to get a decent job if I leave it too long' was a thought never far from my mind, so we left the new nation of Zambia in July 1965.

Note

1 These explanations were part of the process of preparing the entire adult population to take part in formal elections for the first time, both to choose members of their local authority and, most importantly, to elect Members of Parliament in January 1964, who would form the Government which would take the country to Independence in October 1964.

4

MUMBWA, LUNDAZI

Jeremy Burnham

'The best guinea fowl I ever had was simply gutted,
plastered with mud, feathers and all.'

It was mainly because my father happened to know the Chief
Secretary that I was engaged as a Learner District Assistant
(LDA) to work in the Provincial Administration of the Northern
Rhodesia Government. All I remember about my interview is
that at the end I duly passed on my father's greetings, to which
the great man replied, 'Thank you – please reciprocate.' Not having any idea what that word meant I wondered whether I should
kneel, salute or maybe kiss his ring. Fortunately I had developed
some mastery in the art of mumbling, and that got me out the
door.

I was posted to Mumbwa, a small town a hundred miles west
of Lusaka. Soon after I arrived a tall, craggy, unsmiling man,
James, offered his services as a cook. I thought he should have
retired already, but I guessed he'd know what he was about. He
did. I think of him cycling through the bush with me, fearfully
ignorant of what I was supposed to be doing on tour. My District
Commissioner took one look at this soft, pale young man when
I first arrived, straight out of school, summoned his Head
Messenger and told him to send this young bwana off on *ulendo*

(tour). I was assigned a District Messenger, Leonard Kafwabwe, who spoke enough English to get me by, and was told to buy a bike and pack for three weeks in the bush. James knew what to do. I bought a bicycle at the local Indian shop and watched James assemble the food and equipment for three weeks away from any shops. Heaven knows (I hoped) what I would be doing out there.

Turns out we were to tour Chief Mulendema's area. And turns out Chief Mulendema was a benign old alcoholic with little interest in being a Chief apart from the small stipend it brought him to support his fancy. But for this eighteen-year-old LDA he was the first Chief I was to meet, and my only preparation for such an event was in movies I had seen which included a ritual handshake which frightened me a bit. These days everyone does the black double-handshake thing – I often find it more natural than the singular white one – but back then I fudged it. I found myself groping up around Chief Mulendema's armpit, and only the extreme courtesy of the members of the Chief's court pre-vented the occasion descending into farce. They pretended not to notice. The Chief didn't notice – he was already well plastered. James did notice, and patiently taught me how to greet people civilly, including some of the wonderfully liquid ci-Ila greetings which, as in so many African languages, expressed variations on the enfolding theme 'You are seen!' – *Mwabonwa!*

James always wore a red shirt and a khaki chef's hat. He would ride like that, erect, noble and sweating, joining the train of maybe twenty men (never any women) who cycled with me along bush paths, miles and miles from village to village, 'tour-ing' this Chief's area. The train comprised the Chief and his several *Kapasus*, khaki-uniformed tribal functionaries execut-ing the authority of the Chief to be a nuisance in the other-wise rather pleasant and balanced lives of the villagers. Then there was me with three or four District Messengers in their blue and red uniforms (shorts, bush-jackets and knee-length puttees – tedious to do up but great for walking through the thorny bush), adding further nuisance value with this annual crusade. It was part of the deal of living in a protectorate that the inhabitants had to endure, no matter how far away from anywhere they lived, one visit a year from a representative, normally pink, of Her Majesty. And then to complete the entourage there were a dozen or more carriers, bearing on their bikes our tents, bedding, clothes, food, pots and pans, books, medicines and equipment to stock up any schools or clinics that we were to visit on our way. One carrier was also assigned to lug along a curious wooden plank with a large hole in it that I discovered would be perched, flat, on four poles set by the villagers around a hole that they would have dug for the bwana's toilet. I travelled with my own personal toilet seat.

When in the evening we arrived at the campsite which had been prepared for us by a nearby village, 'visiting' several villages along the way, James had the ability to have a fire going and kettle boiling for tea by the time I got off my bike, and have newly baked bread within an hour. The constituents for this bread would have been prepared and kneaded before we left the previous camp in the morning, and would have risen somewhat jerkily on the back of James' bike during the day. His oven was a hole in the ground, in which he lit the fire for the kettle. Once the fire had boiled the bwana's water and heated the surrounding earth he took out the hot embers, put the perfectly risen loaf into the hole, covered the hole with a light metal sheet and replaced the embers on top. It never failed, even in the rain – just make the fire a bit bigger and an umbrella over it all. The best guinea-fowl I ever had was simply gutted, plastered with mud (feathers and all) and cooked without oil or anything in one of James' touring ovens.

I soon discovered that the rifle carried by Leonard was not for our protection but for me to go forth and shoot some animal to feed us. My first kill, an unlucky small antelope called a puku, took five body-shots before it succumbed, and more than that number of misses. I was both exultant and ashamed, and declined my first venison. Everyone else was delighted – puku is tender and tasty.

There were two significant interruptions to my days as an officer of the colonial administration. The first was after a year or so in Mumbwa, when I was called up to serve my four-and-a-half months' army training, in a unit made up solely of Europeans, in Bulawayo, Southern Rhodesia. I was there to defend the integrity of the Federation of Rhodesia and Nyasaland, a short-lived political contrivance that was doomed from the beginning. But I was so politically naive at the time I thought there was some nobility in what I had been called to do.

What can one say about army boot-camp training? It's just like they say – a systematic indoctrination to obey orders without thought. I can still smell the breath of that Scottish sergeant major, staring into my face at a range of 2 inches through his bloodshot, whisky-pickled eyes, yelling full volume at this young man ('57037 – Rifleman Burnham, Staff!') from the North, where blacks and whites were said to mingle in some unsavoury way.

'If I tell you to shoot a kaffir, what will you do?'

'I...I don't know, Staff.'

'If I tell you to shoot a kaffir, what will you do?' (This time with more menace.)

(Silence.)

'Don't bloody stand there all holy, you Government prick. If I tell you to shoot a kaffir, what will you do?' (Up an octave.)

'Shoot, Staff.'

I prayed every night that I would never have to point my rifle at another human being. We were called out several times to be a background presence to the police in political uprisings, but thankfully my prayers were heard.

Back in Mumbwa, I remember a brief conversation with the daughter of the police chief. A bright, buxom girl, she tried so hard with me. Sitting in the pub one evening we were left alone (I always tried to avoid this happening). She turned and asked, 'Do you like kissing?'

'Of course,' I said.

Something probably should have happened next, but it didn't.

'You're as cold as a fish!' she eventually told me, and called me 'Fish' thereafter. Aah, Jeremy, if only...

The second interruption to my bush-station duties was a year later, this time in Cambridge, where I was sent to study Law and 'Colonial Administration'.

Cambridge is in a part of England that is so green and soft it affects the acoustics – any sound that could possibly jar the atmosphere is muted, absorbed, made more civilised by the enfolding lawns and hedges. It's as if the considerate quiet of the college libraries extends through the whole town. I was invited early on to a garden party where we young LDAs from Her Majesty's colonies were to meet up with the British graduates. These were young men straight out of cosseted university life who would be joining us on the one-year course, before leaving England to go out into the wild colonies. Each group was rather nervous of the other.

I found myself clutching a sherry on one of those polite lawns, trying to make intelligent conversation in this hushed air with a couple of these graduates, quite overawed by their erudition (I had gone to Mumbwa straight out of high school, remember). My discomfort kept me backing away from them until my retreat was blocked – I had backed into the rear-end of a young lady. She stood firm. She was talking to another group – I could hear her voice occasionally – she sounded very warm. For the next several minutes I was holding two conversations concurrently. One with the two graduates in front of me, which became increasingly hazy to me; the other through the seat of my pants with the derrière of the girl behind me. That conversation was at first tentative, gradually quite intimate, eventually engaging to meet again.

I'm sad to tell you, I walked away from both those conversations without ever turning to look at my rear partner. I never even saw her face.

A whole year I spent at Cambridge, and those British belles, I tell you...I think I lived in constant pain and yearning. I shared digs with a good friend and fellow administrative officer from Northern Rhodesia, Valentine Musakanya (Chapter 9). Valentine and I both struggled to keep warm through that long British winter. He by staying in bed as long as he dared before classes each morning, I by heading early into town to a small upstairs restaurant with a warm fire that served crumpets – a bread-form that was new to me and totally hit the spot. Apart from making good friends with a couple of the guys from Uganda (one, the son of a Chief, who promised me a royal welcome if ever I were to visit him), only two things remain with me from that year.

One was a tutorial with the dozen or so LDAs (i.e. minus the graduate component of our class) and our political science tutor. He started off by asking us, 'What should happen to make the world a better place?' Sounds like a good, neutral beginning which should get the ball rolling. Silence. He looked around this room of young colonials in disbelief. 'Someone must have some ideas, come on!' We all shrank into tighter silence. Blood out of a stone.

The other was a remark in a lecture from the barrister who was assigned to teach these youngsters due reverence for the law. He was theatrically imposing in his legal robes – we could picture him so elegantly and cruelly tearing into witnesses for the defence. He was very pleased with his ability to spout legal precedent, and one such has stayed with me. Apparently a learned judge in a previous century had made use of the maxim, 'To understand all is to forgive all.' The point our barrister was making, I believe, was that this provides good reason for a court not to delve too deep into the background of its accused, otherwise it would never dispatch society's criminals to prison.

My second tour of duty (oh, those ringing words we British employed to reflect the myth of the white man's burden – 'duty'!) in Northern Rhodesia was in the east of the country, in a small village called Lundazi. After my year in Cambridge I had now been promoted from an LDA to a DO – District Officer. The distinction was real – I now carried the authority to administer justice on behalf of Her distant Majesty. Fortunately I was seldom called on to do so.

Lundazi District runs from the border with Malawi on the east to the Luangwa River on the west, and contains one of the richest game reserves in Africa. What helps is that the Luangwa floods each rainy season, covering the huge plain around it and depositing a rich silt which makes for lush vegetation and abundant wildlife. The larger animals migrate up into the surrounding hills for the three months of the rains.

The Luangwa Game Reserve is unique in this part of Africa in that it still contains quite a large human population – people who have grown up living alongside wild animals. When I was there villagers were still allowed to carry muzzle-loading guns, mainly to protect themselves and their crops from marauding elephants. They were also allowed licences to hunt for the pot a small number of specified animals. Mostly they hunted with spears – those Portuguese guns from a past era were at least as dangerous to the one who fired them as to the target. Of course, there was some abuse but generally the balance was maintained and there was always an abundance of wildlife to satisfy the biodiversity needs of the area and the spectacle needs of the tourists – mainly American.

Two more asides about Lundazi. One is that there were some hyenas who regularly wandered through the village at night, often right past the door of my small rondavel (a round building) – I could hear their snuffling. When they were out in the open they would make their more familiar laughing whoop, which echoed through the night air. When I first moved there, if I had been out at work late I would park the Land Rover outside the rondavel. Once I delivered the vehicle next morning to the boma only to receive a telling-off for having bashed in both the rear brake-lights. I didn't remember any accident, but much of my driving was through the bush – it was possible. But this happened again. This time I noticed the red glass from the lights scattered on the rough ground where the vehicle was parked outside my rondavel, and I investigated the spoor. The hyenas had bitten the lights out – presumably they shone enticingly in the moonlight.

The other is, sad to say, a not-love story. Angela was the nurse at the dispensary down the road. She lived in a cottage just across the way from my rondavel. Irish, sparkly, as ready for love as a man could ever hope for. After my twenty-first birthday party she had taken me home with her. I stood on the veranda outside her cottage, solemnly gave her a kiss, and left. Well, at least I kissed her (just that once).

I spent most of my time those days on my bike – would even ride the 30 yards to her cottage, or more often to the next house along to hang out with the MacBurns. One night Angela caught me on the way past her door to the MacBurns, and said, 'Stop in on your way back!'

'I'll be late,' I said.

'That's OK, stop in anyway.'

It was past eleven when I left the MacBurns. I saw Angela's light still on. I skidded my bike up to her veranda, and there she was through the window, standing with her back to me in the bathroom, naked as a dream. I sat still on my bike, not daring to breathe, looking at that perfectly formed body – the first fully naked lady I had ever seen – wonderful beyond words. Surely she must have heard me skid against her veranda step. She turned, slowly, right around and looked straight at me, a quiet smile, not shy…I turned away and cycled off to my lonely little rondavel across the way. For days afterwards I couldn't meet her eyes.

The Luangwa valley: since there were people living there, and since the Queen had to be duly represented to these people at least once a year, we had to get on our bicycles and cycle around the area on *ulendo*. What a pleasure! Anyone who has cycled a bush path will tell you how smooth it is from all the feet that have travelled it over the years. It twists and turns to be sure, and you have to watch for small anthills which will catch your pedal and throw you off if you are careless, but after a time it becomes a wonderful, swishing meditation. I was often sorry when we arrived at a village, as it would break the reverie of my cycling.

I built up a very good relationship with Chief Chitungulu, whose area I toured twice, each time starting at the Catholic White Fathers' mission station, Lumimba. Father Hébèrt was the young French-Canadian priest there. We would sit into the night on deck-chairs on his veranda, our feet tucked up under us to avoid the attention of scorpions, discussing I don't remember what. His little mission church in the bush was the first where I actually saw people kneeling and mouthing the ritual words (in ciCewa) 'Forgive me, Father, for I have sinned ...'. These were rural peasants, rightly proud men who sustained large families with their bare hands. What sacrilege had my friend taught them? (I didn't think that then.) He tended his flock across the length and breadth of the Luangwa valley on his little 150 cc Vespa, white cassock billowing. A really caring man, as I remember. He died some years afterwards of leprosy, which was rife in that area.

One evening after a hard day's cycling among his villages, Chief Chitungulu and I went out walking in search of guinea-fowl for supper. He carried a shot-gun, I a stick. We startled a flock of these birds, which flew out over a dambo (an area of short grass and no trees where the receding flood stayed longer each year). Our guinea-fowl alighted in a little island of long grass which surrounded a big anthill right in the middle of the dambo. Very convenient, we thought, and strolled out over the now dry dambo towards the anthill. As we came close to the long grass, we heard what I took to be Father Hébèrt's Vespa from the far side of the anthill in front of us. Rats, I thought, he's going to scare off the guinea-fowl. We approached more carefully, the Chief's gun at the ready, hoping nevertheless to bag at least one of the birds. When we were about five paces from the edge of the island, a huge maned head parted the grass and looked out at us. That sound had been no Vespa – it was this lion purring. He was so close he could have been on us in one bound. To make things worse – a lot worse – a couple of females appeared, with several cubs.

We're done, I thought. It's the only time in my life I have felt a physical cold shiver – running down my back from the nape of my neck.

When in the presence of the King you don't turn your back. You move, respectfully, in reverse, slowly. I remembered from somewhere not to try to out-stare the lion – in fact I didn't hold his gaze at all. My friend's shot-gun would have been worse than useless in defence – it was loaded with buckshot to spray wide and hit several birds. It would have merely peppered our lion and angered him.

Well, I'm here to tell the story – and I hope the Chief is still around to recount it, too. We paced back towards the edge of the dambo – far enough, we thought, to break the ritual of the royal retreat – and then walked rather faster quite some way away before we both sat down, looked at each other and laughed hysterically. I can only imagine that the pride had eaten recently, or maybe there was much love-making in the court – hence the loud purring and lack of interest in the proffered meal.

One of my less pleasant tasks on tour in the Luangwa was to shoot elephant that had become a danger to the villagers' crops. Old animals whose teeth were rotten or whose tusks could no longer prise off branches would resort to pillaging fields of mealies (maize) or peanuts as easy takings. One elephant in a night can wipe out a whole year's food supply for a family. I carried a .404 rifle for this purpose, and was always accompanied by a game guard. Game guards were a wonderful breed of men who could track an individual animal through all kinds of terrain, criss-crossing the trails of many other animals, and would then stand as back-up if my shot was not accurate. I only had to dispatch four of these old elephants, but they all bore the marks of several attempts by villagers to scare them off with those ancient muzzle-loading guns. Their hides were ruptured with rusty old bolts and nails that had been stuffed down the muzzles of these guns – festering sores to make these animals' last years even more miserable.

The deal with these old rogue elephants, by the way, was that the tusks were Government trophies – presumably they went off to be auctioned somewhere – but the rest of the animal remained with the village whose crops had been destroyed. Cutting up an animal that size in the bush was no mean task, as we'll see shortly.

In my second year in Lundazi my District Commissioner told me that I now qualified for a commercial elephant licence. For payment of a not very large fee I would be authorised to shoot an animal in its prime with nice big tusks that I could then sell. My salary those days was a pittance, and I longed for a car to be able to make the trip into the Line of Rail occasionally and visit my parents. So I bought a licence, borrowed a .404 and took a week's leave to go hunt me down a couple of elephants.

As I write this now I do so with heavy heart. Then I was a young man out on an adventure, luckily with a game guard, Thembo, to guide me. It took that whole week, walking all day every day, asking villagers, 'Who has seen an elephant with large tusks recently?' We heard of one, and Thembo found and followed his tracks for a day and a half. He had a scar in his right front foot, which I could just discern in his footprint if he had walked on a clear, firm piece of mud. Thembo followed him over mud and rocks, dry sand, through long grass and under trees. 'See where he rubbed there with his back – he's very big!' – I could just make out the slightest of marks on the bark.

Once we knew where he was – we could hear him in the dense bush pulling down branches – the task was to get as close as we could without his hearing or smelling us. When browsing an elephant's eyes are generally cast downwards and focused close to him; he doesn't, like most smaller animals, continually scan the surrounds for predators. So our main task was not so much to keep hidden as to keep quiet and downwind. Thembo carried a little cotton bag of ash that he shook every few paces to test the wind direction.

I won't describe the end – it was in no way heroic. There is no real contest unless you do something pretty stupid. A .404 sends a big lump of metal deep into his brain. What I remember clearly to this day is the sound he made as he went down. A long, deep, sigh. Disappointment.

The disposal of the carcass for a trophy elephant differs from that of a rogue. The 'owner' – that's me – gets the tusks, of course. These are left in the skull for about a week to allow the flesh around them to rot so they can be easily removed without damaging them.

The meat is split evenly between the villagers who come out to do the butchering and the Government. The latter share is sent around to local schools and dispensaries. We were quite some way from the nearest village so it took until next morning for word to get there and the men to start arriving with their knives and axes. Eventually there were about twenty men, and some women, hard at work on the carcass. First of all, out comes the stomach – amazing for me to see the various degrees of break-down as the raw roughage this elephant had consumed moved from one end of his digestive tract to the other. Then all the innards – the liver and heart are the prize cuts and they go to the Chief and headman.

Then Thembo had to ensure that the line around the middle of the animal, length-ways, separating the villagers' meat (the half lying on the ground) from the Government share, was fairly drawn. The Government share had to come off first and that was cut into long lengths that were immediately hung around one of many fires they built, to dry. Then the carcass was turned over and the men cut up their own share of the trophy. By the evening the job was done, and a dozen fires were burning to dry all the meat so it could be carried away the next morning. The elephant's skeleton lay remarkably cleanly stripped, with the tusks now appearing even larger than when I first saw them. As the sun went down that night an assortment of vultures inter-ested in doing a final clean-up of the site was already beginning to assemble in the sky.

And then came the singing. Most of the people in that area of the Luangwa valley belonged to the Lenshina Church. Alice Lenshina was a young woman who had one day gone into trance and when she emerged she told of meeting with God and her mission to save the people of the valley. In addition to her mes-sage she brought back a powerful gift: song. She started teach-ing the people who quickly assembled around her a whole new repertoire of hymns, and they were catchy, lyrical and, very soon, sung the length of the valley. So an unexpected and totally won-derful gift for me that magical moonlit night in the bush, with the smoke from those fires and baying of hyenas and others who had caught the scent of the meat, was about four hours of joyful song from these followers of Lenshina. Anyone who has lived any time in Africa knows the power and rich, deep harmony of African singing. Lenshina had captured the essence of this magic and these villagers released it into the night.

In the morning we awoke to about twenty vultures circling above us, more already sitting ungainly in the surrounding trees, loudly urging us to depart and let them get at the carcass. I wanted to have a close look at this, so had a canvas sheet laid on the ground a few yards away, and as people loaded up and headed off with the meat I slid under the sheet to wait. It took no time at all for the first scavenger to alight on the ribs of the elephant, and for the next hour I had a ring-side view of nature's raucous recycling brigade at work.

Thembo and I went on to locate and dispatch the second elephant on my licence, a somewhat smaller one. I was partly exultant from that night of singing, partly numb from that last dreadful sigh. When I got back to Lundazi I was feted for the largest pair of tusks, both over 100 lb, to have been bagged that year. My feet were painted and I was up-ended in the bar of the Lundazi Castle Hotel – for all I know my footprints are still up there on the ceiling today. I engaged with the celebration but I knew that that was the end of any hunting days for me. The tusks when I sold them raised enough to go buy me a brand-new blue Volkswagen Beetle. Thank you, *nzofu*, that car was a wonderful gift but I wish so much now that I hadn't done that to you.

5

BROKEN HILL, ABERCORN, SAMFYA, MKUSHI, MPOROKOSO

Max Keyzar

'A crunching noise from under my desk...there was a mongoose busily eating a frog.'

Lazalo

My first cook was called Lazalo. Lazalo was quite an old man, thin in appearance and so cross-eyed that it was quite disconcerting talking to him as one never knew which eye to look at. He came with satisfactory if not glowing references; certainly sufficient for the fried-eggs-with-everything appetite of a young Learner District Assistant. He had a wide grin and was impeccably honest. What more could one ask?

My first accommodation in the Broken Hill (now Kabwe) Rural District was a Terrapin, a sort of collapsible box that could be packed up and moved elsewhere when necessary. The box within a box called a kitchen had standing room for one only and included a small gas stove which one had to manoeuvre round to get to a small paraffin-operated fridge. Later, some kindly disposed District Commissioner had a larger, better-equipped brick kitchen built next to the Terrapin, which made life easier for Lazalo. It also gave him a domain of his own and meant he didn't have to limbo in and out of the internal kitchen when preparing and serving meals.

Lazalo's meals were adequate, and since I was a newly arrived District Assistant living in my somewhat spartan box I was fortunately not expected to entertain. While Lazalo provided adequately for my undemanding culinary needs in the Terrapin, when on tour, visiting villages in the bush, he positively shone. Cooking in an earth oven, hastily put together when we arrived at one of our campsites where we would stay for a day or two, he would produce marvellous meals, including sponge cakes – something I never got at home! I never knew how he did it. At the end of my time in the district I returned to the UK to attend a course at Cambridge, and we parted company. I gave him a good reference and was sorry to see him go. I liked Lazalo and he seemed contented in my employ. I hope he went on to prosper.

Mr J

I was working one day in my office at the boma at Abercorn (now Mbala), situated near the southern end of Lake Tanganyika, when I became aware someone was standing in the doorway. I looked up to see someone who looked as though he had stepped out of a novel by Kipling. He was sparse in build, 'stringy' might be a better description, weathered by the sun to a colour not very different from his dark-brown shorts and shirt. He peered out through round-rimmed glasses from under a huge, old-fashioned solar topi and carried a fly switch made of some animal tail. He wore boots but no socks.

His story was rather a sad one. Some years ago he had lent about £10 – a considerable sum at the time – to a person who had been part of a road-grading team then working in the area. The person in question drove a grader – a large machine like an elongated tractor with a big, angled steel blade slung underneath which bulldozed the dirt roads into an appropriate camber to keep them drained, pothole free and in a reasonable state of repair. He had obviously told some heart-wrenching tale to Mr J and persuaded him to part with his £10, promising faithfully to pay him back on his next pay-day. The grading team shortly moved on and Mr J never heard from him again. The road teams moved all over the country and it would have been difficult to trace him.

Mr J, whose sense of honour and faith in the word of his fellow man obviously differed from that of his debtor, could not understand why he had not been repaid, and called in at the boma every now and then to enquire whether the money had yet been delivered. I gather several years had passed by from the time of the original loan to the time he appeared in my office. I commiserated with him, but had to say that I felt his chances of ever seeing the money again were remote. He looked rather bewildered and shook his head in a kind of disbelief and left the office. I have no doubt Mr J continued to visit the boma from time to time sharing his tale with my successors.

The Gamwell Sisters

While at Abercorn I met another 'character' – Africa seemed to be full of larger-than-life characters. I was walking up to the library when suddenly I was confronted by a lady with close-cropped iron-grey hair, dressed in a loose-fitting khaki bush jacket and long trousers, with a sheath knife on her belt. 'I haven't seen you before', she said, and, not unkindly, but with an unmistakeable air of authority, began to interrogate me. When she had satisfied herself she had all the information she wanted she bade me goodbye and went on her way. I found out I had met one of the Gamwell sisters, Hope and Marion. I think it was Marion I had met. They had quite a history of adventure and were widely known. They had settled near Abercorn and I believe one of their projects was to grow a crop from which they hoped to extract an oil called Nindi for use in the perfume industry. I don't know whether the venture was successful or not. I was told that in earlier days they had a venerable old pick-up with a servant who sat in the back whose sole purpose was to jump out with a block of wood when it stopped and place this under a wheel to stop it rolling away. As the vehicle became more decrepit Marion and Hope decided to go to the Copperbelt and replace it with a new vehicle. Having taken delivery of this shiny brand-new vehicle they pulled over to stop at a store or hotel and immediately the servant jumped out of the back and placed his block of wood against the rear wheel!

'Weep'

I had returned from a visit to a Chief in the Samfya District and was preparing a report when a crunching noise came from under my desk. I carefully backed my chair away and gingerly looked underneath it. There was a mongoose busily eating a frog he had caught, with a leg sticking out of each side of his mouth. He looked up and then continued his meal. He stayed in the office that afternoon and followed me to my house when I walked back after work. He stayed around the house and I fed him with milk and meat and we became good friends. His favourite spot was under the paraffin fridge, where he slept next to the glass funnel protecting the flame that powered the fridge. I was very happy to have him around the house as he would have made a meal of any snakes in the vicinity. I christened him 'Weep' as this was the noise he made from time to time. I made some enquiries, as he was obviously used to the company of humans, and I was told he belonged – if such an independent animal can 'belong' to anyone – to someone in the Fisheries Department. Samfya was located on the edge of Lake Bangweulu, where a fishing industry was being developed. Weep was utterly fearless and would go up to a dog many times his own size and investigate. If he didn't like the dog he would chase it, uttering a series of threatening noises. It was amusing to see a large boxer dog running off pursued by the diminutive Weep. Unfortunately his boldness was his undoing as he would go up to anyone in the community to check them out. One day he came out of some long grass to investigate a mechanic working by the grass airstrip and was dispatched by a blow to the head with a spanner. I never heard the full story, whether the person in question panicked at the sudden appearance of this little animal by his feet, or whether he thought he was going to be bitten, or what. I do know that the person in question had to make himself scarce for a while as Weep's 'owner' was understandably incensed. It was a sad ending to another 'character'.

Snakes

Everyone who has lived in Africa has their own snake stories to tell. Here are a couple of mine.

Once when I was on tour in one of the Chiefs' areas in Broken Hill Rural District, we were cycling along a bush path, between villages, in a long convoy consisting of the Chief and his councillors and retinue, together with me and my District Messengers. The porters had gone on ahead to establish our next camp. I was about fifth in line in the convoy. Suddenly everyone seemed to disappear in different directions into the bush around me shouting '*Njoka Bwana! Njoka!*' Whatever kind of snake it was, it was obviously not one to be trifled with, as the odd stray snake we occasionally came across was usually dispatched without too much fuss with a volley of stones or a stick. It was apparent no one was going near this one! I stood by my bicycle, unsure which direction to move in as I couldn't see the snake. It was an unnerving few seconds, which seemed like minutes, with everyone shouting at me and not knowing where to go. Although it was the dry season, tall dry grasses lined the path and obscured the view. Then I caught a movement just off the path and in a gap between the grasses saw about a foot of steel-grey, as thick as my wrist, moving swiftly past me. Not as swiftly as I moved in the opposite direction. I must have been some yards away by the time my bicycle hit the ground! The consensus was that it was a black mamba. I was grateful I was not directly in its path as the black mamba has a reputation for being a nervous, aggressive snake, and will often attack if it feels the way to its home (often in the base of an abandoned termite nest) is blocked. It is also highly venomous.

On another occasion I was on tour in the Mkushi District and had stopped in one of the villages on my tour route to conduct the usual business: discussing with the headman of the village things like the state of the crops, the need for the roof of a teacher's house to be repaired before the rains, why a well was needed in the village, checking who still lived in the village against notes made on the last visit, and so forth. Meanwhile, one of my District Messengers conducted one of the less popular exercises of the visit – collecting taxes. Unusually we had a small Health Team with us, and they had given smallpox vaccinations to some of the new babies in the village and moved on to where our next camp was being prepared.

I had been sitting in the shade under the grass eaves of one of the village houses, and as I came to an end of my business and was preparing to move on I noticed a woman lying on the veranda of a mud house directly opposite being given a drink by another woman. She was obviously not well and I asked what the matter with her was, presuming she was suffering from malaria. 'Oh', came the blithe reply, 'she was bitten by a snake while gathering wood earlier this morning!' 'Why didn't you tell me earlier?!' I exploded. I must have been sitting in the village for over an hour. I presume the reason was a rather fatalistic approach to the problem along the lines of 'Well if she gets better, she gets better, and if she doesn't, she doesn't – what can anybody do about it?' I sent off for the snake-bite kit which had gone off with the Health Team and went over to look at the woman. She was grey in colour with a film of perspiration over her. There was a loose bark tourniquet round her leg, put there with the best intentions but unfortunately completely useless as it was so loose it had slipped down to her ankle. The other woman had been trying to get her to drink from a tin mug in which there was some kind of root, a local *muti* (medicine) I guessed. The victim was feebly pushing the cup away.

Eventually the snake kit arrived and one of the Health Team gave her anti-venom injections, but she died shortly afterwards, probably confirming the belief that our medicine was no more effective than their own.

We cycled on almost immediately afterwards and before we arrived at the next village heard them wailing and bemoaning her death. News travels fast in the bush.

Missionaries

At Abercorn there was a Roman Catholic mission run by the White Fathers. I had very little to do with them, though I did have some interesting conversations with one of the priests. He very kindly gave me a Knox translation of the Bible. It was written in the quaintest English! I still have the copy.

Another missionary was a member of the Brethren called Archie Ross who lived a mile or two out of Abercorn with his wife and family. He was to have a greater impact on my life, which came about as follows.

John Clayton, the boma accountant, lived with his family in a bungalow just below mine and we used to walk up to the boma offices together in the morning. John kept lending me Christian books, and while this was not a subject I was particularly interested in I used to read them, firstly because there was not a bookshop in Abercorn and I enjoyed reading almost anything if it was well written, and secondly because I knew John would ask me how I got on with the book and what I thought of it. John's passion for sharing his Christian faith came about through something that had happened to him not long after he was posted to Abercorn. He had decided to take his family down to Ndola on the Copperbelt to do some shopping, a long journey mostly on dirt roads. He had been driving his family in his VW Beetle when he hit some soft sand on a corner and the car had flipped over. It was pre-seat-belt days, and the children were thrown out of the back window, which had popped out, and they landed on the soft sand. John and his wife, Mary, managed to get out of the car and discovered they were both unhurt. No one in the family had a scratch on them in what could have been a horrendous and fatal crash. Reflecting on this John began to think about what would have happened to him and his family if they had died: in other words, about the meaning and purpose of life. Archie Ross, the Brethren missionary, presented the Gospel to John, and he and his family gave their lives to Christ. It transformed his life and that of his family. Hence his eagerness to share his newfound faith with me. Before long there was a regular worship and Bible-study meeting going on in John's house involving a few local Christians and led by Archie Ross.

John invited me along to the meetings, and while I did not exhibit much enthusiasm, John was a neighbour and I had time on my hands. I went along partly because of this and partly out of curiosity. I found the hymn- and chorus-singing rather boring, mainly because I was unmusical and tone deaf – but Archie's Bible studies I found fascinating. I was soon into a debate with him about evolution and many other subjects, and I would sometimes keep him up late with my questions. His knowledge of the Scriptures impressed me deeply. He would say, 'Well, let's see what the Word of God says about this,' and he would always have an answer from the Bible.

Originally, if someone had asked if I was a Christian I would probably have answered along the lines, 'Of course, I'm English.' In other words I had been christened in the Church of England, attended confirmation classes at school and was duly confirmed, went to church on occasions like Easter and Christmas and generally lived what I thought was a reasonably moral life, meaning that if the pass-mark to heaven was 50 per cent I hoped to just squeeze through as I had done with my A-Levels, despite spending most of my last summer swimming and playing cricket and tennis. However, it began to dawn on me that the issue was not about keeping or not keeping rules, but about a personal relationship. What was I going to do about Christ's claim on my life? I wrestled with this for some time and one night I was woken up by what I believe was God's voice, the only time up to then I had heard his voice audibly. All He said was, 'Max.' It was a very short conversation but I knew then that things were serious and I had to make a decision. Not long afterwards I knelt down with Archie one afternoon in my bungalow and surrendered my life to Christ. It transformed my life. But that, as they say, is another story.

District Notebooks

District Notebooks, usually large, imposing volumes, not little books for scribbling the odd note or two, were kept, I believe, or overseen, by most if not all District Commissioners. They would no doubt by now be of some historical interest. I wonder what has happened to them. I hope many have been preserved. I used to read them with fascination when I could get my hands on them. There follows an extract taken from the Mporokoso District Notebook. Unfortunately, I did not take down the date of the entry, if there was one, but from the style, which would undoubtedly cause some comment these days, it is probably quite an early entry:

African Ideas of God

There undoubtedly has existed for generations and still exists in the minds of the natives of the Mporokoso Division an idea of a great spirit god. Whether this god is considered the god of all countries or a god of a tribe is uncertain – yet in each tribe there seems to exist the idea of a great spirit – unknown, omniscient, all power-ful – the *Lesa Mukulu*. Yet this idea is not propitiated with gifts or sacrifices – can it be that in his agnosticism the native attributes to that Great Unknown power which we comprehend as Nature, the idea of God as we regard it? Is *Lesa* Nature? The Awemba have no individual name to give to the idea – *Lesa* – they cannot grasp it – it is beyond them – and yet there is the *Lesa*. As a title of flattery the native, and not the Awemba only, often speaks of a great chief as *Lesa Mukulu*. Does he mean – imbued with the spirit of the Greatest of All? The *Lesa Mukulu* has no fixed abode – yet there are lesser gods, or are they rather Spirits *mipashi*, which have abodes. To the *Lesa Mukulu* no wife, no children are assigned. To the god *Mulenga* – the tribal god or spirit – who yet has no settled district assigned him – there are allowed his wife and children. *Mulenga* is the God of Hunting. It is *Mulenga* who gives the quarry to the hunter. He is invoked when a hunt is organised. He is even symbolised – but the *Lesa Mukulu* – no! *Mulenga* has his prophets – the *Lesa* – none; still less than *Mulenga* and the *Lesa Mukulu*, yet to be propitiated with offerings, shelters or shrines and sacrifice, are the spirits of the departed chiefs and in a lesser degree the spirits of all ancestors. To certain districts – certain hills, rivers, glades and trees are assigned spirits. Are these spirits, gods in the minds of the natives?

51

They must be carefully tended or ill will befall. Certain men are appointed to care for them. Are these spirits supposed to be the ancestors of the men who tend them? In the time of famine, it is not *Mulenga* or the *Lesa* who is invoked but the spirits of Chitimukulu or other departed chiefs.

Much is to be learnt – little is known – yet it is strange that in each native's heart there is the 'idea' of a Great Unknown! Note however, that no Love – no idea of loving – is felt either for or from the *Lesa Mukulu*.

Rereading this some fifty years since I copied it down in longhand, I find my appetite whetted. If only I had copied more of these gems. But it would have been a lengthy, time-consuming process and there were no scanners or voice-activated iPads in those days, and a young District Assistant had plenty of other activities, work and social, to keep him occupied.

6

CHOMA, LUSAKA, CHALIMBANA

Judy Mitchell

*'Malcolm built up the most comprehensive collection of
Zambian moths and butterflies at that time and discovered a
number of new specimens.'*

Our first posting, for three years, was to Choma, where Malcolm
was to begin his career in the Overseas Civil Service as a Cadet in
the Provincial Administration. The town lies half-way between
Lusaka and Livingstone, serving the farming community and
a base for many agricultural advisers and other civil servants.
Choma straddled the railway line and the main road, and along
the main road there were a number of multi-purpose shops, as
well as a bank, a butcher's (with front and back entrances), a
doctor's surgery, the boma not far away and a hospital on the
edge of town run by nuns; milk was delivered daily by a farmer
not far out of Choma. In addition Choma had a golf club and the
equivalent of a leisure centre: tennis, swimming pool and club
house with a hall, stage and bar. With a fairly large community
of Europeans, and hardly any mixing of the races, it was all in all
not unlike life in a small English town.

Of course, with a house-servant, life was not quite the same.
It was wonderful to have someone to clean the house, to do the
laundry, to make sure that the wood-burning stove stayed alight,

to keep the fire burning under the barrel for hot water and to do most of the cooking. Keeping the paraffin fridge alight was altogether another problem, my problem. We inherited this very temperamental and horrible contraption, which needed a lot of care and attention, with much cursing, but it was so hardy that we had it for nearly two tours. For the first few months much of my time was spent settling into our first home: getting the house ship-shape, making many cushion covers for Government furniture and curtains for a three-bedroomed house, then making maternity and baby clothes. We both used 'the leisure centre' frequently, and when I gave up tennis because of pregnancy, the nine-hole golf-course, just over the railway line from our house, lured Malcolm away from tennis for frequent games of golf.

A few months after Andrew (our eldest son) was born I decided I had had enough of golf-widowhood and often joined Malcolm on the golf-course, with Andrew in a push-chair, but I continued to play tennis. Outings in the evenings for bridge and dinner parties involved Andrew sleeping in the back of our car – not to be contemplated anywhere these days. We took our only holiday during our time in Choma when my parents visited us, and we travelled with them for two weeks on a whistle-stop tour down memory lane around Southern Rhodesia: my parents started their married life near Salisbury (where I was born) and spent ten years in different areas of Southern Rhodesia. The trip was fairly arduous, with four adults and a baby in a smallish car, and long distances to travel.

During our first few months in Choma I went with Malcolm on some of his tours, travelling by lorry to the area and usually cycling between villages when we had set up camp. I was always greeted with pleasure and smiles (and probably curiosity). I thought it a rather grand way to camp, having camp-beds, latrines and someone to do all the cooking and clearing up – not at all like Girl Guide camps back in England. I worked as a temporary secretary in the boma on a couple of occasions to cover annual leave – good to keep my hand in. Not long before Independence and in the absence of the DC, we were instructed to provide lunch for President-to-be Kaunda and some of his entourage during his tour of the Southern Province. That created a bit of a stir in the household, wondering what he ate, whether he'd like wine or beer to drink, how to seat everyone around the dining table, what to talk about (in my case, at least). We weren't dismissed immediately, and so I suppose it passed muster. Independence for Zambia was celebrated during our time in Choma, and in due course our first Zambian District Commissioner was appointed.

On our way back to Zambia after our first home leave, we were almost at the end of our drive through Southern Rhodesia when we heard on the radio in a café, where we were having lunch, that UDI had been declared and that borders would be closed. We dashed to the car and drove at speed to get through the border just in time.

After a few weeks in Lusaka our second tour took us to Chalimbana, where Malcolm was on the staff of the local government training centre with two other Europeans. With petrol rationing introduced not long after that, we were really confined to base, relying on someone else to do our weekly shopping in Lusaka. Fortunately we three families had small children to care for, a swimming pool for occasional use, tennis-courts and of course good weather. With some help I took up gardening (the glut of runner beans put Malcolm off them for ever), continued with sewing and shared time and activities with the other two young families. Here we (at least Malcolm) experienced at first hand a distant rural health clinic (presumably nearer than Lusaka Hospital) – Andrew had fallen against a door jamb and split his forehead open, requiring a good array of stitches.

I had another spell as temporary secretary to cover annual leave, but more importantly, though, Malcolm found that one of his colleagues, Frank Schofield, was also interested in butterflies and moths. This started a huge part of his life in Zambia, during which he built up the best and most comprehensive collection of Zambian moths and butterflies at that time and discovered a number of new specimens. During those few years of petrol rationing, almost all collecting and breeding was done 'at home', with traps and lights installed in the garden and a bedroom set aside for a caterpillar farm and other necessary paraphernalia for collecting. Even I had to become involved when Malcolm was away on business. Malcolm's next appointments were to the Local Government and Finance departments in Lusaka, taking us to the capital or nearby for the rest of our time in Zambia. Andrew started at an infants' school, which Fiona (our second child) misheard and called the Elephants' School.

At this time we acquired a dog, Brutus, a black Labrador, the runt of the litter. He was great fun and quite daft, but he had a marvellous grin when greeting us, wagging his whole body in delight. Later we moved to a property out of town, beyond the airport, which we called 'the farm', and there Brutus was at his daftest: his favoured pastime was to try to dig snakes out of holes, coming out the worse for wear several times. Twice I noticed that he had been spat in the eye by a cobra, and I had to administer a wash to his eyes, but this left him blind in one eye. His worst encounter was when he was bitten on the head by a puff adder. I administered snake serum, and he shot off into the bush for several days. He came back eventually, a pretty sick dog, and over the weeks the flesh on one side of his face withered away, giving him a very lopsided look. He didn't learn from this encounter and continued to risk his life. Much later, when we lived back in Lusaka, Brutus felt he had to defend his property from all other dogs and was not afraid to confront and be mauled by visiting dogs. In the end he ended up with cauliflower ears as well. Not a pretty sight.

The farm was a good place to live, apart from the snakes. We had a large chicken house, and so I went into chicken farming in quite a big way – selling eggs and chickens (when they had finished laying) to any local people coming to the door. We had a large orchard of oranges, lemons and mangoes, pawpaw trees, a row of mulberry trees and a large banana plantation – one had to be careful of snakes there. In addition we had a swimming pool, which was constantly full of little beetles and such and whose pump frequently broke down. The drawback was that the property was a good distance from neighbours – one family opposite and everyone else a car-drive away. Andrew went to a school not far away, Silver Rest School, and Fiona followed him in due course, by which time he was at school in England.

While we were at the farm the first of my part-time jobs came along. This was home-based, typing out on Gestetner skins a manual for rural health workers. The next job was with a small company run by an entrepreneur importing goods, and I took work home to be typed up. I remember having to hurry a particular job to be delivered to that company on my way to hospital for the birth of Ian. Both Fiona and Ian were born in the same ward at Lusaka Hospital, but immediately after the birth of Ian we were moved to the new hospital – a much cleaner and more sterile place.

When Ian was about fifteen months old, I was travelling home with him when I was rammed by a car coming out of the airport road while I was driving straight on towards home. Fortunately there were plenty of police around, as President Kaunda was about to arrive, and we were scooped up quickly to get out of the way and whisked off to hospital, together with the chap driving the other car (who, needless to say, had no insurance). I had a broken wrist and broken ankle and Ian a broken leg and a cut or two on his head (no seat-belts in those days). Fiona was at school miles away, and so the first thing to do on arrival at the hospital was to phone friends near the school to ask if they would collect Fiona, go home to get her night gear and take her home with them, because I didn't know how long I would be. We were kept in hospital overnight until suitable staff were on hand to set bones.

Guess where Malcolm was! Hundreds of miles away in Mwinilunga on a butterfly- and moth-hunting trip. I told people in his office *not* to try to contact him since he would be on his way home the next day. But they did. Towards the end of the day, in the middle of absolutely nowhere, local police, with great efficiency, found him and told him of the accident. Incidentally, they made no mention of Fiona: only that Ian and I had injuries. So Malcolm gathered everything up and drove to a local rest-house to get a bit of sleep before undertaking the hundreds of miles back to Lusaka, worrying all the way about us and wondering what had happened to Fiona. The accident took place on a Friday afternoon, and he drove all day on Saturday, to arrive at the hospital to find that we had been discharged. He then drove back home to find us all together, to his great relief. Sadly, his beloved MG sports car was too damaged to repair, but Ian and I were very lucky to escape severe injury.

Soon after this accident, and while I was still in plaster, we moved back into Lusaka. There were no servants' quarters in the area we lived in, and so we helped our house-servant to finance and build a very small house on an estate on the outskirts of the city. His plot had a stand-pipe and nothing else. During this time I had my last job in Zambia – working as secretary for a solicitor. His firm certainly moved with the times: I think we had one of the first word-processors in Zambia, a huge piece of machinery.

Malcolm's next and last appointment was Director of Elections, a post he fulfilled with much appreciation from the President. He took every opportunity when required to travel on business in parts of Zambia to enlarge his collection of butterflies and moths. What few short holidays we took during our time in Zambia usually involved travelling to remote areas, camping somewhere near water but also to the rest-house on the Nyika Plateau via Malawi. Our trusty Peugeot 404 Estates usually coped very well with the roads. In all our time with Peugeots (three tours) we had only three mishaps with them. On one occasion we had started for home during a bank holiday weekend in the Mwinilunga District when we suddenly saw a wheel racing away in front of us – it was ours. On another occasion we had not one but two punctures. We had to set up camp by the side of the road for me and the children, while Malcolm thumbed a lift to 'goodness-knows-where' with a wheel tucked underneath his arm to get it mended. We were not far from a village, and so all the locals came to watch us while we waited for twenty-four hours or so for Malcolm to return. The only other time there was a problem was when the clutch leaked, and all we could do was to drive in one gear all the way home, hundreds of miles. That took a long time. Our Peugeots (always 404s) served us very well, so much so that we have had nothing but Peugeots ever since.

We could not stay in Zambia for ever, and after twelve very good years we made the difficult and sad decision to return to England with our three children to start a new way of life. Malcolm wanted to keep his wonderful memories intact, and so unfortunately we never returned.

7

MPOROKOSO

Mick Bond

'A job of immense variety and responsibility, playing one's part in ensuring good government and pushing local development on all fronts for the benefit of the local population...a suicide career.'

Why had I joined HM Overseas Civil Service and gone to Northern Rhodesia in the first place? When I was fourteen we had a lodger staying with us who was on a London University course in Colonial Administration, preparatory to going out as a young District Officer to what was then Nyasaland. I became fascinated by his descriptions of what he imagined the work would involve. Of course it was coloured by all the concepts of imperialism and British arrogant superiority of which we have long since come to be embarrassed or ashamed – but one cannot change history. Above all it seemed to be a job of immense variety and responsibility, playing one's part in ensuring good (if at times paternal) government, maintaining law and order and pushing local development on all fronts, for the benefit primarily of the local population and only coincidentally to satisfy any British interests. I then decided, at that tender age, that this was a most attractive career for me to pursue.

By the time I was actually interviewed at the Colonial Office in late 1960, Northern Rhodesia certainly appeared the most attractive of the remaining dependencies and I had accepted that I was embarking on a 'suicide career', to help achieve the morally unchallengeable and inevitable transition to independence. I undertook the Cambridge Course in Colonial Administration in 1961/2, continuing to be a member of Jesus College, where I had been an undergraduate. I certainly concentrated more on the language than on the other subjects, even rendering into ciBemba 'Pericles' Funeral Oration' from Thucydides! The abiding memory of the course was of the camaraderie – we all got on with one another so well.

Wendy and I married in Cambridge in April 1962, and immediately Valentine Musakanya (Chapter 9) and Dave Alexander (Chapter 21) came to join us in our terraced house. Our parents took our impending departure most calmly in the circumstances; after all, we were off 6,000 miles into the (to them) unknown for at least three years. This was especially true of Wendy's family, while my parents had had several years to prepare themselves for it.

On 5 July we sailed, along with many others from the course, from Southampton on the *Transvaal Castle* for the fourteen-day cruise to Cape Town. A three-day train journey followed from Cape Town to Livingstone, where we were met by D'Arcy Payne (Chapter 2) with a load of immigration and other bureaucratic paperwork. Arriving at Lusaka on 22 July, we had our luggage all conveyed to a PWD (Public Works Department) store and were housed for four nights in the main Government rest-house at Longacres. We had reached our country of destination!

A brief period of intense socialising and shopping in Lusaka followed, with a lot of generous help from 'old colonial hands'. There was a reception for all our group and wives at Government House (now State House), where we met the Governor, Sir Evelyn Hone, his Deputy, Richard Luyt, and several current Ministers. The Provincial Administration, which we were in, came under the important Ministry of Native Affairs – an embarrassingly colonial name but one which at least emphasised that local African interests were deemed paramount. We Cadets also had to spend most of a morning being shown around the Secretariat offices (the Civil Service hub) to fill in forms or to be introduced to important people; and one afternoon was taken up with touring around the houses of various VIPs to sign their visitors' books – it was all exhausting and fairly confusing.

On the shopping and other practical sides one old hand introduced our wives to Lusaka's main shopping street, Cairo Road, whose name conjures up Cecil Rhodes' ambition of extending Britain's imperial sway all the way from the Cape to Cairo. We had to open a bank account, buy up an enormous bulk-order of goods and get a paraffin fridge and four 44-gallon drums of paraffin, ready for life in a rural area. On 26 July we thankfully left Lusaka and flew to Ndola and then by an old Dakota to Kasama, where we met our DC, Ian Macdonald, and his wife; she was going off to the UK the next day to put their children into schools, so we never got to know her. He, with his moustache and keen eyes, looked very military and efficient, but was pleasant enough. In the evening we were entertained by the Provincial Commissioner for Northern Province, Peter Clarke, and his wife, and met most of the other members of the Provincial Administration in Kasama. This was a much smaller, friendlier and more informal group than we'd met in Lusaka, and naturally they had more immediate interest in and for us.

The next day, Ian Macdonald drove us the 110 miles to Mporokoso. This was where we were to spend our first two years in Africa, the first two years of married life and for me my first paid employment (apart from National Service). Over the two years we were there, 1962–4, we fell in love with Mporokoso, as a station and as a district, and that intense feeling was probably enhanced because it was our first posting and we were learning so much all the time. It is certainly true that even today we still have clearer recollections of people and events and scenery from Mporokoso than from any of our subsequent postings. It was, and has remained, *ku mwesu* (our home). And arguably it was to be the happiest two years of our lives.

Geographically, and to a large extent socially, Mporokoso was divided by the grass airstrip; the most frequent user of this was our 'flying doctor' friend, Derek Braithwaite, calling in to see and pay his staff at the small clinic. VIPs used it, as well, but it was a comfort to have it there for any emergency, too, and we always kept it well maintained. On the north side of the airstrip were the Government offices and the low-density (i.e., European, with one exception) staff houses. Immediately on the south side were some medium-density houses for the middle-ranking African civil servants, plus a Catholic Mission, a small clinic and, later, a new prison. Behind this row were the District Messengers' lines, houses of other boma employees and, further on, the primary school, with its staff housing on site. To the side of this area small African stores lined the road which led west to the next boma at Kawambwa. Yes, even those few sentences imply correctly that, apart from the few storekeepers and Mission staff, all residents in the township were Government employees.

When we first arrived the European officers were:

- the DC – Ian Macdonald, now a grass-widower as his wife had left to take their children back to schools in the UK;
- the DO (Cadet 1), a year my senior – Jeremy Collingwood and his wife, Margaret;
- the SBO (Special Branch Officer) – John Cochrane, a bachelor;
- the Game Officer, when he wasn't tramping through his beloved reserves – the bearded, irascible and teasing Leslie Allen and his wife, Jean.

With our arrival as DO (Cadet 2), the number rose to eight in total.

Changes occurred. For example, Ian Macdonald left in November 1962, to be replaced as DC by Alan McGregor; Alan was younger than Ian, more liberal-minded and easier for us to get on with both socially and at work. Alan himself went on leave in early 1964, to be replaced by Angus McDonald, whom I was to meet again in both Chinsali and Lusaka. The Collingwoods were sent to Abercorn (later called Mbala), always regarded as a plum posting, in early July 1963. Their replacements, Max and Ursula Keyzar (Chapter 5), had been with us on the Cambridge Course, but they too left in April 1964. So by the time we were moved to Chinsali in July 1964, Angus, the DC, was probably the only European officer left on the station.

The senior African civil servants at the boma qualified for medium-density housing. They included: the quiet and very industrious Medical Assistant; the District Agricultural Officer, a large, competent and very industrious officer; two Senior Clerical Officers, one of whom I next met when I was in Mongu and he was DS (District Secretary) Sesheke; the elderly Accounts Clerk (in my first month I sat at his elbow and learnt book-keeping and trial balances from him); and of course we knew all their wives.

Other non-civil-servant Africans we saw fairly frequently included Eleazar Namweleu. He was a senior *kabilo* (traditional adviser/counsellor) to Chief Mporokoso, and also a great lay preacher. Eleazar was an old muBemba who spoke perfect high-class quasi-Dickensian ciBemba, with clear diction and beautifully rounded phrases interwoven with the metaphors and proverbs in which the language is so rich; he was a joy to listen to, and I seriously attempted to emulate his style.

I remember, too, many of our smart District Messenger force – probably around sixteen in all. All the Senior Messengers were ex-askaris (soldiers) who had served with either the Northern Rhodesia Regiment, or the KAR (King's African Rifles), in Abyssinia 1941, Libyan Desert 1942, Burma 1944 or Malaya 1952–4; they wore their rows of medal ribbons with pride. I can still recall most of their names.

The DC's house was inevitably the largest and had a guest-wing for the fairly frequent visits of civil servants from elsewhere. It had been built at the very beginning of the century and had a lovely and well-cared-for front garden and a great view west-wards; some 550 yards from it, across a grassy wilderness, was the boma garden from which we could often get fresh vegetables, and a *mushitu* (grove of tall trees at the source of a stream) in which a swimming pool had been created. At the rear of the house was an *insaka* (shelter) beside a tennis-court – an amenity most old-style DCs had constructed at their bomas for free, with the available prison labour (Chinsali had a golf-course instead).

Next to the DC's house and alongside the road was the boma itself, i.e., the District HQ offices. The building was old, thatched and full of bats in the roof, with its ceilings sagging under the weight of accumulated and odoriferous bat droppings. Behind it was the thatched prison. This was a semi-open prison, in that the exercise yard was merely enclosed by a spindly hedge. Secure? A prisoner once ran away; the others immediately ran after him, caught and hauled him back and beat him. 'You don't do that here: it'll give us all a bad name!' Of course, regular wholesome meals could make a spell in prison very welcome for some unemployed and undernourished villagers. A new boma and new prison were built during our first nine months, and the old buildings were demolished; it is a pity they were not preserved as historical monuments. (The DC's house, built 1901, and another old house are now preserved as such.)

From the boma eastwards there was a lovely 110 yard avenue of tall blue-gum trees. The first large plot on this side was where the new boma was built in early 1963, its open-square design intentionally built around a beautiful spreading tree. There followed seven houses, all facing the airstrip: the one at the end was ours. Beyond this was just thick bush and a gravel pit.

That two-bedroomed little house, the first proper home of our own in married life, was all we needed. It had a prolific pawpaw tree at the side. Within the first few days Wendy had taken on a cook (Black Mpundu) and a house-servant (James), on recommendations from other officers, and a young orphan, Jimmy, to do the gardening. Fairly soon we had created a vegetable garden at the back and constructed a chicken house. It took rather longer to get the front garden looking reasonable, within its semi-circular driveway – an unnecessary amenity as we didn't have or need (and couldn't afford) a car for our first three years, and went locally on foot until we could afford a bicycle. At the end of every garden was a small two-roomed house for one servant and his family – in our case, Black.

Mail and meat came once a week from Kasama on the bus; groceries, newspapers and other supplies arrived once a month from Lusaka. This meant that we had to wait some three weeks before we received responses from parents to our letters, and maybe a month before we heard of an event on the wider world's stage such as the Cuban crisis. But we didn't feel deprived of anything of real value.

On Saturday afternoons, tennis (in whites) on the court behind the DC's house was virtually compulsory; the best silver teapot was brought out for interval refreshments and the wives took it in turn to bake a cake. Ernest Cruchley often cycled over from Kashinda Mission to join us in this, and when his wife Kathie came she sometimes taught the other wives how to cut their men's hair.

We certainly enjoyed a full social life. The successive bachelor DCs were especially generous in their hospitality and, of course, invited all the few Europeans along when they had visiting civil servants to stay with them. Monopoly and bridge were quite common evening entertainments. Sometimes the White Fathers came across to one of us; I recall Father Deslauriers tucking his arm through his rosary to play games of rounders with vigour on the airstrip.

Despite the impressions the previous paragraphs might have given, we were all breaking the old racial and class barriers in socialising. The DCs and the Collingwoods hosted several parties which included all the senior African staff and their wives, and we danced. Wendy put on a hilarious New Year's Eve party in our small house, to which all the African staff and friends listed above came. And we had several to meals with us on other occasions. Senior Chief Nsama and Chief Shibwalya Kapila both felt able to drop in on us casually several times, and we had easy chats with them over either tea or beers without a hint of awkwardness on either side (Shibwalya Kapila as an ex-teacher was happy to converse in English – or, for my language benefit, to switch in and out of ciBemba in a teasing fashion – while with Nsama I had to stick to ciBemba). We went to the school plays and concerts and I became involved in school sports and the Scouts.

On the official work side, the day started at 7.30 a.m. on Monday to Saturday, with the DC inspecting the parade of District Messengers and, in consultation with the Head Messenger, allocating them their duties. These might be for the day or for a week, when those being sent off to distant parts on their bicycles might need to draw an imprest, in order to hire local gangs for bridge- or road-repairing jobs.

My main regular responsibilities included the supervision of the boma accounts, including weekly checks, the monthly receipt and counting of cash sent to us on the bus (!), and running the monthly pay parade for all DMs and junior boma staff. I was also involved with the NA (Native Authority) Treasuries, carrying out monthly checks of draft trial balances. This normally entailed visits to the NA headquarters at Chishamwamba, Nsama and Mukupa Kaoma.

The checking of all Native Court records and the collection of fines imposed was another task. (Local Customary Law was upheld/encouraged so long as it was not incompatible with English legal ethics.) I was also responsible for the NA Buildings Programme, which meant I had to inspect the progress on all constructions, pay over the Government subsidies on them and prepare estimates/plans for the following year. I was also Transport Officer concerned with matching staff needs with available vehicles and checking the regular maintenance of vehicles.

Additionally, my main one-off exercises included: running a district-wide film-show tour to explain the voting procedure for the first (limited suffrage) elections in October 1962; running the Census over the whole district in June 1963; planning constituency and polling area boundaries from the Census figures ready for the (first full suffrage) 1964 elections; and running and supervising the first complete district-wide registration of voters for the 1964 elections. I also ran a Native Courts' Staff course and two one-week refresher courses for District Messengers and *Kapasus* (NA Messengers), giving them talks on Native Authorities and taking them for drill. In addition I assisted the DC in negotiating with the six Chiefs on the plans to create a new District Council (local government), to involve them together with elected local politicians. I was also Secretary of the District Education Authority.

Village tours were highlights for me – very instructive and great fun – although I was not permitted to undertake one until I had gained some experience. I went by bicycle with the senior NA staff, three DMs, two or three *Kapasus* and about ten porters; and I always took Black, my cook. I had only three tours: two covering Chief Mukupa Kaoma's area and one Chief Shibwalya Kapila's area, with the Chief himself.

My diary's day-to-day record of what I found and did in each village on these tours makes fascinating rereading for me, and of course I still have copies of my formal twenty-page tour reports. I should like to have toured with Chief Mukupa Kaoma, but he was away at the House of Chiefs each time. My diary has this entry regarding my tour with Chief Shibwalya Kapila:

> [In one village] I talked for a long time on development and probably made my best speech so far, the Chief expanding on my themes in forceful terms. He is a good speaker. He talks fast, excitedly and with conviction, playing his audience along with a great sense of humour and then crushing them with his climactic point...The Chief came round to my tent for supper with me and we had a good long chat on all sorts of subjects.

During our first six months the school for the blind was being built, at the White Fathers' Mission across the airstrip from our house, and we watched the progress with frequent visits. Trachoma and river blindness were quite prevalent, especially in the lower-lying northern parts of the district. Initially the school took about a hundred children, but it was planned to double in size later. Some 20–30 per cent were albinos. These usually had a progressive visual impairment caused by lack of pigmentation, rather than full blindness. Wearing sunglasses seemed to offer some benefit to them, yet we had no idea why the albino gene should be so common in this region. Father Carrière, who ran the school, was marvellous with the children, and so innovative. He conned a gullible business company into giving him a film projector (!), saying 'We like to give the blind children every experience,' though really it was for the benefit of the boma. We have so many happy memories of this place and of Father Carrière. The Governor formally opened the school in May 1963.

The size of the district was around 9,460 square miles. It contained the areas of three tribes and six Chiefs: two Bemba (Mporokoso and Shibwalya Kapila) and two Lungu (Mukupa Kaoma and Chitoshi) on the high ground, and two Tabwa (Senior Chief Nsama and Mukupa Katandula) below and north of the Muchinga escarpment. The two Lungu Chiefs were subordinate to Senior Chief Tafuna in Abercorn District.

Mukupa Kaoma was always my favourite *musumba* (Chief's headquarters) and I visited it more than any other place – seventeen times in our first year, Wendy being with me on four of these occasions. My impressions of the place and of the Chief are shown in this quotation from my diary entry for 11 September 1962, my first visit there.

> Mukupa Kaoma is a really beautiful spot; a neat *musumba* with a fine office block, and the whole village very well irrigated. There's a lot of building going on, a dispensary and some individual voluntary building under the supervision of Duncan Banda from the Rural Development extension team. Having finished the accounts with Anthony Chipasha soon after lunch (the Lungu have almost no money!), I looked round all the building projects with the Chief. He is a most impressive person, only young middle-aged, intelligent, and well in command of what is going on in his area. He does a lot of work in the office too, and thus gets double respect from his people, from the older people just as a Chief, from the younger and more educated ones as an administrator too. In the evening I went for a walk round the *musumba* with my camera. The little rest-house there is in a most perfect spot, perched on the crest of an escarpment with a magnificent view for 40 miles south, and a bubbling waterfall within a stone's throw. It's a joy to go there.

The northern, Tabwa, part of the district, lying below the (northern, west–east) Muchinga escarpment, was the most interesting. For a start, it had two game reserves.

Mweru-wa-Ntipa is a lake and swamp system that has been something of a mystery as its water level and salinity fluctuate so much. This is not entirely explained by variation in rainfall levels. In fact it has been known to dry out almost completely. What is more, sometimes its waters flow slowly through the Mofwe dambo into the Kalungwishi River, while at others they flow from the river into the lake. The Mweru-wa-Ntipa Game Reserve, which included the lake, was one of the least known.

What I vividly recall is that, as soon as we entered the reserve, the geology and botany changed. Woodland was replaced by dense and impenetrable thickets of lower bush. This I later learnt was the rare 'Itigi-Sumbu thicket vegetation', a variety endemic to this region; the only other place with the same variety is in central Tanzania. Typically it is made up of over a hundred plant species woven together so tightly that a person is unable to walk through them. Even elephants forcing their way through these thickets barely leave tracks as the shrubs spring back to their original position. (This area was, in 2012, being actively researched by Kew Gardens experts, fearful that it may disappear.)

Kaputa, at the north end of the reserve and lake, was just a small outpost of the Native Authority, but it had an 'unofficial' dispensary. It was 'unofficial' in that it had been built by a former DC of Mporokoso out of his 'roads budget', to help our good friend the Provincial Medical Officer, who then had to juggle his accounts to provide drugs and medical aids for this 'non-existent' dispensary. Kaputa was only some 12 miles from the Congo border to the north, and the dispensary received many patients from the Congo who had no such facilities (it has now been replaced by a large hospital, still catering for numerous Congolese).

Some 20 miles along the road eastwards was the International Red Locust Control Service (IRLCS) station at Kangiri – another unusual topic of interest in the district. The areas surrounding Lake Mweru-wa-Ntipa and Lake Rukwa in southern Tanzania have for centuries been breeding grounds for red locusts. The vegetation on the west and north sides of Mweru-wa-Ntipa is especially favourable for locust breeding; records show there were widespread plagues in the years 1892–1910 and 1928–33, with swarms migrating from these lakes to the Congo and elsewhere. The IRLCS was formally established in 1949, with headquarters in Abercorn.

The eastern shores of Mweru-wa-Ntipa supported a flourishing fishing industry, despite the irregular cyclical decreases in the lake's water level. There were several large and attractive fishing villages along the banks. Kampinda was the main source of fish exports from the lake, having the best dirt-road access from the south and so attracting the most traders – which in turn encouraged more activity by the fishermen themselves. The lake supported a large population of hippos and crocodiles, too, and was a paradise for those keen on spotting birds and waterfowl.

Near Chief Nsama's *musumba* was the interesting village of Abdullah bin Selemani, This was one of only three recognised 'Swahili enclaves' in the country – a legacy of Tippu Tib's slave-trading operations; the others were near Ndola (its 'slave tree') and at Sumbu. The residents had a mosque, all claimed to be Muslim (many dressed accordingly) and all understood kiSwahili; but they mostly spoke ciBemba and called themselves Tabwa.

We went to Sumbu on the shore of Lake Tanganyika quite often, combining business with pleasure. It had a very small resthouse, a jetty, a petrol pump, fish-sheds and one lone European resident (an ex-White Father who had had to leave holy orders after marrying a local girl), an NA clerk collecting fish levies and not much else. It was idyllic. One came out of the reserve to the top of an escarpment, from which there was a magnificent view across the lake. We bathed, despite the water-snakes. Several animals came down to drink at dusk and dawn, and the noise of nearby hippos lulled us to sleep.

The other delights of the district were the waterfalls, particularly the series of five magnificent falls on the Kalungwishi River.

All in all, Mporokoso District was one of the most varied and attractive one could find, and we had two wonderful years there.

8

KABOMPO

Tony Schur

'I managed to get hold of some specifications for a basic airstrip but was faced with the problem of having no funds for its construction.'

It was some time before I realised why my sausages tasted different from those I had been used to. It was because they had spent two days travelling from the Copperbelt to Kabompo through the African heat on the twice-weekly bus.

Kabompo boma is the headquarters of Kabompo District in the North Western Province of Zambia. To get there you had to travel for 300 miles along a dirt road from the Copperbelt mining town of Chingola, which lies on the country's main north–south road and rail system. Although the road was reasonably well maintained, it could become difficult to use during the rainy season, when the bus could take even longer to reach us. Twenty miles before the boma all vehicles had to drive on to a floating pontoon so that they could be pulled by hand across the Kabompo River, a major tributary of the Zambezi.

Because of its remoteness the boma had been chosen as the place where Kenneth Kaunda, then leader of the main African political party, had been held in detention in 1959, when fears grew that serious unrest could arise over the continuation of the

Central African Federation. Five years later, following what had become a pattern in British colonial Africa, Kaunda became the first President of the newly independent Zambia.

The district was home to about 30,000 people, who were spread fairly thinly over some 10,000 square miles of poor sandy soil and thick bush. Most families supported themselves through subsistence farming, with some men earning money from working on the Copperbelt or in the mines in South Africa. There was also a limited amount of trading in food and other local products, some of which was done on a barter basis. Generally, people were very poor.

Being a small place and distant from anywhere else, Kabompo boma did not have an electricity supply or a telephone connection, although we were fortunate to have a piped water system, which had been installed a few months before my arrival. Previously, people had had to carry water up a steep bank from the river, on whose bank the boma was built.

Apart from the bus which brought and took away our mail, our main means of communication with the outside world was a radio telephone link with the provincial headquarters in Solwezi and the other districts in the province. This link was scheduled to be open for an hour in the morning and an hour in the afternoon. A small diesel generator, which had to be started by hand, was used to charge the batteries which powered the radio.

The administrative team in Kabompo was small. For my first few months, for example, there was only Dick Beck, the District Commissioner (DC), and me. Later we were joined for short periods by others, including Progress Mulala, an African District Assistant (DA), who was soon promoted to be our District Officer (DO) before being posted elsewhere as one of the country's first African DCs, and then Stephen Napier Bax, a British DO, who had previously served in Kenya. After a few months with us he was transferred to the Secretariat in Lusaka. We were also assisted for separate periods by Mark Sheldrake and Douglas Clarke, two young DAs from the UK. Mark had been in Kabompo before I arrived, when he had been stabbed (see below), and had then been away doing his National Service in Southern Rhodesia. After a few weeks he was moved away to another post. Douglas was later transferred to Eastern Province, but not before he had organised a successful Agricultural Show attended by the Hon. Elijah Mudenda, Minister of Agriculture in the pre-Independence Government.[1]

In the early months of 1964 Dick Beck, who by now had become a good friend, retired and was replaced by a new African DC, Ackson Mwale. The team was completed by a small number of male clerks, who looked after the book-keeping, filing and typing, and by eighteen or so District Messengers, who had the powers of police constables, but who were answerable to us. Some of them had served in Malaya with the Northern Rhodesia Regiment during the emergency there and wore their campaign ribbon with pride.

Also at the boma were a Community Development Officer (CDO), who together with his wife ran the Development Area Training Centre, which taught a range of skills to both men and women, and an Agriculture Officer, who left after a few months on being posted elsewhere. The CDO was replaced on retirement by D'Arcy Payne, who recounts some of his experiences in Chapter 2. For some of the time we were also joined by, successively, a British buildings foreman and a South African roads foreman.

Kabompo was unusual for the diversity of its community, with members of nine different tribes living within its borders. Some of them had come into the district in the distant past from the Congo to the north; others were more recent arrivals from Angola in the west; and some had connections with Barotseland, a distinctive area of Zambia to the south of Kabompo, and now renamed Western Province. Each of these tribes, of which the most prominent were the Chokwe, the Luchazi, the Lunda, the Luvale and the Mbunda, had more members living outside the district than in it.

The difficulties between the tribes were evident in two main ways: a resistance to the authority of the Senior Chief by some of the tribes, particularly those who were more recent arrivals in the district, and a historic rivalry between the Lunda and the Luvale.

The Senior Chief in the district, Sikufele, who was also head of the district's Native Authority, was an Mbunda with links to the royal family of Barotseland, which in the past had included the area of Kabompo District in its territory. There were two other Chiefs, Chiyengele, another Mbunda, and Kalunga, a Luchazi, both of whom had authority over small parts of the district. The Luchazi, who were relative newcomers to Kabompo, did not accept Sikufele's authority, even though many of them lived in his area. The Lunda by contrast, who had been in the district for a long time, did support him. Thus the tribes tended to split into two factions, with the Luchazi and Luvale, who were opposed to the Senior Chief, on one side, and the Lunda and Mbunda, on the other.

About six months after I arrived, matters between the two sides came to a head. It had become the practice for many members of the Luchazi and allied tribes who lived in Sikufele's area to take their cases to Kalunga's court, which was closer to them than any of Sikufele's. The policy which we had to implement was to reinforce the authority of Sikufele and the Native Authority. Behind this policy was the British colonial practice of governing by means of Indirect Rule, which meant that instead of merely imposing our will directly, as other European nations did, we managed affairs through indigenous institutions in the form of Chiefs and their councils. One of the aims behind Indirect Rule was that the Native Authorities, which the Chiefs and their councils had become, would evolve with our support into democratic local authorities.

Our aim was to establish a new court in the part of Sikufele's area that was occupied by those Luchazi and Chokwe who had been making use of Kalunga's court. As part of this process the DC, Senior Chief Sikufele and I, accompanied by four Native Authority members and the Senior District Messenger, held a meeting at the site of the proposed new court to seek a nomination for a Luchazi Court Assessor. The principle that the court and the area in which it was situated would continue to be under Sikufele's jurisdiction was not up for discussion. After a peaceful start some of those attending the meeting became agitated and

Plate 1   Cambridge Course photograph, 1962

Back (L to R)   AC, AC, David Taylor, John Shaw, Max Keyzar, AC, AC, Robert Humphreys, AC, AC

Middle (L to R)   AC, Jeremy Burnham, John Theakstone, Neil Morris, Richard Pelly, Mick Bond, John Woodmansey, Jim Lavender, John Edwards, Paul Wigram

Front (L to R)   AC, Lazarus Mwanza, AC, AC, Tony Schur, Hugh McLeery (Course Director), Course Secretary, Malcolm Mitchell, Stephen Karamagi, David Alexander, Valentine Musakanya

Absent   Tony Goddard, Jonathan Leach, Peter Moss, D'Arcy Payne

AC denotes member of Agriculture Course

Plate 2a   Kabompo boma, 1964

Plate 2b   Inspecting District Messengers, Mkushi, 1960

Plate 3a   Old house, built in 1904, Mporokoso

Plate 3b   DO's house, Kabompo, 1962, new style

Plate 4a Prison inspection, Mkushi, 1960

Plate 4b Swimming pool, Mporokoso, 1963

Plate 5a   On tour: erecting the tent, Kabompo, 1963

*Plate 5b   On tour: 'one found only the very old and women and children in the villages',
Mkushi, 1960*

Plate 6a   On tour: an ideal village, Mkushi, 1960

Plate 6b   On tour: citimene – *garden in the bush prepared for sowing millet in the ash, Mporokoso, 1964*

Plate 7a   On tour: the millet harvest slowly becoming flour, Kasama, 1964

Plate 7b   On tour: and so on to the next village...

Plate 8a   District Messenger and prisoner on the way to the boma

Plate 8b   A welcome lift, Kasama, 1964

aggressive. We decided the most sensible course was to retreat, in the process of which a few members of our party were man-handled and threatened.

It was agreed in discussions with the Provincial Commissioner (PC), Hugh Bayldon, that we needed to re-establish our authority and that of the Senior Chief and Native Authority by mounting a show of force in the area and arresting the ringleaders of what had in effect been a riot. And so a few days later a party of about a hundred people including District Messengers from Kabompo and other districts in the province, a platoon of the Police Mobile Unit from the Copperbelt, some other police and a few *Kapasus* (similar to District Messengers but employed by the Native Authority) gathered at the boma to prepare for the exercise. The plan was for a dawn raid into the area with the DC in charge, supported by the PC and a senior police officer.

During the day before the raid I was sent to the area with three Messengers, ostensibly to carry out some road work but with the primary aim of gathering some intelligence. We heard that a mass meeting of Luchazi was planned. On the way back we had to deal with half a dozen trees felled across the road. Later that evening my task was to supervise the fuelling of all the vehicles which would be used the next day. The boma petrol pump, which was inside a compound surrounded by a high wire fence, was hand-operated by Daniel, our store man. As it was dark I decided, in an act of staggering idiocy, to light a paraffin lamp so that we could see what we were doing. There was a loud explosion, which startled Daniel, who was lame and walked with the aid of a stick, to such an extent that he was over the top of the 8-foot-high fence and on his way to safety in the blink of an eye. Fortunately, he was unhurt and neither the pump nor the vehicles were damaged, so that we were able to complete our task.

My next act of over-enthusiasm occurred the next morning. We set off before dawn in around fifteen vehicles for the area where the riot had taken place. My job was to be at the rear of the convoy, making sure there were no problems out of the sight of the DC and PC, who were at the front. As we neared the villages, where arrests were planned, the Messengers who were with me excitedly pointed out a man watching us from about 50 yards away. I was told he was Mbowela, one of the leaders of those most opposed to the Senior Chief. Assuming without a moment's thought that he ought to be arrested, I chased him across the dambo, caught up with him as he was trying to cross a stream and jumped on top of him. The Messengers, who had followed, then took him back to the Land Rover.

Meanwhile the main force had met some resistance from some of the villagers armed with knives and clubs. This was overcome at the expense of a few minor injuries, and a number of arrests were made. At a stop to regroup, Mbowela, whom I had transferred to a lorry, caused a commotion which the DC and PC came to investigate. It turned out that he was not on our list of those to be arrested, since we did not have evidence that he had been involved in the riot. He was, therefore, released and given some money to compensate him for the damage caused to his trousers during his capture. Needless to say, the PC had a few words with me about my contribution to the exercise.

I got into hot water again during the trial of those we had arrested. The cases were heard in Balovale (now renamed Zambezi) by a Resident Magistrate, who had been flown up from Lusaka for the hearings. When giving evidence as a witness for the prosecution I was called to order by the magistrate for arguing over-enthusiastically with the lawyer who was defending the accused. I was reminded that I was there to answer the questions, which were being asked on behalf of the court, and not to take part in a debate. At the end of the trial most of the defendants received short prison sentences. Unfortunately this was not the end of the matter, for shortly after they were released the new court-house, which had been the source of the trouble, was burnt down.

What struck me later, reflecting on this whole incident, was that the policy of Indirect Rule did not work effectively in places such as Kabompo, where a sizeable part of the population did not accept the authority of the Senior Chief nor of the Native Authority, which was closely associated with him. It seems to me, looking back, that the administration of the district and its development, both economically and administratively, was held back by the continual need to deal with these tribal difficulties. [Appendix 2 contains more information about Native Authorities and Indirect Rule. *Ed.*]

Matters did improve, however, during the months leading to Independence, as the Native Authority was reformed. New councillors were elected, the Chiefs ceased to be members and the authority's base was moved from where the Senior Chief had his headquarters to the boma. These changes enabled the new authority to become more widely accepted. At the same time a new court was established, peacefully, close to where the riot had taken place, under Sikufele's jurisdiction but with a Luchazi Court Assessor.

Happily, life as a Cadet in Kabompo involved much more than dealing with the effects of tribal difficulties. A major part of our work was concerned with administrative matters. These included touring areas of the district for a couple of weeks at a time accompanied by a whole team of people, usually including the local Native Court Assessor, representing the Chief, the court clerk, a Native Authority councillor, a boma clerk, a District Messenger and a *Kapasu* as well as my cook and several carriers, who would take all the equipment, including my tent, each day from one base to the next. In the villages we visited we would listen to matters the headman and his people wished to raise with us, talk to them about topics we wanted to discuss, take a census, encourage the payment of taxes, visit any local schools and check how the crops were growing.

At one stage it became clear that in one area the cassava crop, which was the major source of food in the district, was failing. In conjunction with the Native Authority we arranged to bring in a new variety of cassava plants to replace those that were dying, as well as supplies of cassava meal to ensure there would be enough food until the next harvest.

Crops could also be devastated by herds of elephants and, if the problem was severe, the Game Department would be called in to shoot one in order to drive the herd away. I was offered the chance to join one of these exercises. Having had some practice shots with the rifle I had been lent in order to get the feel of it and to test its sights, I travelled with a game guard to the village, where this particular herd had been causing problems. After camping overnight we set off early in the morning accompanied by a local tracker. Several hours later we caught up with the herd, which was spending the daylight hours in a patch of thick bush. As we got closer I could hear a loud pounding sound. At first I thought this must be coming from the elephants, but then I realised it was my own heart beating with the tension and excitement. We then had a clear sight of the one which was to be our target. I fired first, as agreed, with the game guard's shot following almost immediately. Sadly the animal did not fall there and then but fled with the rest of the herd. We spent the rest of the day and most of the next day tracking them so that we could dispatch the one we had wounded. I then had to return to the boma, but the game guard and tracker continued their search, finally finding the animal dead a day or two later.

One of the responsibilities of the DC and his team was to work with the Native Authority and help it to evolve into an effective local government organisation. In my case this meant I had to spend time once a month checking the authority's accounts, probably the only task we had to carry out for which we had had no training on the Cambridge Course.

We also had overall responsibility for law and order. Although as a Cadet I was authorised to hear cases as a Class IV Magistrate with the power to impose very small penalties, I never had an opportunity to act in this capacity. I did, however, perform the role of prosecutor in two cases, achieving a conviction in one but not the other. Another important responsibility was to carry out regular checks of the records kept by the different Native Courts to ensure that the cases heard did not contravene the regulations governing the courts or go against what we believed to be the principles of natural justice.

One of the larger sums of money we received each year was for the maintenance of roads and bridges. Supervising the repair or replacement of bridges was an occasional activity I enjoyed.

They were constructed using the trunks of trees which grew near to the site of the bridge, using wooden pegs cut from branches to lock the timbers together. When finished they had to be strong enough to carry the weight of a loaded lorry, but with sufficient spaces between the timbers to allow the swollen river to flow through during storms in the rainy season. I was always impressed by the level of skills and know-how displayed when this type of work was carried out.

About half-way through my time in Kabompo I was given responsibility for constructing an airstrip. This arose because the hostility between the Lunda and the Luvale had given rise to an unfortunate incident a few months before my arrival. Because of a central Government policy that only one local language could be used for teaching in each school, a Lunda man, who objected to his daughter being taught in the Luvale language, removed her from school. This was in contravention of the Native Authority's requirement that children of her age should attend school. The father was, therefore, made to appear before the Native Court at the boma.

On being found guilty he became aggressive and threatening and was, therefore, immediately taken before Dick Beck, so that the case could be reviewed. A fracas broke out, in the course of which he escaped and went off into the bush pursued by some Messengers. Tragically the episode ended with the deaths of the father and one of the Messengers. What saved these events from having wider repercussions was the fact that the Africans most deeply involved were all members of the same tribe.

During the commotion both Dick and Mark Sheldrake, who had gone to his assistance, received deep stab wounds. They were taken to the only doctor in the district, who worked at a small mission hospital about 20 miles away. It became clear that the only way their lives could be saved was by having them treated at a major hospital, but this presented a problem in that there was a risk that they would not survive the journey along a hundred miles of dirt road to the nearest airfield. Fortunately there was for the first time ever a helicopter in the province, working for one of the mining companies. This was quickly made available to transport them to Balovale, from where they were flown to Lusaka in an ambulance-plane. Both made virtually complete recoveries.

The difficulty of transporting Dick and Mark to hospital after this incident had made us realise that we needed to find a way for small aircraft to get in and out of the district. I managed to get hold of some specifications for a basic airstrip, but was faced with the problem of having no funds allocated for its construction. We decided to use an existing straight stretch of road, about 5 miles from the boma, as the basis for the runway, on the grounds that the area was already partially cleared and the earth was compacted from having been driven over. The road itself was easily diverted around the site. Trees were felled and stumps removed from the prescribed areas at the sides and ends of the runway with the co-operation of some of the boma prisoners, and fan-shaped areas at the two ends for the aircraft approaches were created by reducing the height of the trees that stood in the way. Finally, the driver of the big Roads Department grader, who was working on the main road through Kabompo, was persuaded to spend half a day smoothing the runway. A few days later, with some whitewashed planks marking the strip and a newly acquired windsock flying, the plane coming to test the facility arrived, and after flying low down the length of the runway to inspect it, made another approach and landed safely. The landing-ground was then given a basic operating certificate and is still in existence today.

One of our main concerns was to promote economic development. This was not an easy task. Although many of the people in Kabompo were energetic and forward-looking with a wide range of skills, there were few natural resources and the district was a long way from the main centres of population. Over the years many ideas had been explored. One of the skills of the local people was fishing, so the possibility of starting up some fish farms was investigated. However, the distance from Kabompo to the Copperbelt and the fact that the markets there were already well supplied meant that an investment in this activity was unlikely to be successful. Expansion of groundnut production was also felt to be unsustainable for the same reasons. The growing and curing of Turkish tobacco appeared more promising, and a small number of trial schemes were set up. We also brought in the services of an apiarist to advise local beekeepers on how to increase the production of honey and beeswax for sale. Nurturing colonies of wild bees and harvesting their products was a well-established activity in the district. It is pleasing that this industry has developed further in recent years, and that Kabompo honey has been exported to the UK.

At one stage we were offered some sheep of a superior variety with a view to improving the quality of the existing stock in Kabompo. I volunteered to collect them, as the trip would enable me to have a weekend away, staying in Kasempa with Paul Wigram, whose reminiscences are set out in Chapter 16. The evening before my return we loaded the sheep on to the lorry, counting them carefully so that I could sign a receipt for them. Half-way back I thought I ought to check that they were all safe and sound, as it had been a cold night. To my horror I found that one had died. In my panic I decided that the best course was to get rid of it, and so I seized it by all four legs and hurled it into the bush. I spent the rest of the journey worrying how I was going to explain the loss of this expensive creature to the DC. Expecting to have to confess to my incompetence immediately on my arrival back at Kabompo boma, I found the DC was away from his office. We, therefore, unloaded the sheep and, counting them, found that I had returned with precisely the right number. It was some days before I told anyone the full story.

Adventures with vehicles seemed to be a recurring theme of my time in Kabompo. Returning on another occasion with a load of concrete culvert pipes after spending Christmas in Kasempa, I was distracted by a young dog I had just acquired and drove off the edge of the road. The ground was soft as it was the rainy season, and I was unable to coax the lorry back on to the hard surface. Remembering I had just passed a village, I walked back to it and found the men in good form, as they were still celebrating the festival. Although I could not speak Kaonde (the language of the people in Kasempa district) and they had no English, we managed to agree that they would help me sort out the problem. With the aid of trees cut from the bush we managed to roll the culvert pipes, each of them extremely heavy, off the lorry and then lever the vehicle out of its resting place. The hard task of rolling the pipes back up the trees leant against the side of the lorry then took place. After paying my helpers the agreed sum we parted the best of friends. My difficulties with that journey did not end there, however, for I ran out of petrol just short of the Kabompo River crossing and had to sleep in the cab until the pontoon began to operate again in the morning. I then had a 3-mile walk to a mission run by the Plymouth Brethren, where I was able to borrow some petrol to get me back to the boma.

On another occasion I was returning with a Messenger from a visit to a remote mission station in the north of the district, when the engine of the ancient Land Rover we were in spluttered and died. I suspected that one of the jets in the carburettor had become blocked with dust, because the previous day I had been driving through waist-high grass. The vehicle had no tools, and to complicate matters a wall of fire, several hundred yards long, was being blown towards us from where the local people had been burning grass. The Messenger, who had run back to the nearest village, managed to borrow a screwdriver and some bicycle spanners. With these it was a simple matter to dismantle the carburettor, blow through the jets and reassemble it. We drove away just before the fire reached the road, grateful for the motor maintenance training I had received on the Cambridge Course.

I was, however, unable to make the necessary repairs the next time I had a problem with a vehicle engine. About 30 miles from Kabompo boma, on the way to Balovale with half a dozen Messengers, the engine of the vanette began to make a loud metallic sound. Stopping to investigate, I found that the engine had lost its sump plug, with the result that all the oil had drained away. I had no means of making telephone or radio contact with anyone to obtain help, and it could have been two or three hours before another vehicle came along. As the purpose of the journey was to take reinforcements for an imminent operation to make some arrests following a tribal dispute at Chavuma on the border between Balovale and Angola, I decided the best course was to try to get to a mission a few miles further on, where I might get some assistance. The engine started and, to my surprise, we managed to drive slowly all the way to the mission, where I was able to persuade the missionary in charge to lend us his vehicle, which we used to get to our destination and back. The engine of the boma vanette was, unsurprisingly, a write-off.

At Chavuma I found myself taking part in an event which had an element of farce. On the evening before the planned exercise, three of us crossed the border into Angola for discussions with the Portuguese authorities, who were anxious about the situation. Arriving at their boma we found that none of them could speak English, while none of us could manage any Portuguese. And so it came about that these important dealings between representatives of the British and Portuguese empires were conducted in schoolboy French, which one of them and I could just about manage.

In January 1964 a general election was held to elect the members of a new National Assembly, which would take office straight away, and a president, who would assume power after Independence in October. This election was the first in which everybody over the age of twenty-one had been able to vote and attracted huge interest. In the weeks before, I made several visits to different parts of the district to explain the voting process to well-attended meetings. As many people were unable to read, the ballot-papers incorporated representative symbols chosen by the different parties. On the day of the election long queues formed at the polling-stations as people waited patiently to record their votes. This was a remarkable sight, and it was good that, except for one small incident of fighting between members of two of the parties, the whole election campaign in Kabompo was a peaceful affair.

A few weeks after the election I decided to resign when I heard that the new Government had chosen to release from prison a number of people, whom it described as political prisoners. It seemed to me that those concerned had actually been convicted of criminal offences and that to release them would undermine the rule of law and set an unfortunate precedent for the future. A futile gesture? Probably. Certainly one in which idealism triumphed over realism.

Shortly before I left Kabompo I had a chance meeting with Mbowela, whom I had leapt on in a stream in my early days in the district. He was very friendly and grinned broadly. I was not sure whether this was because he was pleased that I was going, or because he remembered our first meeting with amusement. I like to think it was for the latter reason.

Note

1 Elijah Mudenda later became Finance Minister, then Foreign Minister before holding the post of Prime Minister for two years.

9

CHINGOLA, ELISABETHVILLE (KATANGA), LUSAKA

Valentine Musakanya

'I have found out that although I love Zambia so much, I perhaps love a truthful approach more, because only the latter will make her truly free.'

Although they had little money, Valentine Musakanya's family were determined that he should receive a good education and he was sent to Kutama, a leading African school in Southern Rhodesia. Joining the pre-Independence Civil Service he rose to the highest level available to an African before being recommended for promotion to District Officer and attending the Overseas Services Course in Cambridge. During his time in the Civil Service he studied for a degree by correspondence course with Fort Hare University in South Africa.

After Independence he held a number of senior posts in the public service of the new Zambia, including Cabinet Secretary and Governor of the Bank of Zambia. In 1980 he was arrested on suspicion of being involved in a planned coup attempt. Together with others he was convicted of treason in 1983 and sentenced to death. Permanently damaged physically by his time in prison, he was acutely upset by one further indignity – not being allowed to attend the funerals of his parents. In 1985 he was acquitted on appeal on the grounds that the only evidence against him was a confession which had been obtained by torture. He died in 1994.

It was perhaps inevitable that he would fall out with President Kaunda and other members of the post-Independence United National Independence Party (UNIP) Government. He was a highly intelligent and independent-minded man with firm views on how government should work and how a newly independent nation should be helped to develop. In 1968 he resigned from the post of Cabinet Secretary when he became aware of plans to politicise the Civil Service. Four years later he was removed from his position as Governor of the Bank of Zambia after he submitted a defence of the multi-party state and an independent Civil Service to a Commission set up to develop a new constitution.

The following passages are extracts from Valentine Musakanya's writings, which he began secretly whilst in detention and did not revise.

Early years in Northern Province

I was born in 1932 at Nkunkulusha's village in Kalundu country of Bembaland...Kalundu is that large piece of land to the west of Kasama...The land is a watershed between the Lukulu and Lubasenshi on the one hand and the Bangweulu on the other. It is a low plateau from which perennial cool and really beautiful streams, protected by magnificent tree groves called *mishitu*, flow into these two rivers...

Schooling...was mostly reading, writing (on the floor of the thatch-roofed classroom open on both sides) and some arithmetic. Very little time was spent in class in a day, because in addition to working in the teacher's garden and sweeping the school area, we had to have enough time for cooking and drawing water from the stream which was a good distance away.

1944 to 1949: Copperbelt

In early 1944 my mother returned to the village expressly to take me with her to [Kitwe]. Wusakile [a township in Kitwe] was a vast, treeless habitat of tens of thousands of people in 2,000 box-like corrugated roof huts standing in rows one after another. It was a new African mine compound or township built since the beginning of the war. The decision to build the new housing was expedited by the African strike of 1939 ... Previously the mines did not cater for African labour with families; miners had to leave their wives at the village. Were it not for the intervention of World War II, the situation would have possibly continued like this and the history of Zambia could have accordingly been different. The advent of the war increased demand for copper as a strategic metal, but at the same time reduced the flow of European labour to the mines. In the circumstances, the high turnover of African labour induced by the non-availability of family accommodation became an obstacle to the war effort. The disturbances further emphasised African labour instability. Thus, the mines began to encourage employees to have their families join them and started building 'appropriate' housing. Wusakile was built between 1940 and 1942 for married employees, leaving the old compound exclusively for bachelors ...

There was at that time compulsory education on the Copperbelt. Accordingly, I had to be presented to the school as soon as possible. I was taken to Wusakile African School, where Mr Thawe was taking over from Mr Harry Nkumbula as Headmaster.[1] I went on the first day and thereafter faithfully moved with the early morning stream of school-going children, only to turn away with friends into the nearby bush to trap birds. We would be back by the end of the day's school session to join the others going home. I played truant in this way for a couple of months, until the Attendance Officer reported that I had never attended school. My father, who was on a night shift, promised to take me to school the following morning ... When we reached the school, I was led directly to the Headmaster's office, where he demanded that I be punished in his presence forthwith. I was mercilessly caned by Mr Nkumbula. He was somewhat soft afterwards and tried to console me, asking me why I did not like going to school. In defiance, I had the courage to tell him that it was because they put me in Sub A when I already knew how to read. He laughed and brought out some Bemba text which he gave me to test my reading. With much annoyance and injured pride I read (recited!) every chapter given to me from Sub A to Standard I books. They were very impressed with my reading and my diction. The Headmaster said that they should first try me in Sub B. I was quite happy with this decision.

After three months in Sub B it was decided to move me to Standard I. This frightened me because I did not really know how to write and there would be an examination in four months' time. Accordingly I began staying at home when not at school, just to practise writing. I failed Standard I and had to repeat in the 1945–6 school year. I soon found the trick to writing and took the lead in the class. In 1946 I went to Standard II and in 1947 to Standard III, still top of the class. After four months, I was promoted to Standard IV. There was a row about this, but quite a few of my teachers thought I was ready for the Standard IV examination. I passed Standard IV in May 1948 with nearly 100 per cent marks. This turning of a new leaf may sound rather dramatic but given the circumstances I do not think it was...I was given a tremendous morale boost by the promotions, and wished to meet the challenge...

The Catholic church in Wusakile was perhaps the most important social centre in the compound, with regular daily activities...Since the majority of the residents were from Northern Province, the majority of practising Christians were also Catholics. So most afternoons I was at the church and I served at Mass in the morning. A new library [was] set up at the Welfare Centre, accompanied by a literacy campaign by the Government. Having learnt to write Bemba, I quickly learnt to read and write English. I became obsessed with reading and tried to read every written matter I came across, including newspaper pieces found in the public toilets. I began to spend a lot of time in the Wusakile Welfare Library. I gained the confidence of the librarian, Mr Henry Kapata, so that he exceptionally allowed me to borrow any books I wanted, in return for sitting in for him in the library on Saturdays whilst he was away for a drink...

My father, despite his lack of money, was prepared to sell everything he had to send me for higher [upper primary] education. To him nothing mattered more. One day he returned from work with a bandaged arm. When I asked him what had happened, he un-bandaged the arm and showed me a wound. He said, 'I quarrelled with the white man boss and he stabbed me with a pencil; I could have beaten him dead but he is powerful because he works with the pencil. You too make sure you work with the pencil!'

Valentine was then sent to Chikuni, a leading Roman Catholic school in Southern Province. After spending one day there he returned home to attend Kitwe Main School.

The year I spent at Kitwe Main School stands out as one of the great hardships I and all the boys from Wusakile endured. The school was 7 miles away and classes started at 7.15 a.m. To get there on time we had to leave Wusakile well before 6 a.m. There were classes in the afternoon ending at 4 p.m. and therefore there was no lunch at home for us; there was usually no money for lunch. Therefore, apart from the fatigue of the daily trip, there was daily hunger...I would probably not have withstood a year at Kitwe School had my father, seeing my utter weariness each evening, not bought me a bicycle. It was an enormous sacrifice for him and the other children, but it revolutionised my school attendance routine and gave me a feeling of coming of age...It was at Kitwe Main that, through Civics classes, I began to learn about the organisation of society, and complaints about such, a combination of which I slowly learnt to be politics.

1950 to 1953: Kutama

I wasted no time in trying to find another school to go to. 'This time,' my father said, 'as far away as where the Europeans come from, so that you do not run away.' He decided to try Kutama in Southern Rhodesia, where he had an old friend who was school chaplain. He set matters in motion and in early 1949 I received an acceptance for Standard VI, to start in January 1950...My ambitions and, indeed, those of my father for me to go to a better school had absolutely no financial realism. My father's annual income was £23.10s.0d, whereas my upkeep at Kutama was to be £26. It was easily the most expensive school for Africans in Southern Rhodesia...My father withdrew £5 from his savings. I had to sell the bicycle and seek contributions from my uncles. The years I spent at Kutama have been a lasting and forming influence on my life to this day to such an extent that I have had a feeling that I hardly learnt much that is really new since then...

Most holidays were spent at the school, working with the Brothers on various school projects...We spent these quiet holidays at manual work and in often serious philosophical discussions...we became obsessed with Rousseau, Voltaire, St Thomas and modern philosophers, whom we read more for self-esteem than for full understanding...The school was run on the basis of individual responsibility and liberty. You were given the school rules and told that you individually were expected to discipline yourself in the observance...

One had a feeling that the years 1947–1950 were the Northern Rhodesian African renaissance period. Material development was to be seen everywhere; mines were expanding, attracting many from the rural areas for urban employment. Government and the mines launched new housing programmes...The radio, as Central African Broadcasting Corporation, Lusaka, came into its own...African education was given its first big push by the expansion of upper primary schools and Munali being built.[2] An effective campaign for girls' education was launched, side by side with an adult literacy campaign. On the economic front, there was the introduction of co-operatives, and the colonial administration began to talk about community and economic development. Politically it was the turning point, the ANC [African National Congress] was formed and the African Representative Council became vocal.

1953 to 1961: Civil Service

Valentine returned to the Copperbelt in 1953. After trying various jobs he joined the Provincial Administration as a Senior African

Clerk, before being promoted to more senior positions, eventually being given responsibility for two sub-districts in Kitwe – Wusakile, where he had lived as a child, and Mindolo. He also began to study for a degree by correspondence course with Fort Hare University in South Africa. During this period the Zambia African National Congress (ZANC), under the leadership of Kenneth Kaunda, broke away from the ANC. ZANC later changed its name to the United National Independence Party (UNIP).

My functions as a boma clerk consisted of the collection of Native Tax, writing *Chitupas* (Identity Certificates), typing for the District Officer, acting as an interpreter and preparing statistics and returns on various subjects...

Until [the formation of ZANC], politics to me were essentially theoretical and impersonal, in that I had no contact with any of the public organisers and office bearers of the ANC who, at least in Chingola, operated at a different level and would, even if I endeavoured to speak to them, not welcome my company...ZANC at its formation appealed to the level of the more enlightened at organisational level...My involvement [in ZANC] was early though distant, partly because of being a civil servant in the first place, but also my nature in avoiding association with mass opinion or organisations.

[In 1959, as resistance to the Central African Federation was reaching a climax I was] instructed by the District Commissioner to purchase a quantity of food and store it for the weekend at the boma. I concluded that there was possibly to be an Emergency (which had already been declared in Nyasaland)...I warned Sikota Wina of this possibility, who was of the opinion that as a journalist, he was unlikely to be affected...Days later, when the Emergency was declared and ZANC banned, he was picked up[3]...That night, District Messengers and police glued on to every door in the compound stickers announcing 'ZANC *Aferatu*', meaning 'ZANC is dead'...Practically every house owner, instead of removing the sticker, carefully cut off the *Aferatu*, leaving a free advertisement for ZANC, which became a household word, even to those who had never heard of the party...

I was from every point of view apart from blackness an oddity in Mindolo Compound. Contrary to my expectations that in Kitwe I would find company amongst my childhood friends, I found none. We had developed in the years of my absence along divergent routes. Those I met were established as miners like their fathers before them, and we found each other strange in our ways.

1961 to 1962: Cambridge

Having been awarded his degree in record time Valentine was recommended for promotion to District Officer and selected to attend the Overseas Services Course in Cambridge.

As much as I was not excited by going to England *per se* I really looked forward to setting my foot in Cambridge as one of the world's foremost shrines of knowledge...Unfortunately such exhilaration as might have been there was effectively muted by problems...of finding suitable accommodation...Digs-hunting became a formidable and heart-rending task. We read advertisements, which were always plentiful, first thing in the morning and started off to the various addresses we thought suitable knocking on door after door. At each door the landlady emerged with exquisite politeness and would sometimes ask us in, but upon looking at us, and before we made our enquiry, she would say 'Oh, I am sorry. I have just let out the rooms. Poor things, if only you came ten minutes ago!' This was repeated at virtually every door...It soon painfully dawned upon us that there was a racial bias which became aggravated by our being a couple. To satisfy ourselves that racial prejudice indeed had something to do with the landladies' attitudes, we enlisted assistance of some NR European students...to look for digs on our behalf. On the first day of this strategy our friends came back with several acceptances...When in each case we went there by ourselves or in company of the friend who found the digs, the landlady was absolutely embarrassed and was obliged to withdraw the offer...I finally decided that there was only one way to solve the problem, by changing the market...We moved higher and looked for a two-bedroom flat in a more expensive bracket. A Reverend gentleman, a Fellow at one college, rented us a nice flat at a nice price...

Since at that time development economics were very much in vogue and theories were mushrooming in every college, lectures on it were most popular...Professor Lord Kaldor was particularly controversial...An apparently dedicated socialist but also a committed Keynesian economist, he was a rather popular economic 'trouble shooter' for young and newly independent countries whose heads of state were in the habit of calling him to devise a cure to some economic ills (usually inflation and prices). His advice inevitably included exorbitant taxation which desperate Governments eagerly implemented but [which was] inevitably followed by popular unrest and, in some cases, [the] fall of the Government. When tackled on this rather bizarre reputation he candidly replied that in each case he had given the Governments concerned alternatives, with the probable consequences of each, but they all preferred the alternative with consequences of unrest which they hoped they could handle...Professor Austin Robinson was also popular for the theory on public finance – also Keynesian. Rostow's theory of 'take-off' was a hit especially to those of us from, or going to work in, developing countries who saw it as the ultimate solution...Even the British recruits going to the colonies at this dusk of the empire took cold comfort that their mission would be different from that of the colonial pioneers; it would be administering economic development and therefore a better future for the colonials. With this in view members of the course did, in addition to the economics, put effort in studying elements of agricultural economics.[4]

1962 to 1964: Katanga

Returning from Cambridge, Valentine was posted for a short period to Isoka in Northern Province as a District Officer before being seconded to Britain's Consulate General in the Katanga Province of the Congo, where he worked with British civil servants.

Elisabethville...was in turmoil; the war of secession of Katanga which started in 1960 was still going, but more furiously with the UN's final push to unseat Tshombe...Elisabethville was unsafe[5]...

I saw a wonderful rich country fall to pieces, ravaged by foreigners and its leaders. Ignorant men as leaders whose greed and hunger for purposeless power [made them] puppets of international politics and insensitive to the rape of their country and the rapidly growing misery of their people...The Congo was a frightening forewarning of what might happen in other parts of the continent, all of which was galloping towards independence...

Tshombe was right in contending that Katanga's place was in the southern sphere of central Africa either as part of it or independently in it. The fact that Katanga provided revenue to the rest of the country 2,000 miles away was more a ground for secession or federal relationship than union. Since Tshombe's [aims] and those of the Katangese could not be fulfilled, Zambia's relationship with the Congo should aim at increasing its sphere of influence over Katanga in the interests of economics and trade.

1964: Ministry of Foreign Affairs

Valentine's next task was to help establish the new Ministry of Foreign Affairs. At this time the country was in a period of self-government leading up to Independence. UNIP, which had won the general election held in January 1964, was the governing party, with Kenneth Kaunda as Prime Minister.

As we were finalising, the Minister called me into his office in which I found a stranger in most unpresentable apparel, to wit dirty and tattered. I was informed that the individual should be appointed a Counsellor and posted specifically to Washington. I was astonished but was prepared to give him the benefit of the doubt. I took him to my office for interview only to find that his incompetence in English alone could not qualify him for the Foreign Service. I reported back to the Minister and told him that the man was not fit from every practical point of view.

I was informed that my opinion was quite wrong, what I saw was merely a good cover for the high intelligence activities the Party had trained him for [for] many years. He had to go as instructed. He went only to prove a disastrous disgrace in Washington. He was withdrawn within six months and never heard of since.

1964 to 1968: Cabinet Secretary and Head of the Civil Service

After serving for a few months as the newly independent Zambia's first Director of Intelligence, Valentine was appointed Secretary to the Cabinet and Head of the Civil Service.

Faced with demands for some 'spoils' by their followers the Cabinet must have looked upon the Civil Service with distaste as an obstacle and also as an elite group which was reaping where it did not sow. It developed into an uneasy but inevitably antagonistic coexistence between the Party and the Civil Service. Furthermore since at the time an opposition party ANC existed, the professed impartiality of the Civil Service in administration became a sore point to UNIP, who feared that if ANC was not seen by the people as vanquished and had no power to give favours, it could reorganise to give them a serious challenge at the next elections. Regularly I received reports and requests from Ministers that such and such a civil servant was ANC and must be dismissed or not promoted. Civil Service regulations could not, however, entertain such requests...

Rarely are reasons of our state of backwardness ever sought at home within our midst or attributed to our own actions or omissions. Often no sooner have we denounced those we allege...conspire against our progress than we approach them for more development assistance...We fought for our independence on the justification that only we ourselves can order our affairs to our best advantage. Independence meant entering the world arena of nations, each with its own interests, some of which would conflict with our own, but that we would rationally secure our own in that arena, at the same time respecting those of others in order for them to respect ours...To shift that responsibility on to 'external' forces each time things go wrong is condemning oneself and the nation to childishness and inferiority complex...

What the administration needed most was better-educated personnel and not political propagandists. I was, it is now clear, talking at cross purposes with the President's intention, which was the total politicisation of the administration to ensure [the] Party['s] and his own continuity in power. My motives were to meet political power halfway but ensure the eventual creation and stabilisation of a national administration to serve the people impartially and equally, so the politicians might come and go. To contemplate the latter situation was being hostile to the Party. I was expected to think of UNIP as a permanent institution for all the people and should therefore create an administrative structure such that any change of Government by another party would be impossible or be done only at the peril of great confusion.

1969 to 1970: Minister of State

Unhappy with plans to reorganise the Civil Service, Valentine resigned at the end of 1968. He then accepted an appointment as a nominated Member of Parliament and Minister of State for Technical and Vocational Education. During this period he was responsible for the development of new technical colleges and the creation of Orbit, *the science magazine for young people (see Chapter 17). He also learnt to fly.*

I have found out that although I love Zambia so much, I perhaps love a truthful approach more, because only the latter will make her truly free. In this particular controversy I am convinced that the opinion I have expressed is not a minority one as such, but one held by many well-meaning and understanding citizens and, if fully explained, acceptable to all our people...The views and the highly emotional indignation directed against 'Mini-Skirts' could be dismissed as ridiculous and a waste of words, but for the fact that the campaign is being waged in the name of 'our culture – our way of life'...

Those who desire that as a public policy…our national dress comes down to the knees or ankles are unfortunately looking at us through the eyes of the colonial era…On their arrival the colonisers and missionaries found our nudity incompatible with their trade and contrary to the religious doctrines preached by the missionaries. Accordingly they dispensed calico either freely or for little labour…As time went on…we copied and accepted the 'Bwana's' dress…The type of reaction exhibited against the 'Mini-Skirt'…is a compound of [the] inferiority complex we ex-colonial people continue to live up against…My thesis is that cultural conservatism is in inverse proportion to economic and technological development; the more culturally intolerant a nation is, the less capable it is to advance…

It also dawned on me with sadness that in Parliament, and consequently the country, the Independence struggle leaders had changed, if not lost, their roles as national leaders. They were now privileged leaders or dispensers to a small group of followers with them in Parliament, who in turn [had] a few of the Regional Office to keep happy…After [the] achievement of Independence the common platform was swept from under their feet and, left with all the trappings of power, they were at a loss of how to use it for [the] immediate and future good of a nation-to-be.

1970 to 1972: Governor of the Bank of Zambia

In 1970 Valentine was appointed Governor of the Bank of Zambia.

The core of the problem is that developing countries suffer a peculiar dilemma: they are catapulted into, and wish to run, a modern post-capitalistic state whose legitimising symbols are free social service – education, health, social security, subsidised housing, foods, transport, etc., price control, punitive taxation, workers' participation and state industries – without recognising that their economies are in a pre-capitalistic state of development…They give away free goods and services which they neither produce nor possess, and bottle up initiatives necessary for higher production and narrow or remove altogether the base for local currency revenues. The policies frighten away international capital so that for every venture the state has to find its own foreign exchange. In the circumstances [the] prescription of the IMF, which often includes [a] demand for devaluation, will become routine, but sustains the patient in a state of subconsciousness. World Bank soft loans will never create a base for a take-off, but add to foreign indebtedness which sooner [rather] than later will have to be paid...

To world bankers and many Western Governments, an LDC [Less Developed Country] is 'stable' if its people are ruled by a repressive, undemocratic and corrupt dictator. It would appear that for bankers and Western and Eastern Governments democracy is a bad risk for money in LDCs, particularly African ones.

His time at the Bank coincided with a period of political change. Simon Kapwepwe, who had been Vice-President, resigned in 1971 admitting he was leader of the newly formed United Progressive Party (UPP). The following year the UPP was banned and a Commission was set up to recommend a new constitution. Valentine's submission to the Commission included the following comment.

A claimed justification of our Enquiry is that many-party political systems are not suitable for Africa, but One Party ones [are]. This statement gives a feeling of peculiarity as Africans – that we are a world apart. Why do we think that we are so peculiar in our problems as Africans...It is probably because this is the easiest way to escape criticism of our actions and failures...It is...peculiar why we should idolise political mechanics as a special African identity and accept everything else as liable [to] being copied from the world at large...In the absolute and practical sense, [our] government machinery, economic operations and mobilisation apparatus are non-African and [so] inevitably [is] our political reaction [to them] even if we profess these to be independent and peculiar to ourselves...

He also advocated:

- the clear separation between political policy making and Government administration, and an independent Head of the Civil Service;
- the limitation of Presidential role and powers, and the appointment of a Prime Minister as the Head of Government;
- the publication of the records of public service institutions to prevent corruption or bribery;
- specific guarantees of civil liberties;
- educational qualifications for Members of Parliament.

1972 to 1978: Working for IBM

Following his submission to the Commission Valentine was removed from his post as Governor of the Bank of Zambia.

On 26 June 1972 I was for the first time since leaving school unemployed and had no plans for new employment. I was 39 years old and at that age, unless one is in a rush, one does not go round knocking office doors enquiring for employment. Moreover Zambia's employment market was not only small but virtually monopolised by the state...The few large companies still outside Government control were foreign and all frightened to incur the Government's displeasure by employing someone publicly denounced by the State. Above all, I had no specific qualification other than [as] a senior administrator whom most international companies could only employ for mercenary motives of influence [rather] than genuine belief in the individual's capacity for efficient contribution...

I knew very little about IBM but soon discovered the enormous organisation that it was...I was first interviewed by the District Personnel Manager, next by an Area Personnel Director from Paris, then by the Area Manager, also from Paris...The period from October 1972 to 1977 was [one] of intense travel for me. I spent at least half each year away from home on courses, conferences and work overseas and in Africa. I had to be in Nairobi once a month, in Paris at least once every quarter.

When Mozambique became independent in July 1975 it came under me and I had to be there at least once a month. At first I welcomed this new way of working. Firstly it kept me away from Lusaka [although] even during my absence reports...were being made as to what I would have said at the Lusaka Flying Club...I was personally happy to be out of it. It, however, meant that I considerably lost touch with a lot of goings-on in Zambia...

By 1976 I was travel weary...I was asked to move to Paris in a higher capacity and at most comfortable remuneration. I stalled on this offer because I could not face the prospect of working and living in Paris...Finally the assignment was reduced to segments of three months at a time...I prepared to leave Zambia on 28 July 1977 for my first three months in Paris...But on 26 July I was called to Aaron Milner's office – then Minister of Home Affairs – to be told that, on instructions from the President, he had to withdraw my passport with immediate effect. When I pressed him about the reason, he showed me the President's letter which was a mere directive that he withdraws the passports from me [and three others]...he had been given verbally a reason by Kaunda that the persons concerned were known or reputed to speak ill of the Zambian Government and Kaunda himself during their trips abroad. I was extremely angry about this move and more so about the allegation....I could never recall voicing criticism against Zambia whilst abroad.

1980 to 1983: Arrest and Detention

It was 3 a.m. on 24 October 1980. I asked, 'Who is there?' 'Police,' the reply came. With my wife by my side and both of us in our sleeping clothes, I opened the door. We were confronted by five policemen, two in plain clothes and three in Paramilitary combat uniform armed with rifles. One in plain clothes, armed with a revolver pointing at me asked, 'Are you Musakanya?' I said, 'I am.' 'We have come for you,' and with that he pushed himself and the other uniformed men inside the house. In a second all five men were standing in the hall. The military took up quick positions in the hall and the sitting-room. The man with the revolver spoke. 'First of all, we have to search the house. We are looking for firearms and documents only. No one in the house should attempt to get out. This property is completely sur-rounded by armed men'...

We got to Force Headquarters about 3.30 p.m. The No. 2... said to me, 'Mr Musakanya, we have been instructed to detain you.'

'What for?' I asked.

'We do not know, some people will be talking to you in the next few days.' He gave the papers to the team leader who signed and handed me a copy. It was a police 28-day detention order...After my wife left, I had to wait for my arresting offi-cers, sitting on that bench inside the charge office...The bench which I shared with two youths was hard; as the night wore on, it became harder and colder. I could not stand up for fear of the space being taken up by those standing...I felt extremely tired and cold. The constable on duty saw this and appeared embar-rassed and pitiful. At 1 a.m., he came and said, 'Old man, I think you'd be better off if you could sleep in that car near the cell. It is an impounded car and is open. Lock yourself in'...

The shocking reality that, after all, I had been arrested started to dawn on me. I sat taking it all in until my wife came about 8 a.m. [The Assistant Superintendent in charge of my arrest] came about 10 a.m., put me in his car and drove me to Lusaka Central Prison...I was taken to cell No. 15 – the 'VIP' cell of [the] prison...I was the 23rd inmate in a cell of 16.7 feet × 16.7 feet, with two tiny windows plus the squatting toilet stinking to the heavens. I surveyed my new abode. It consisted of 4 two-tier bunks for beds, obviously improvised from scrap iron angles, presum-ably by some enterprising earlier inmate. The wall was lined with six small bundles of tattered cotton waste which were supposed to be the bedding and covering. The wall was hung with a litter of plastic bags containing the belongings of the inmates...

[A] was picked up from his cell at about 8.00 a.m. on my sec-ond day (26 October) at the prison...Just after lock-up, [A] was returned, accompanied by warders and a plain-clothes policeman to pack his belongings. He looked extremely exhausted, puffed in the face and with a hoarse voice. He was whisked out...A week later we heard about him through 'prison telegraph' whispers, that he had been thoroughly tortured and had to be sent to the Annex Hospital for treatment. There was no means to confirm this...On 31 October [B] was taken at 2 p.m. for interrogation...He was not to return until 6 p.m. the following day. He was a moving ghost, eyes puffed from lack of sleep. He could not speak, his mouth and throat were dry and sore. He slumped into the bunk. There was total silence as everyone in the cell visually examined him. He could not even answer my question of 'What happened?'...

The following morning 2 November 1980 at 2.30 p.m., plain clothes police came for me...I was pushed into the ambulance (with tinted windows) and driven away to Lilayi Police Training School. When the doors of the ambulance opened at Lilayi the vehicle was already surrounded by armed Paras. I was led to the entrance of the officers' mess building by two of the Paras with guns...six inches from my back...I entered a large room 20 feet × 20 feet. It was plain except for a small rickety table near the wall by which an enormous man sat on a small chair. There was another chair opposite him. He was fumbling with two pieces of paper. As the door shut behind him and me I noticed two Paras, again armed, in the two corners beside the door...

My interrogator lifted his eyes (as red as a cobra's) and motioned me to the upright hardboard chair in front of him and under the lamps...A few minutes later three other interrogators entered...As the interrogation opened in earnest (it was to last from 3.30 p.m. to 5.30 the following day [the interrogators] most, if not all of whom had Eastern European training in interrogation...ignored any subsequent trial and the relevance of their questions to the evidence. They were keen on a confession under pressure; they had a fairly good story about a possible plan for a coup from their earlier interrogations but nothing substantial about my involvement. They were, however, convinced that I or [B] was the mastermind...The main question and refrain was the alleged meeting at [B]'s house and what was planned there...

I still denied because I never attended a 'meeting'. However, the fact of the situation as I recall was that...in February 1980 or maybe early March I had met [B] at the Lusaka Golf Club when I was looking for a bottle of wine...[B] told me to pass his house and have some over the weekend...the next weekend I passed there. I found him within the lounge...Some minutes later [C] arrived with a bottle...It was at that time I realised that [D] was there all the time drinking a beer because he greeted [C]. We opened the bottle and I went to get a glass and returned to the lounge to talk to [B] while [C] and [D] talked outside about the stupidity of shortages which had led people to be smuggling wine...At this point I went outside and said, 'I know a way without violence...let me just ride with him [Kaunda] in his helicopter and talk to him...He would sign the papers ordering change of his Government.' The conversation rumbled on...This could possibly have been the meeting but [C] had not asked me to attend a meeting...

While in detention Musakanya issued a public appeal entitled 'A Call to Reason' which included the following paragraphs:

Before and after we were arrested Kaunda and others have made public statements that we were dissidents, plotters and enemies of the people of Zambia. In contrast, nothing has been heard...of our views and what our dissent is all about. We have come to the conclusion that our major offence – even perhaps our betrayal of the people of Zambia – has been our complete silence about the many wrongs...that have been done in the name of the people of Zambia by a clique that has monopolised ruling power in Zambia for the last eighteen years.

We feel, therefore, that since we are already imprisoned we might as well...give our innermost views about the political situation in Zambia. We believe...in the democracy of the people and not of a minority called One Party; in utmost freedom of the individual – even at the risk of anarchism. Only a nation of free individuals can advance...Accordingly: a multiparty system and opposition are not only necessary but are inalienable rights of man to enable him to express his views and contribute to his own advancement.

Notes

1 Harry Nkumbula later became President of the African National Congress (ANC) political party.
2 Munali was the leading African secondary school in the period before Independence.
3 Sikota Wina was a prominent politician who became a Government Minister.
4 Austin Robinson was a distinguished Cambridge economist who had worked with John Maynard Keynes. He taught economics to the Overseas Services Course and was married to Professor Joan Robinson, also a leading economist at Cambridge. Walt Rostow was a United States economist, whose work *The Stages of Economic Growth*, published in 1960, set out a theory in which countries achieve economic growth by passing through five stages of development, of which stage 3 was called 'take-off'.
5 Elisabethville is the former name of Lubumbashi, capital of the Congo's Katanga Province. Moise Tshombe (1919–69) was President of the province and declared it independent of the rest of the Congo at the time the country became independent in 1960.

10

MWINILUNGA

David Taylor

'Senior District Messenger Kalan Fundamukanwa was a friend of mine and a delight.'

On average, in a district, there was an establishment of about twenty-two to twenty-five District Messengers. They were the DC's eyes and ears and they did the job of a police force where there was none. It was a prized job and when, once in a blue moon, a vacancy came up, we were inundated with applications. The Head Messenger enjoyed enviable patronage; his choice was not the last word but it carried great weight with a DC who knew what was good for him. A reasonable standard of spoken and written English was essential, but the most important, and indefinable, quality seemed to be that the candidate should 'fit in' and that he should become an enterprising member of the Head Messenger's team. Once chosen (I cannot remember that there was any formal training whatsoever), he was issued with a uniform which he accepted with pent-up excitement, given a loan if he needed one to buy a bicycle and provided with a pair of handcuffs to loop onto his leather belt. From the very next day, the law awarded him formidable powers of arrest over anybody, of any colour or station, while the DC himself had been given none. Then, as he went along, he was shown how to salute, how to lift his feet in a very approximate military fashion and he learned his job from his colleagues.

Senior Messenger Kalan Fundamukanwa was a friend of mine and a delight. Taller than most, lean and a bit floppy, he had a gap-toothed smile which threatened to blind him; his salute was beyond correction and had been given the benefit of the doubt because there was simply no alternative. It could be construed either way; it was an airy blessing in which all were invited to share, or it was a personal and mutinous insult. As one warmed quickly to Kalan, it became an endearing part of him, but high-ranking visitors to the district were sometimes less than enchanted. There was more to Kalan than met the eye, he was far and away tougher than he looked, his loyalty and stamina were inexhaust-ible and his local knowledge was vast. He was, when we needed one, our lone ranger and he got his man – every time.

Kalan brought in to my office a man who had been sent by his headman to report, as the law required, an accidental death. Kalan had already provided himself with the correct volume of the village register and it was put in front of me, open at the right page. The dead man, it was said, had been out in the bush with a friend when he had stepped on a snake which had retaliated sharply. It was not a venomous snake but a very large python and, although between them they had recovered themselves and killed it, I was told that the one who had been attacked had collapsed from what seemed to be shock. Death from snakebite of any kind was, in fact, very rare and, apart from the fact that the story was at the edge of probability, it was too pat, too elaborate. It was saying all the things that the white man might be expected to fall for and so I started to ask a few questions. Kalan, looking at me from behind the sitting villager, began to smile and seemed to be telling me that he, too, thought the story very fishy. The snake got bigger and bigger as I persisted and so did Kalan's smile.

'So, what had happened to the body?' I asked, and the answer was all wrong. They were a long way from home and his friend had buried him where he died and dug the hole with the axe which they had with them. The second bit of the answer was just credible but the first was not. There was no way that the dead man would have been left there for long. The village, as a team, would have brought him in for proper burial and they would have done this regardless of the time and effort which it took. If he was still out in the bush, then there were others who didn't want it known how he had died.

I thanked the villager for coming in and he disappeared, looking relieved. Kalan stayed behind and didn't wait for me to speak. 'I will go and find out, Bwana,' he said and I agreed it was a good idea. He came, by easy stages, to attention, knocked together one of his cheerful blessings and went off to his house to get ready for a journey.

Some time later, I watched through the window as Kalan said his goodbyes to the Head Messenger and then, one by one, to each of his colleagues in the Messengers' shelter. There was gentle clapping and murmured words, the fingers of both hands were put between those of each friend in turn and the junior in rank or prestige bent both knees as a sign of deference. The formalities done, Kalan was ready to go.

It was towards the end of the rainy season and Kalan was heavily dressed. The uniform for the bush included a wide-brimmed hat and a heavy full-length serge overcoat, both in black. A cape, black boots and black knee-length puttees completed a doleful image. He mounted his bicycle, arranged the folds of his coat and, with a rain-proofed roll of bedding and clothes across the back of the bicycle, pedalled slowly away. He had a long way to go and this was not a race. Watching his shrouded back as it receded, I was glad that I was not the one he was on his way to see.

Days went by and stretched into nearly half a month. From time to time, when I noticed that Kalan was missing from the morning parade, I remembered where and why he had gone but his mission had largely passed from my mind when, after a knock on the door, I suddenly found him looking down on me, his habitual smile creasing his face and still in his heavy coat and hat. He leaned forward and with evident relish, produced from his handkerchief a roughly spherical lump of beaten lead and put it on my blotter. It was about a third the size of a golf ball and looked unwholesome; there were bits sticking to it and I finicked it around with my pen. 'Go on, Kalan, what is it?' He was enjoying his joke. 'It is the snek, Bwana.'

'Snek? Come on, friend, what are you saying?' Still milking his joke and smiling hugely, he reached outside the office and produced a truly wicked-looking contraption. It was a home-made gun fashioned from a length of old piping, well over half an inch in diameter, one end of which had been crudely beaten and welded closed. It was bound into a rough wooden stock and the firing mechanism had been contrived from a nail and a flint held in place by a web of elastic straps cut from the inner tube of a car tyre.

Kalan then proudly introduced his prisoners. They included the village headman and a woeful lot they looked, loosely roped and handcuffed to the bicycle which, between them, they had pushed for three days while their warder sauntered along behind. Just how he had managed to keep them in one place during the nights they had spent on the way, I didn't ask.

A hunting expedition with a murderously illegal weapon had gone terribly wrong. Walking in single file, the owner of the home-made gun had been carrying it over his shoulder and, with outrageous confidence in his workmanship, pointing backwards straight at his friend. When the elastic slipped, the death of his companion must have been mercifully close to instantaneous; he had, quite literally, been blown away. For the survivor, the horror and panic of that moment, alone with his mutilated friend and a long way from any help, can only be imagined. He was still plainly stricken by what he had done when, looking at his feet, he mumbled his plea of guilty and went to prison for a shorter term than the offence should have carried.

Just how Kalan had broken the story, I never knew, but he had taken the village headman and the other guilty parties back to the scene and made them dig up the remains. Undeterred by the putrefying mess which they uncovered, he had poked about with his fingers for the 'snek' and then wrapped it into his handkerchief. The party was then called upon to carry the long-dead corpse back to the village, where it was decently reinterred.

The headman and the others who had connived in the cover-up did not go to prison. They, too, owned up and were fined at a level at which it is probable that many in the village paid a share.

11

CHINSALI

Mick Bond

*'Carrying out the orders we had been given to burn
the village left me numb and angry.'*

On 13 July 1964 I was told to transfer with immediate effect
to Chinsali. My task there was to help ensure that the instructions of Prime Minister Kenneth Kaunda, relating to the Lumpa
Church, were implemented.

The Lumpa Church had been founded by Alice Lenshina
in 1953. According to John Hudson in his book *A Time to
Mourn*:

> [T]he original impetus came from a real or imagined
> spiritual experience. Alice Mulenga Lubusha was a very
> ordinary village woman from Kasomo in her early thir-
> ties. Later she became known as 'Lenshina', a vernacular
> version of 'Regina'. Both she and her husband Petros were
> uneducated. Kasomo was close to Chinsali, and within the
> Lubwa sphere of religious influence.

Chinsali was the centre of the Lumpa movement. The Revd
Fergus Macpherson, who was a missionary at Lubwa, has
written a detailed account of Lenshina's 'spiritual experience'.

On 18 September 1953 Alice came to seek an interview with him at Lubwa. She stated that she had been taken ill and died not once but four times, each time 'rising again' when mourning had begun. At her last 'rising', which seemed to have taken place on Monday, 16 September, she stated that she had been called by Jesus to go and meet him 'at the river'. Jesus, she said, had shown her 'a sign' and told her to go and visit the *Abena kubuta* (the white people) at Lubwa, who would have a message for her. She recounted her 'rising from the dead' and said that Jesus had taught her some *inyimbo* (songs, hymns) and shown her *Ibuka lya Mweo* (the book of life). Then Lenshina told Fergus that Jesus had sent her to him and that he would have a message for her.

Fergus answered that he could pass no verdict on her record of her strange experience but 'inasmuch as you were given life and health again when you were, as it were, at the gate of death you should give thanks to God and serve Him from now on with your whole heart.' She agreed and promised not only to attend worship regularly but also to gather people for prayers at her village.

Initially the Mission expressed faith in the genuineness of Lenshina's vision, and relations with her and her growing number of followers were amicable. The missionaries felt it was important to keep the group within the Church. But the relationship gradually deteriorated when it became obvious that Lenshina was moving towards the formation of a separatist Church with its own teachings, some of which were inconsistent with those of the Mission. Reports of baptisms by Lenshina herself were particularly disturbing; people began to travel long distances from other districts such as Lundazi, Mpika and Isoka to seek baptism. Lenshina insisted that those seeking her baptism should first discard any witchcraft materials they possessed, to be purified. Piles of surrendered materials soon accumulated at Kasomo. It is clear that this cleansing ritual was highly attractive to the local people and was probably the main reason for the astonishingly fast growth of the support for Lenshina and her embryo Church.

During 1955 there was a final schism when Lenshina defied attempts by Lubwa to correct her unacceptable practices. She and her husband were suspended from membership of the United Church of Central Africa, to which Lubwa now belonged. At the same time Lenshina and Petros were declared heretics by the Catholics, who were also affected by defections. By the end of 1955 Kasomo had been visited by around 60,000 people, and they were still arriving at the rate of some 1,000 per week. Churches had been set up over a wide area of Northern Province and in Lundazi, and even on the Copperbelt. The Church now became known as the 'Lumpa' Church, from the Bemba word for 'excel' or 'surpass'.

In 1958 an enormous church, or cathedral, was built in burnt-brick at Kasomo and thereafter the village was called Sione (Zion). A crowd of about 5,000 attended the opening. In accordance with the movement's name the building's dimensions surpassed those of the largest local church at Ilondola Catholic Mission by being a foot longer and wider. By 1959 the Church's estimated membership was at least 100,000; in Chinsali alone it had 60 churches and a membership of 35,000 – more than half the population. Lenshina, however, refused to register the Church under the provisions of the Societies Act. In a much more serious challenge to authority, some Church followers disregarded customary law by forming new villages without seeking the permission of the local Chief. Widespread disorder occurred in 1961 throughout the Northern Province, arising from the nationalist campaign for independence – the period of 'cha-cha-cha'. The Lumpa Church tried to keep out of the campaign, preaching against involvement in politics. But inevitably it was affected. In the run-up to the 1962 elections many people abandoned the Church to join UNIP (Kaunda's United National Independence Party). In 1963 throughout the province UNIP followers were demanding party cards and intimidating those who did not possess them. Alice allowed her followers to burn their UNIP cards; this was regarded as an insult to UNIP, but was not a misdemeanour. Trouble soon started, and escalated into a tit-for-tat cycle of aggression and retaliation. By mid-1963 more Lumpa followers began to move into their own separatist villages for greater safety. These new settlements were founded without the approval of the Chiefs and were considered threats to security, and fanned suspicion.

Following incidents which occurred over Christmas 1963, Dr Kaunda (then Minister of Local Government) attended discussions between UNIP and Lumpa local leaders, at which it was agreed that the Lumpa followers should be persuaded to return to their old registered villages. Eleven 'peace teams' consisting of Lumpa Church deacons and UNIP Rural Councillors toured the district in January 1964. These tours undoubtedly contributed to the restoration of peace after the Christmas incidents, but the basic antipathy between the two groups remained. There were no signs of the Lumpa followers returning to their old villages; on the contrary, they consolidated their huts and gardens in the new settlements and were clearly determined to stay.

After another serious incident on 26 June 1964, when a young Lumpa boy was cuffed by his UNIP uncle for not attending school, the police were attacked by 150 men armed with spears and had to open fire in order to effect their withdrawal. This unfortunate clash brought to a head all the suspicions and tensions which had been simmering beneath the surface since the beginning of the year. Dr Kaunda, now Prime Minister, flew to Chinsali on 13 July and informed Alice Lenshina and her deacons of the Government's decision that all Lumpa 'illegal' settlements were to be vacated within one week and the inhabitants were to return to their original villages.

This was the point at which I came on the scene. The Prime Minister had given the Lumpa followers a deadline of just *one week*, from *13 July*!

Why me? I'd passed my Advanced Bemba exam and perhaps was thought fluent enough to argue in ciBemba with the Lumpas. As with the 1914 predictions of World War I being 'all over by Christmas', I was told this would merely be a short secondment for perhaps a fortnight, three weeks at the most. We should just be prepared to 'camp' in an empty house containing merely the usual basic hard furniture. So, on the morning of 14 July we set off in a Land Rover – Wendy and our sixteen-month-old first-born, Alastair, and James, our house-servant – for the six-hour drive to Chinsali. I knew nothing of the past events in Chinsali and had barely heard of the Lumpa Church, so I could be said to have arrived with an open mind, or just a blank one.

My tasks were to persuade the Lumpa followers to accept the Prime Minister's orders, and arrange with them when and where they wanted transport or food; to liaise with their old villages to which they were to go; to open up and run as a transit camp the emergency prison at Chinsali; and to liaise with the police and Special Branch on the reactions of all sections of the community.

From 16 to 19 July I visited eight Lumpa villages, accompanied by one or two District Messengers and on several occasions by two sections of a Police Mobile Unit platoon. A police officer was always present when his forces were represented. I spent an average of two and a half hours in each village, trying every argument I could think of to persuade the people to move and tackling their objections. Before proceeding to villages I always checked recent police patrol reports regarding the attitude they had found there. In most of these reports the villagers' attitude had been recorded as 'hostile, truculent, uncooperative', etc. I suspected that if such attitudes had been assessed correctly it merely indicated that the police were regarded with suspicion or quite natural dislike (they always went armed), or that they had not won the villagers' confidence by speaking in ciBemba. I recorded such phrases as 'reception friendly and fairly interested', 'reaction friendly but adamant'. At no time did I feel the slightest uneasiness nor could I perceive any tension on the part of the villagers. They were willing to argue, and they appeared to have all the arguments on their side except the main one – that this was a Prime Minister's order they were being told to obey.

It soon became my practice to visit the villages without a police presence, unarmed and with just a Messenger. I had a splendid Senior DM, Julius (I cannot remember his surname), who was not only an ex-askari with a good row of medal-ribbons but could also drive, so I could send him off on a short errand while

I carried on talking in a village until he collected me. He came with me (poor chap) almost every day; if it was not good policy to monopolise him in this way, at least we built up a great relationship of mutual trust – which at times was needed to get us through unharmed.

The Lumpa villages were all *so* impressive. Their appearance was exemplary; just what we thought, on tour, every village should aspire to. All the houses were built in neat rows, their grain-bins likewise, and their *fimbusu* (pit-latrines) were also in rows behind their houses and nicely thatched. It is true that most villages had defensive stockades, which were off-putting, but they, too, were neatly built. It made me sad that we were forcing them to leave such excellent places to return to old villages where the rest of the inhabitants did not show such domestic pride.

It was a mentally as well as physically exhausting time. After the usual greetings in a village, I would sit on a *cipuna* (stool), identify a deacon or headman, and then start trying to persuade them. It was just as well that I knew my Bible, as they would so often throw out biblical quotations to justify their stance and I had to think of another biblical sentence (in ciBemba) for a counter-argument. But if I couldn't persuade them to agree to a move, at least the arguing was friendly and done with humour; I was enjoying myself at this stage.

But the deadline came and went.

The PM was away in Cairo when the deadline passed, and nobody in Lusaka knew what the next stage should be. The Permanent Secretary, Len Bean, directed that patrolling and constant visits should continue during the next week as before, and in the circumstances this was the only possible decision. To have stopped patrolling suddenly would have created tension. However, local politicians began spreading the word that 'the PM has said move by the 19th *or else*!' and that dire retribution would befall the Lumpa villages after the deadline. Soon it was being said that 'the next time our UNIP Mobile Police come to visit your village they will come to kill you'. I myself experienced the reaction to these threats on 22 and 23 July when visiting villages. There was no sense of aggressiveness towards me, but an atmosphere of uncertainty. Entering one village I was immediately asked, 'Where are the police? Are they hiding behind the trees preparing to kill us?' And in another village, 'We know you are all right, but if we see the police we know they will be coming to kill us.'

On 24 July a routine Mobile Unit patrol was ambushed as it entered the Lumpa village of Chapaula. Two officers, Inspector Smith and Constable Chanda, were speared to death and the platoon withdrew under cover of fire. The next day the DC, supported by police reinforcements, attempted to reason with the villagers and to persuade them to lay down their arms. Firing commenced and the village had to be taken by force and destroyed. Events then moved swiftly. Word of this incident spread at once and the Lumpa followers assumed that war had been declared against them. Most of them took to the bush and made reprisal raids on neighbouring villages, burning and killing. Another police officer, Inspector Jordan, was killed and Inspector P. Hopwood was wounded when their patrol to investigate reports of arson and murders was ambushed 10 miles east of Mulanga Mission. Soon after this the security forces in the district were increased (almost overnight) to two regular battalions of the Army (Northern Rhodesia Regiment at that stage) and no less than 10 platoons of the Police Mobile Unit, and a Provincial Operations Committee (ProvOps) was set up.

While the police patrol went to Chapaula on 24 July, I went to two large Lumpa villages in the south accompanied by just the faithful Senior DM, Julius. In my absence, news of the Chapaula deaths flew back to the boma in the form '*Bwana mutali* (the tall officer) has been killed.' James, our cook, heard this and at first naturally assumed it referred to me! Fortunately, he used his common sense and made some more enquiries before giving the news to Wendy, who was now six months pregnant. Inspector Smith, whom I'd met a few times, was the same height as me and apart from his uniform we could have been mistaken for each other. All the same, it was a relief to Wendy when I returned home that evening, unscathed.

I well remember Inspector Jordan, with his large droopy moustache; in fact, I had had drinks with him and other police officers the evening before his ambush. I also knew well the little bridge across a dambo where the ambush had taken place, as it was on the way to the large Lumpa village of Chilanga which I visited often. The villagers had attacked the patrol with spears as it was crossing the bridge; Jordan got out of his Land Rover to fire at them, but his Sten gun jammed (as they sometimes did) and he was overrun; the rest of his patrol fled. The spot was immediately given the name of 'Jordan's Drift'.

The week following the deaths of the police officers was a period particularly fraught with tension and danger. Police patrols continued to visit all the Lumpa villages, and so did I. But I was keen to go without an armed escort and with a semblance of peace. My main aims in that week were to persuade the Lumpa followers to calm down and refrain from further reprisals, to dispel their belief that the police were 'UNIP police' (as local UNIP leaders were claiming), to assure them that the door was still open for them to get assistance in moving from their present villages if they would do so in accordance with the PM's orders, and to gather intelligence.

Accompanied only by the ever-trusting and trustworthy Senior DM, Julius, I managed to get round most of the district in four days. On paths leading to Lumpa villages we would often find their sentries, looking for early signs of any police patrol. Our first shouts to them would usually be: '*Awe mukwai, lekeni mafumo, poneni mfuti panshi, tuleisa mu mutende*' ('No, drop your spears, put your guns down, we come in peace'), and usually we could then move into discussions with them. They certainly felt it was a war situation and in any future conflict they must strike first; moving from their villages was quite out of the question, and all my attempts at persuasion were useless.

Chilanga was a very large and well-laid-out Lumpa village, east of Mulanga Mission and near the Muchinga escarpment. On my first visit, I remember, the reception was quite friendly and we had the longest argument based on biblical texts. I now chose to revisit it once or twice, since its inhabitants were probably those responsible for both Inspector Jordan's ambush and some of the reprisal raids in the surrounding area. In two small villages beyond Jordan's Drift, places he had been on his way to investigate, we came across the grisly evidence of reprisal raids: houses burnt, some with the residents trapped inside; corpses, now bloated and smelling, lying nearby where they had been overtaken in their flight and speared (we saw similar sights in the north-east, too). We experienced other incidents and sights around Chilanga which remain vividly in my memory; Julius agreed with my decision that, because of their nature, they should for ever remain *fya munkama fyesu* (our secrets) and unreported; if they were known by any higher authority, this would lead to questions or formal inquiries and certainly to a ban on my movements without police escort – preventing my future peaceful contact with the Lumpas. They remain our secret, for which I feel no shame, though they have often haunted me. We knew we were taking calculated risks, but we survived.

With the Army's two infantry battalions now camped beside Chinsali airstrip, the decision was taken on high that all the Lumpa villages must be taken by a show of force and Alice arrested. The critical stage had been reached.

It was planned that the two worst obstacles, Sione and Chilanga villages, should be 'cleared' on 30 July. While the DC went with 1NRR (1st Battalion, Northern Rhodesia Regiment) to Sione, I went with the 2nd Battalion (2NRR) to Chilanga. I have recently been reminded through email correspondence that Peter Moss, another of our Cambridge Course colleagues, was seconded at very short notice from Mkushi to Chinsali as an additional DO, and in the following pages I have with his permission inserted some of his comments on events.

At Sione the DC with Peter and the Army used the same procedure as at Chapaula when recovering Inspector Smith's body. As soon as the troops were in position in front of the village, the DC spoke through a megaphone saying that if the villagers wanted peace, they had to obey Government instructions. He repeated this message four times. Then some Lumpa supporters who had been hiding in the grass attacked the troops, who promptly opened fire. The Battalion Commander then gave the order to advance into the village. It was met by fierce opposition. Bows and arrows, spears and firearms were used, the villagers (men, women and children) fighting with complete disregard for their lives in the face of automatic weapons. Fifty-nine men and seven women were killed; 110 were wounded, given first aid and then transported to Chinsali Hospital.

I left Chinsali on 29 July with 2NRR and we camped overnight at Mulanga Mission, ready to move to Chilanga early on the 30th. Chilanga was the largest Lumpa village in the district, having over 300 huts. It was responsible for the deaths which Inspector Jordan's patrol had gone to investigate, and the subsequent ambush. As a result morale locally was low and over 300 UNIP villagers were gathered at Mulanga Mission for protection when we arrived; over the next week this number increased until at its maximum I estimated it to be 3,200. I then led 2NRR to Chilanga. The village seemed deserted, the residents having fled into the bush at our approach, but I was convinced until we actually entered it that a trap was prepared. I, therefore, spoke at some length through a megaphone outside the stockade to the imagined crowd inside. We burned the village, as directed, and took all the food and cooking utensils which we could carry (two lorry-loads) back to Mulanga for the refugees there – and to deny these means of sustenance to the Lumpas in the bush.

Some might regard the method of these operations as bizarre. The Army was, quite correctly, 'acting in support of the civil authorities'; so, at Chilanga, I was the lone civil authority (plus Julius) with a whole battalion supporting us!

All accounts I heard of the Sione operations praised 1NRR for their control of fire. The Commanding Officer, standing next to the DC, would observe Lumpa supporters taking aim with their weapons and just direct the fire of a sergeant or marksman by saying, e.g., 'Man on the left anthill, take him out; man aiming, right-hand group, take him out.' But when several men, and women, just charged, there was no alternative but to stop them in their tracks. We heard stories that Alice had promised her followers that their faith made them immune to bullets, that she had handed out 'passports to heaven' and that some villagers were seen to be standing on top of anthills and 'waving their arms in order to fly to heaven'; such stories about fanatics might not be implausible, but exaggerations did abound.

But Peter was personally present at Sione, and his comments are as follows.

For the record I helped out the DC in Chinsali in three episodes over a period of three or more months: the first included being close to him throughout the Sione assault, actively participating not only as a learner/spectator but also in some of the operation itself. I was present when the Army rocketed a house near the 'cathedral' where they thought Lenshina was hiding. I walked down a line of at least 100 corpses which the police had laid out in the sun, and which were then loaded on to trucks and buried in mass graves near Chinsali boma. I think the number usually mentioned may refer to a rush of many villagers en masse straight on to the first burst of machine guns, when the words 'be careful, they are using bows and arrows' were recorded, and not the other shootings that took place elsewhere in the village.

As for our actions at Chilanga with 2NRR, I was of course relieved that we had not needed to fire, but frustrated that we had not tried to surround the whole village first and had, therefore, allowed all the villagers to escape into the bush. The Commanding Officer, understandably, would not risk sending his men far into the bush in very extended lines for such a manoeuvre. While I spoke through my megaphone, he stood beside me with his pistol at the ready. Carrying out the orders we had been given to burn the village left me numb and angry – to be party to the total destruction of the finest African village I had ever seen (or would see). In useless consolation I took the enormous village drum as a personal memento, and we still have it.

Returning to Chinsali I immediately had to check how effective my preparations were for handling the 411 Sione survivors in the 'cage' (the emergency prison). Food and blankets were distributed at once, and we had on hand hospital staff who inspected individuals for injuries and checked the hygiene issues (toilets, etc.). The abiding memory is of the ghostly silence: faith in their immunity from bullets had been shattered, perhaps their faith in Alice Lenshina had been dented, certainly they found it incredible to be in their present plight. This silence continued for days and was especially eerie as the majority of those in the 'cage' were women and children; they were in severe shock.

For the next week both Peter Moss and I alternately led 2NRR to all the other thirteen Lumpa villages and systematically destroyed them. On these occasions I found no village occupied and there was no fight.

But Peter had a very different experience at one village on 4 August, leaving him very sore if not traumatised, as he has recounted.

> I was dealing with a huge massively stockaded settlement somewhere not far from Shimwaule. I was with 2NRR battalion and ten or twelve platoons of the Mobile Police. I had only spoken a few words in ciBemba through the blue regulation loud hailer when the occupants opened fire with muzzle-loaders and bows and arrows, at which point I made the announcement that the Civil Authority had to hand over its responsibility to the military. All military hell broke loose! Many villagers, old and young, were killed and wounded.

> After Sione and this action, in which I thought the Army and its new recruits had behaved badly, I recall having a long discussion with the DC in which I said that we did not seem to be approaching the problem in the humanitarian PA (Provincial Administration) way which we all understood. I felt by then we were probably going too far and had lost our way by carrying out these military coercions. He sent me to see my own PC in Broken Hill, who told me bluntly either to resign or to go back and follow orders...I followed orders and, working as far as I could within the

system, managed to save some lives...I took a few days' break in Mkushi where I was DO at that time. Returning to Chinsali I was with the Army again, and joined them in an operation against a Lumpa stockaded village on the Luangwa escarpment, which turned out to be deserted (all except for a scared cow elephant).

Recently, Peter has made the following comments on his Chinsali experiences, agreeing with me that it was difficult to approve of what was done.

It was a deeply traumatic experience for me. I had become a proficient Bemba/Lala speaker and like the rest of us was working at grassroots level – so much so that I believed strongly that we were getting it VERY wrong. I had gone to see the PC because I thought that there should be a high-level change in approach to the problem. I was profoundly shocked by the whole thing, but I do not think the DC could have handled the situation any better than he did. Soon after these tiring events I returned disillusioned to Mkushi. After the Lumpa campaign I vowed never to have anything to do with public administration again, and thus began my move in 1965 to the Department of Game and Tsetse Control.[1]

The next phase was the hunt for Alice Lenshina herself. On 1 August, two days after Sione and Chilanga, Senior Chief Nkula reported that two Lumpa deacons had come to tell him that Alice wished to surrender and was at Mwanachanda village. On 2 August I, therefore, set out with two companies of 2NRR for Mwanachanda, in the marsh area near the Chambeshi River, west of Chinsali and Sione. I repeatedly asked ProvOps if I might go alone on this mission, but my request was refused. My view was (and still is) that if Alice wished to surrender, she would want to do so to the Chief or to the administration who knew her, not to armed forces who had just fought at Sione; she would be lacking confidence, and would need to be approached openly and with no semblance of trickery. This exercise failed, as I knew it would, because she took fright on hearing the approach of 300 soldiers through the trees, and much time was wasted in trying to get information as to her whereabouts from the villagers there. In fact, she left the village not five minutes before we entered it, dropping her handbag on the path. A few days later she did, however, surrender in Kasama District.

Meanwhile, the scenes of fighting and massacres had shifted to Lundazi District, where horrific atrocities were committed. Tony Goddard was there, and his personal account in Chapter 14 covers the early stages.

While I was out and about so much during that first month in Chinsali, I confess that I saw little of Wendy and young Alastair. I am sure I told her only the barest minimum of what I was up to, to minimise any worries on her part; I'm also sure that I had full confidence in her being able to make the most of her situation 'back at the ranch'. She tells her own stories in Chapter 17.

The Lumpa Church had been banned but various problems remained after the military actions had been finished. On the administrative side there was the problem of rehabilitation, both of ex-Lumpa followers and UNIP villagers who had lost their homes. On the security side it was necessary to account for all ex-Lumpas who had deserted their villages at the time of the Army attacks and had taken to the bush. Obviously, these problems went hand-in-hand.

The administrative aspects of rehabilitation included: deciding who should or should not be allowed to return from the 'cage' to their villages; the issue of clothing, food and blankets to those in the 'cage' or others in the district who had suffered; the building of new and larger villages where ex-Lumpas and UNIP followers were to live side by side in harmony; persuading UNIP refugees at Chinsali and Mulanga to go back to their own villages or join these new settlements; starting agricultural projects such as tobacco, as well as subsistence farming, at the new settlements and elsewhere; reintegrating children into the schools; checking on medical supplies and outbreaks of diseases, as well as public health in the 'cage' and in the new settlements;

and informing the security forces of any ex-Lumpa gangs known to be still at large.

Peter and I dropped leaflets from small aircraft in early August over most of the bush areas where we suspected ex-Lumpas to be hiding, urging them to return at once to their old registered villages.

By late August I estimated that over 4,000 ex-Lumpas had returned to their villages, largely as a result of our leaflet air-drop. During tours around villages in that period I certainly came across many who had somehow returned at some time without having passed through the 'cage'. My problem was to see that they integrated well into their old society. They were still afraid at this stage, and not warmly received by UNIP followers. Whenever I visited a village they remained in two distinct groups, both to greet and to listen to me. This I half expected and it did not unduly worry me; I felt time would heal this antipathy.

In the Mulanga area I had, above all, to ensure that no revenge was taken and that the refugees did not take the law into their own hands. Neither side was on the offensive but each side was in fear of the other. A delicate and gradual process of 'forgive and forget' had to be started, although its success could not be immediate; hatred would only prolong the tension. I felt we would succeed better if we could play it our way and were not being constantly thwarted by directives from ProvOps Kasama or MainOps Lusaka, who were not on the spot.

Confidence was just being built up nicely and the crowd at Mulanga were well under control when Simon Kapwepwe, then Minister of Home Affairs, visited Mulanga by helicopter on 14 August and made a speech, which destroyed all the work we and the missionaries had so far accomplished, renewed the hatred and encouraged violence. Various headmen with whom I discussed it immediately afterwards said Mr Kapwepwe had told them to go and hunt the Lumpas and to kill any that they saw. The situation was clearly explosive, and I went straight to Chinsali, where I handed a précis of Kapwepwe's speech with my comments to my Permanent Secretary, Len Bean, who I understand handed them to the Prime Minister. The PM visited

Mulanga four days later and told the people the exact opposite of what Kapwepwe said and thus brought the situation back to where we wanted it.

When Kapwepwe made his speech at Mulanga I was in the area but not close. He had just finished speaking when I arrived, and I was given the précis of his remarks by a White Father who was present. I still have the signed original of this. It was also a lucky coincidence that I found Len Bean at Chinsali on a surprise visit by air from Lusaka, and was able to update him in person. I was, however, embarrassed when Colonel Welsh of 2NRR, who was there too, told Mr Bean that 'Mick is the only person around here who knows what's going on'.

2NRR had left Chinsali on 31 August. I was still busy for the rest of September trying to locate ex-Lumpas in the bush and visiting many villages to monitor progress on 'reconciliation'. I was determined to get the surrender of those ex-Lumpas still at large, but the only way was to make contact with them and win their confidence. They had been afraid of the security forces and might have been afraid of me, too. Accordingly I went unarmed (except on two occasions when I carried a loaded revolver, carefully concealed in my shorts, in case I had to defend Julius and myself), accompanied only by the good Julius and a couple of guides chosen from those ex-Lumpas who had already surrendered to me and with supporting transport waiting at Mulanga. Once I was accompanied by a CID officer from Kasama who wanted to see my reported methods. On five occasions I made contact with groups in hiding who were prepared to accept me and showed neither fear nor aggression. In all, 246 surrendered to me over a three-week period and came in. A final 400 surrendered at Chief Lundu's *musumba* (Chief's headquarters), just inside Lundazi District, on 20 September.

My records are vague on our next family episode. It had become all too clear that we were required in Chinsali for the 'long haul'. It must have been in the first days of September that we returned briefly to Mporokoso to pack and move on a permanent footing to Chinsali. The optimistic secondment for 'two weeks, three at the most' had now lasted for at least seven.

The DC and his wife were due to go on leave in mid-September. PC Peter Clarke and many of the older colonial civil servants were leaving at or before Independence. Who would become the next DC Chinsali? We were told that the position had been offered to several officers of some seniority and experience and they had all declined this 'poisoned chalice'. I found myself left in charge, as the man on the spot – or in the wrong place at the wrong time – and, after 'acting' for a couple of weeks, was confirmed as District Commissioner as from 14 October 1964 at the tender age of twenty-seven, maybe the last expatriate to be confirmed a DC before Independence. I had no DO or other supporting officer, only clerical staff and of course Messengers. We moved into the DC's house at the end of September, just in time for the next major event – Wendy was safely delivered of Ruth Bond in the Kasama Cottage Hospital on 6 October.

Scarcely had we adjusted our domestic life to this new and beautiful arrival than Independence was upon us, on 23/24 October. I arranged the main ceremony in front of the boma, with the District Messengers lined up on parade beside the flagpole. The DM I'd instructed to play his bugle was fairly drunk by midnight, and his rendering of the Last Post as the Union Jack was hauled down was scarcely recognisable. The new Zambian flag was hoisted, and I had to lead the assembled spectators in singing the new National Anthem; I was surprised and disappointed that few of the leading local politicians seemed to know all the words, but Wendy and I sang with gusto. The fireworks display was rather a disaster; the man in charge of it dropped a lighted cigarette or match into the box of fireworks and most of them went off at once, with squibs darting all over the place. It could have been just amusing, but 165 yards below our boma terrace was the 'cage', and panic seized the ex-Lumpa inmates, who thought the shooting had started again!

I should mention that all DCs had received secret instructions earlier in October to make sure that before Independence they burned all files held which were marked 'secret' or 'strictly confidential', so that there were no later recriminations. This was exceedingly repugnant for me with my views on historical evidence, but orders were orders and I complied. But before burning them I painstakingly copied by hand all the main contents of the secret intelligence reports.

On the organisational side of my life a lot changed, either at once or over the next few months. The Provincial Administration was now to be called the Provincial and District Government; DCs were renamed District Secretaries; we already had a Magistrate, to my relief, but he soon had also to take over the supervision of the local customary courts; the police were now, in theory, entirely responsible for law and order, and two of my DMs were transferred to them; the Prisons Department took over responsibility for the normal prison from me (but not the 'cage') and another seven DMs transferred to this new organisation, to carry on what they had been doing under me; the Ministry of Finance became responsible for the boma accounts and my accounts clerk. But the largest burden taken off my shoulders in all these reorganisations was the supervisory responsibility for the new Rural Council, when a Local Government Officer was posted to Chinsali at the end of the year.

If some people were confused about the meaning of Independence because they still saw me, a European, in the boma office, I went out of my way to let it be known that I was now an officer of the *Zambian* Civil Service. Yes, I found a DS's responsibilities were less than a former DC's. But because of the nature of Chinsali it was more difficult for me than other District Secretaries to divorce myself entirely from responsibility for security matters, given the need for very close co-ordination between rehabilitation, famine relief, police activities and intelligence work. So I chaired the District Intelligence Group and sent off the weekly secret Intelligence Reports to the (now) Resident Secretary in Kasama. I may add that the new Resident Secretary, Mr Baker, seemed to have complete trust in me and never interfered with me – the old colonial adage of 'trust the man on the spot'. I got on very well with him, never abused that trust, and reported to him regularly.

A senior civil servant and ex-DC, Hugh Thompson, had been appointed to a new post of Rehabilitation Officer. He came up from Lusaka and opened a camp at Kotito in Mbala District. He and I then liaised closely. Any ex-Lumpa in my 'cage' who, as agreed by the Chief's representative and a local UNIP official, was still unfit for a return to his/her home village or a new settlement, was transported off to Kotito. Here they were 'de-indoctrinated' (I suppose along the lines of de-Nazification in British PoW camps) until they were deemed to have become acceptable to a Chinsali community. It was a mammoth logistical task and one demanding detailed records of those sent, those returned, those left in my 'cage', those left in Kotito, etc. It took up a lot of my time, but it was necessary. My annual report for 1964 said, '1,700 ex-Lumpas passed through the "cage" between August and 20 November when it was closed; of these, 750 were transferred to Kotito.'

In early December Hugh Thompson informed me that Dr Kaunda, now President, would be coming to Chinsali with most of his family, partly to spend Christmas with his mother and partly to review the progress on rehabilitation. As the DC's house was the largest in Chinsali, Wendy and I 'would have the honour' of accommodating the Kaunda family! We had to rush around making lots of domestic arrangements. We could cope with the President, Mama Kaunda, their youngest four children and a nanny in our house; an ADC and two older Kaunda boys were to sleep in the Magistrate's house next door; and two empty houses were kitted out for Hugh Thompson and several Cabinet Ministers who would be coming, too. State House cooks would travel up by car from Lusaka, to help Wendy and Black.

Come the day, all went very smoothly. As Kaunda's plane landed at the airstrip, I had the amusing task of lining up the reception party. As DS and therefore the President's local representative, I took precedence; I asked the various Cabinet and other Ministers to sort themselves out into whatever order of precedence they mutually agreed, and they entered into the humour of the occasion. Back at the house, I had the Head Messenger ready to raise the Presidential Standard up the flag-pole as we arrived.

The evening meal was a great success, although I cannot recall all the details; present were the Kaundas, the Resident Minister from Kasama (Robert Makasa), Hugh Thompson, two Cabinet Ministers and ourselves, eight in all. Wendy helped our cook to bake a loaf in the shape of a fish eagle, the national emblem, laid it on a mini-flag of Zambia and invited Kaunda to cut off the eagle's head. The atmosphere was very relaxed: conversation flowed easily, even when it inevitably touched on the present problems of reconciliation and rehabilitation. I do remember being encouraged to tell the President exactly how I saw the situation – even if I displeased Robert Makasa with my criticisms of local UNIP officials. I described how long the process took in a village to build up mutual tolerance between UNIP and ex-Lumpa residents, and how one insult from a drunken UNIP member could destroy all the good work and bring us back to square one. He understood entirely and sympathised.

At some stage, either that evening or in the morning, Wendy had a great time with Mama Kaunda. Her twin babies, one of whom (Cheswa) we should meet again forty-eight years later, were about ten months old while Ruth was two months, and the two mothers merrily swapped babies to cuddle and quieten them.

The President and his family went off in the morning to Lubwa, to visit the grave of his father, David, who had been one of the early missionaries there and had come from Livingstonia in Malawi, and then went on to see his mother at Shambalakale Farm. Yes, it had been a great honour for us to entertain the Kaundas. Whenever we met again in my later career, the President used to greet me cheerily with 'Ah, Mr Bond, my tallest civil servant'.

The district was quiet and back to normal until 19 January 1965, when large numbers of ex-Lumpas decided to leave the district. Nearly all ex-Lumpas from the eastern border, totalling about 2,000, gathered into one large group and migrated south-eastwards over the Muchinga escarpment. For over a week they were not traced. Eventually many were found and came to Chief Mukungule's Court in Mpika District, together with some from Chief Chikwa's area who had been living in the bush for six months since the Lundazi incident. We had located them by spotter aircraft and had dropped leaflets for four days running. Their condition was miserable, and many had to remain in hospital for some days to combat the effects of malnutrition and starvation.

This was the time when I had to go off into the bush again for days on end, after doing several flights in a spotter aircraft and a few landings from a helicopter. On the ground my base was the isolated *musumba* of Chief Lundu, 15 miles beyond burnt-out Chilanga and on the edge of the Muchinga escarpment. With Julius again and local guides we walked all day for several days, trying to locate the migrants. That was the area in which we expected them to be, as further north we had come across a trail of possessions they had discarded (including a sewing-machine or two!) as they became exhausted and hungry. The berry season was over, there was no game on the slopes, they would be starving, wet (it was the rainy season) and in fear. We went down and across innumerable gullies, with memorable views over the North Luangwa Game Reserve in the distance, but with little success at first. At last we did come across a few small, frightened groups and they were encouraged to indicate where some larger groups were. In the end I managed to persuade about sixty to follow us back to Lundu, where I had lorries waiting.

Chinsali District did contain one very special place – *Shiwa Ngandu*. A whole separate chapter could deservedly be written about Sir Stewart Gore-Browne, how he built and developed the *Shiwa Ngandu* estate (written about in *The Africa House* by Christina Lamb) and more relevantly to us, his major contribution to Zambian Independence. I will be brief.

I was privileged to know him because Shiwa was in our district. I called on him perhaps half a dozen times in 1964, mainly to check there were no troubles in the vicinity. I found excuses to go more often in 1965, and took Wendy once to meet the 'old man'. His library was where I used to be given an 'audience' with him. One occasion, probably in December 1964, was in connection with his citizenship. He had of course opted for Zambian citizenship at Independence; but in those days this involved his renunciation of British citizenship. In that library I as a magistrate had to witness and countersign his renunciation and, when it came to it, he had an understandable struggle with the emotions. The balcony which led off this room gave a glorious view not only of the well-maintained gardens with their lovely trees but of his beloved lake in the distance, too. And on the flag-pole was the old man's personal standard – a *cipembele* (rhino) on a green background. I also recall him showing me in the long gallery the photographs of which he was most proud: one was of King Edward VII, personally signed by King George V as a gift from him for Sir Stewart's part in the lying-in-state of King Edward VII; the other showed him in full cavalry uniform on guard at one corner of the late King's catafalque.

In July 1965, I handed over to a Zambian DS and we packed to go, exhausted, on leave. Mama Helen Kaunda (KK's mother) attended our farewell party. Stopping for a couple of nights in Lusaka, I felt very ill. This was diagnosed as a bad case of hepatitis A. I was certainly a frightening yellow colour when my parents met us in London.

So many images of the 'Chinsali episode' have remained indelibly imprinted in my mind, yet, second only to Mporokoso, Chinsali was 'our home' and we had come to love many aspects of it.

What irked me, then and since, was the general perception by others who linked the name Chinsali only with the dramatic events of July–August 1964, totally overlooking the aftermath. For me, the next ten months had also been of great importance, if frustrating and less dramatic, as we relentlessly pursued the uphill task of trying to achieve reconciliation in the villages; our efforts in this seemed generally to have been undervalued. Later in life I came to learn that this is the common fate of those dealing with the aftermaths of conflicts, e.g., Rwanda, Bosnia, Sri Lanka, Darfur; in today's jargon, they 'fall off the radar'.

Note

1 *A Visitor's Guide to the Kafue National Park Zambia* by Peter de Vere Moss was published in 2013.

12

LUWINGU, SAMFYA, BROKEN HILL

Kate McRae
(formerly Fiona Morris)

*'The most important person on any boma
should be the DC's wife.'*

One bright spring morning, with considerable trepidation I leave
Neil with baby Bluebell, now aged four or five months, a heap
of instructions, a bottle of juice and a can of baby food and take
the train from Cambridge to London.

The Women's Corona Society has arranged a series of talks
for the wives of new Colonial Officers shortly to be posted overseas; it will obviously help Neil's career if I participate.

I may even learn something useful – but I'm still a nursing
mother and it's the very first time that I've EVER left my baby.
In pigtails, a home-made winter coat, Scholl clogs, my old grey
sixth-former's skirt and Neil's thick woolly socks I'm hardly the
essence of colonial chic.

What do I remember from that informative day?

1. PALM NUTS ARE FULL OF VITAMINS, AND THEIR OIL
    MAY BE GIVEN TO UNDER-NOURISHED AFRICANS
    This information was no use at all in Northern Rhodesia: I
    never went near a market selling palm nuts; and I wouldn't
    have recognised a palm nut if I saw it.

However, in Ghana nearly thirty years later I learned: palm oil is a potent laxative; so, never let a cook put palm oil on your *fufu*; palm wine is delicious drunk from a calabash and the later in the day, the higher the alcohol content of the palm wine.

2. STORES OF FOOD SHOULD BE LOCKED UP BECAUSE COOKS STEAL

   This information was indeed true: but it seemed so insulting to Africans in general, that I did not at first lock up my storeroom, and lost the best part of 100 lb of sugar.

   (It only takes a teaspoon of sugar to make a loaf of bread.)

3. STAFF (COOK, GARDENER, ETC.) SHOULD BE HANDLED FIRMLY

   This information was irrelevant: I mostly had only one cook/house-servant; gardens are looked after by boma staff or prisoners from the jail; cooks already know how to wash clothes if you give them bar soap; it was impossible for someone like me to handle Africans firmly.

   But in Ghana I danced the night away with some of them.

4. A PROPER DINNER CONSISTS OF AT LEAST FOUR COURSES

   This information was impractical: I didn't have enough crockery for four courses; I'd never eaten a four-course meal myself and wouldn't be able to plan one; food was difficult to obtain; Neil's salary was too low for us to afford entertaining.

5. MATCHING LINEN TABLE NAPKINS SHOULD BE FOLDED INTO WATER LILIES, WHICH IS SOMETHING EASILY TAUGHT TO AN AFRICAN

   This was also impractical: I had no idea how to fold a napkin into a water lily; I had no linen napkins.

6. WHEN EXPORTING A PIANO, MAKE SURE IT IS FULLY TROPICALISED

   This information was irrelevant: where would I get the money to export a piano?

When I eventually did get a piano through friends in Livingstone, I found I needed an adjustable spanner to tune it – and I needed to know a bit about piano-tuning.

However, there was a happy ending: I arrived home to find a miraculously contented baby, and a very proud father.

* * *

The most important person on any boma should be the DC's wife. She should stand right behind her man, calm him down when the administrators in Lusaka, the clerks in the office or the locals in the villages have driven him crazy and dissuade him from some of his more foolhardy decisions regarding clinics, vegetable markets, missionaries and the issuing of Land Rovers to European staff so they can go down to the Copperbelt to do their Christmas shopping.

I remember three such wives of people in power: two were DCs' wives and one was married to a PC.

The first I encountered was a PC's wife in Kasama, where we stopped for lunch, after leaving Lusaka and before reaching our first posting at Luwingu. She was tall, big-boned, black-haired, dressed in a smart black or navy frock, and frighteningly, crushingly bossy. The baby was noted and I was given advice on how to get the red dust off her. I think she was taken from me during lunch and handed to a big-bosomed African servant to be kept amused. I certainly had two hands to eat with, even if I wasn't sure how to handle the cutlery.

I remember being shocked at how smart the dining-room was: gleaming silver, snow-white table linen, sparkling glasses – and servants who moved silently, were spotlessly clean and knew what they were doing. I was definitely served avocado pear first. I had never seen or tasted one before. This one was creamy, slimy and cut up into strips. I forced it down with lots of dry bread and tried not to heave. There was also sherry, and probably wine. Since I didn't normally drink in those days, I must have turned squiffy. I certainly did not enjoy myself, even though the host turned out to be quite a dear.

The second wife I met was Jill, wife of the DC Luwingu. She was probably the best of the bunch: short, tough, well-bred, mannish. She was totally in harmony with her tall, wispy, aristocratic, fairy-like husband who was said to be related to the gentry. She wore short-sleeved check shirts and neatly-pressed slacks. She didn't speak, she barked. I imagine she must have been capable of driving an ambulance, firing a gun or leaping into the saddle and riding a horse. She was reputed to have reversed a car into her two-year-old son and fractured his skull.

Jill's big skill was organisation. She was top of the pecking order and she got us all lined up behind her in rank order. When the Governor-General of the Federation of the two Rhodesias and Nyasaland turned up on an official visit, she worked out who could be expected to entertain him for what portion of which day – and who could not (i.e., me), and she distributed our tasks accordingly. She taught us to curtsey. When the actual big event happened, I stumbled over the doorstep – we'd practised in the garden, where there hadn't been a doorstep – and I completely forgot my curtsey. But I had other things on my mind: I was newly pregnant, and I had just finished sewing my dress from a piece of Grandma's silk and I was afraid it was going to slip off my shoulder. The event was evening cocktails. And when Jill produced dinner for the GG afterwards, she made him egg custard for pudding, saying that the poor man was probably tired of all the fancy food people gave him and would enjoy something simple – and I believe he did.

Jill gave dinner parties for those of us whose husbands were part of the administration; she carefully avoided feeding Police, Roads and Drains and Waterworks. From her I gradually absorbed how to set a table, how many courses to have, how to turn limited foodstuffs into something new and palatable and what a local cook from the village could – and could not – be expected to do. So different from my childhood meals in the kitchen at Ealing, and occasional Sunday roasts with Grandma. From my pool of relatives, only Great-Aunt Marie (ex-Barbados, three husbands, drank like a fish, taught me at age five to play canasta) could have matched Jill for chutzpah.

I remember being utterly amazed by upper-class table manners. When the soup was a little bland, Jill said, 'Cook wasn't at his best when he made this' and tossed the entire contents of her sherry-glass into her soup-plate, advising us to follow suit. When a DC from another boma recited my father-in-law's poem about the sexual urge of the camel during dinner, following it up with a joke about a bishop who dangled his balls in the gravy, Jill couldn't stop laughing.

Jill was followed by Mary. She was large, soft and jolly, a gentler woman than Jill but equally competent, and married to a small, fierce, soldier-like person. She had been a midwife and was a mine of information (comforting, sensible information) about pregnancies and babies. She was also willing to give us injections if the doctor sent the stuff out by Land Rover in a Thermos. She once delivered her cook's wife's baby by lamplight in a *cimbusu* (latrine) and saved its life when it got stuck, with the cord wound round its neck.

Mary and I had babies two days apart (my second, her first) and she let me weigh mine on her kitchen scales. She wasn't as experienced a boma wife as Jill at that stage, but I'm sure she would always have kept her head in any emergency and, having been a ward sister, she knew all about keeping her end up in a managerial hierarchy.

*   *   *

Having now arrived at the beginning of old age and survived two decades of decadent living as an expat in Hong Kong, as well as two icy winters in vodka-soused Mongolia, I am no longer easily shocked. But when I look back to myself at the age of twenty-three, the product of an all-girls' school and a parson's daughter to boot, I can see how incredibly naive I was, and how totally confused as to what was expected of me. I had no idea what was 'done' and what was 'not done'; I collected scraps of advice from other wives and applied them when I could, making a none-too-successful patchwork.

Everything was new to me: the climate, the seasons, the servants, the spiders and snakes; ordering food two weeks in advance so it could be delivered by refrigerated truck; getting goods on tick and paying the tradesmen later; being totally cut off from radio or newspapers and rarely getting post; living without electricity, running water or a telephone; using powdered milk and a paraffin fridge; recognising and treating the various kinds of diarrhoea; meeting my very first Paramount Chief and my very first White Fathers.

An older, more motivated me might have occupied my time wisely learning ciBemba or sketching; but in those days I was content to talk to the baby (herself now a TEFLA teacher in her fifties) and sew baby clothes for her young brother (who now works with computers in Hong Kong). Now and again I dipped into my father's Kipling but unfortunately I didn't like his Hardy. It seems to me (now) that my life (then) was quite addled by baby clutter. I've tried to pick my way through the debris and remove whatever could have happened at any time, in any place, to any mother. What remains below is what seems to me to be uniquely African, and of its time.

Seersucker

First, there is my seersucker blouse, carefully crafted by hand from a length of my grandmother's fabric. I remember Baranabba, my first cook, coming to me in despair. Having dampened the blouse several times and compressed it mightily with a pair of flat irons, he declared himself quite unable to get the bumps out of the cloth. For those of you who have not encountered this once-fashionable fabric, seersucker is made out of intentional rows of bumps, which is what makes it such a unique sort of cloth.

Putsi Fly

There is a rule about what to iron in Africa. All garments made of natural fibres must be ironed if they've been hung outside to dry, because of the putsi fly which lays its eggs on damp clothes, from where the maggots can burrow into the warm flesh of their host animal. My cook already knew this. But a child's winter pyjama suit is relatively thick. So if it's hung in the sun inside out and then turned the right way before ironing, there may still be fly's eggs in an inside seam, which have not been cauterised by the iron's heat. My memory concerns a bright red boil on my baby's shoulder, whose head I pierced with a darning needle. When I gently squeezed, instead of the expected pus, I was greeted by the head and shoulders of a large wriggling maggot. I had to pull the whole creature out without squashing him, and pack the crater left behind with acriflavine cream. Luckily, I had read the instruction manual.

Christening

The new baby's christening may not have been uniquely African, but it was certainly un-British and a far cry from Clare College chapel, where baby number one had been baptised. He was born shortly before we were to leave Luwingu on posting; the DC's wife had also had a baby the same week as me, so we arranged a joint christening in her garden. The ceremony was performed by an itinerant parson and our baby was christened Malcolm Gregory.

I remember nothing about the food at the christening: not making sandwiches nor boiling eggs. I certainly wouldn't have risked baking a cake. However, I did provide something of value: the font. I had a splendid cut-glass salad bowl from the Bonanza Stores in Ealing Broadway – which remains treasured and unbroken to this day. The parson said it was ideal: he didn't need a lot of water for just two babies. Afterwards I caught him tipping the water away in the flower bed and (since water was precious and had often to be carried a long way) I asked him why. He said that, because he had blessed it, it was now Holy Water, and it would have been quite wrong to give it to the cook.

Marmalade

Since our trees were loaded with oranges and I had nearly a whole hundred pounds of sugar, I decided to make some. I took out my grandmother's cookbook and borrowed some large saucepans, chased the cook out of the big dark kitchen annexe and set about boiling oranges. When the mixture was ready, I poured it into the white enamel baby bath to cool and set, and gave the pans to the cook to wash and return to their owners. Unfortunately I didn't know the difference between Seville oranges, which contain pectin which helps marmalade to set solid, and Rhodesian oranges, which are totally unsuitable for jam-making. For several days we had custard and runny orange sauce for pudding. Eventually the mess started to ferment and was thrown out. The baby bath remained a hideous shade of yellow for ever.

Fried Baby

After the culinary problem with the marmalade, I had another: the inadvertent near-frying of the baby. He was brand-new, straight back from hospital and clearly going to have red hair. Obviously he had to be kept out of strong sunlight. After his morning bath and breakfast, I put him in the pram under a fly-net and wheeled him beneath a shady tree. Being recently fed, he wouldn't wake up for at least three hours. I carefully did the maths, triangulating sun and shade, just as I'd done for our first baby in Cambridge. You may have guessed what happened next: within ten minutes the baby was squawking his head off, scarlet in the face. Glancing at the sun, I realised it had moved in completely the wrong direction and started cooking the baby instead of moving him deeper into the shade. Some eight years before, when I had reluctantly dozed through geography lessons, I recalled a teacher mentioning that if you lived in the southern hemisphere the sun appeared to rotate anti-clockwise. Somehow I'd already been in Africa ten months and not once noticed the sun.

Snake

My African memories would not be complete without a snake. This one arrived after lunch when both children were napping. The cook was howling in the garden, and when I opened the door wide to see what was wrong with him, the snake slipped past my bare feet and into the dining-room, where it took shelter amidst the thicket of chair legs under the dining-table. It wasn't a little adder-like thing but green, seriously snaky and about 5 feet long.

Luckily, there was an alternative way to the children's bedroom which bypassed the dining-room, so I shot down the corridor, slammed their door shut and stuffed Beatrix Potter books into the crack at the bottom of the door to keep the snake out. Then I raised the mosquito gauze and popped Bluebell out, onto the flower bed, tucked the baby under one arm and climbed out myself.

We went to the boma to get Daddy, a Messenger who understood about killing snakes and a big stick. The snake turned out to be a green mamba.

Elections

My final memories concern the elections. Just before they took place, Neil went on a tour of the swamps to register the voters so that there would be some sort of electoral register, however incomplete. To my delight, I was allowed to travel with him and take the children.

When we were back in Samfya, the wives (around twenty of us) were summoned to the boma and asked to help co-ordinate the electoral data. We worked in pairs, dictating, typing and checking list after list of names. I typed each man's village after his name. I typed 'Chief Mwansakombe, P.O. Mwewa' until my fingers were dropping off.

Later the people of Zambia had their president and they had their freedom. I remember standing outside my bungalow in the night air, listening to frenetic, crazily happy drumming echoing off the lake, and wondering what Kaunda would mean for Africa – and for us. At that time I felt very apprehensive, and scared of what 'they' might do to 'us'.

It was only years later, with VSO, that I learned to love Africa.

13

MAZABUKA, LUSAKA, BALOVALE, SOLWEZI

Robert Humphreys

*'This was Africa as I had always imagined it in
my childhood dreams.'*

*Throughout my time in Northern Rhodesia I kept a record of
my day-to-day experiences. The extracts below, which are taken
from my diary entries, are supported by notes giving additional
background information.*

Tuesday, 28 October 1958

Lightning flashed, thunder roared and the rain fell in a solid wall
of water. I had just stepped off the north-bound mail train from
Livingstone in what seemed to be the middle of nowhere with only
6d in my pocket. I was somewhat inappropriately dressed in grey
flannel trousers, a blazer and wearing my old school tie. I had with
me a suitcase and gun case and was sitting on my father's battered
old metal uniform box trying vainly to shelter from all that nature
seemed to be directing at me personally. Welcome to Mazabuka.

I had turned nineteen in September and had been
appointed as a Learner District Assistant by Her Majesty's

Colonial Office to serve in the district of Mazabuka in the Southern Province of what was, then, Northern Rhodesia. I was hot, wet, apprehensive and terribly alone; feelings which were only to last for a few moments for a Land Rover swept through the rain and mud and I was rescued by the District Officer. I was whisked off to the District Commissioner's house, where I was introduced to the District Commissioner and his wife. From then on there was no time to feel sorry for myself as I was taken under the wing of the DC's wife and organised and prepared for life in Africa.

Thursday, 16 April 1959

The DC asked me to accompany him to Lochinvar, a huge cattle station on the Kafue flats, as he wanted to check on some game guards. He also told me to bring my gun. When we arrived, we reported to the manager and told him we were off to the flats. On our way down we passed a small herd of wildebeest and hundreds of red lechwe. We met the game guards and then set off after the duck. I managed to bag four and the DC, who on his own admission was not a keen shot, made some valiant attempts; in shooting at a spur wing goose he managed to hit a vulture. It was a truly wonderful place; flat as a pancake with a huge expanse of water stretching in one direction and rolling grass land in the other all under an enormous sky. Roaming over this paradise were herds of countless red lechwe and zebra with scattered herds of eland. Outnumbering all these animals were the birds of every sort, which flocked onto the flats in their millions. This was Africa as I had always imagined it in my childhood dreams.

Saturday, 18 April 1959

I woke at 4.00 a.m. and cycled to the boma where I met the District Assistant and the Messengers and we were shortly joined by the police contingent. We were off on a beer raid. When we arrived at Lubombo it was still pitch dark so we split up and began searching the houses for illegal beer brewers, their product, prostitutes and unlicensed dogs, not necessarily in that order. Soon after dawn we had rounded up some of each. The beer was contained in 44-gallon oil drums and the contents were tipped on the ground, much to the annoyance of all the villagers. It was only when a few very large ladies dashed forward and started trying to lap up the beer before it soaked into the mud and slipped and slithered in their attempts that everyone began to see the funny side. A potentially nasty situation was avoided and good humour once again prevailed.

Before leaving England I had received my call-up papers for National Service; these arrived about a week before I was due to sail. After frantic phone calls I was assured by a very smug voice on the other end of the line that I needn't worry because the Federation, being still under Her Majesty's jurisdiction, would catch me at the other end. Sure enough, my papers duly arrived and on Monday, 24 June 1959 I found myself, along with a group of equally lost and apprehensive characters reporting at Heany Barracks, the HQ of the Royal Rhodesia Regiment outside Bulawayo. There followed four and a half months of intensive basic training, which after a very rude awakening, typical, I suspect, of all military training, turned into one of the most interesting and entertaining parts of life up to then.

I returned to Mazabuka after my basic training and heard that I had been chosen to go on the Overseas Services Course at Cambridge. My tour was extended for a further six months, which I spent working at the Secretariat in Lusaka; a very boring time.

After completing the course at Cambridge, during which time I married, my wife, Jane, and I were posted to Balovale in the North Western Province.

Monday, 29 October 1962

At 2.00 p.m. I went to the boma and met Tommy from the Water Department, who was to be my 2 i/c for tomorrow's election. We hung around for the African clerk and when he didn't arrive we went to his house and found him tight as a tick clutching two radios and a bottle of gin. There was nothing for it but to report him to the DC and set off without him. We travelled in grand style to the pontoon to cross the Zambezi only to find the operator had gone AWOL. After hours waiting in the boiling sun he lurched towards us breathing out fumes strong enough to strip paint. We got across more by good luck than anything else and finally arrived at Muyembwe. We immediately set to putting up posters and polling-booths and then paid off the labourers who had built the camp.

Tuesday, 30 October 1962

Election Day and a 5.00 a.m. start for us. We shaved using a bucket looking at ourselves in the wing mirror of the Land Rover as the sun rubbed its eyes and poked a tentative finger through the trees. At 6.15 a.m. the UNIP representative arrived. We formally sealed the ballot-boxes and kicked off at 6.30 a.m. Everyone was very well organised and came through in a steady stream. At about 9.15 the Special Branch Officer arrived to see if all was going well and sold me a couple of tickets in the election sweep which he was organising. By 10.30 the penultimate voter had finished leaving only one woman to go. She, poor thing, was eight months pregnant and was last seen 15 miles away struggling with her bicycle in the sand. We were powerless to help as we could not possibly be seen to be favouring anyone. There was nothing left for us to do but sit and wait until 7.30 p.m. We chatted and listened to the African Service of the FBC (Federal Broadcasting Corporation) on a wireless one of the messengers had brought with him. In the afternoon Tommy and I played cricket with a bit of wood and Masuku fruit. Eventually, after a rain storm we got on with the necessary reports and it was then that we found Tommy had issued a whole book of Lower

European National votes instead of African. It was too late to do anything about it and poor Tommy had visions of spending a life sentence at Her Majesty's pleasure. At last 7.30 came and we were able to seal the boxes and depart. The pontoon wasn't working so we crossed the Zambezi in a dugout canoe hoping against hope that we would remain upright and not tip ourselves and the precious boxes into the river in the pitch dark.

Tours here were always on foot because of the deep sand in the dry season and the floods in the wet, making cycling impossible. A typical tour in the Balovale District consisted of the District Officer, a couple of Messengers, the DO's cook, the African Court Clerk for the Chief's area where the tour was taking place, the *Ngambela*, who was the Chief's 2 i/c, a couple of *Kapasus* (the Chief's Messengers) and about twenty-four African carriers, who carried all the camping equipment. Food was either bought from the villagers en route or, in the case of the rains, was bought in advance in Balovale and sent out to villages along the proposed route to await arrival.

The purpose of going on tour was for the Administration to be seen by the villagers as actively administrating. On arriving at a village, all the inhabitants were called together by the *Kapasus* and Messengers, the headman was formally greeted by the DO and then the roll was called. Every man in the village had his name entered in a huge ledger which was kept by the Court Clerk. As his name was called out he was asked to give the number of his wives and children, the number of dogs, chickens and livestock he possessed and how many bicycles. Dogs, bicycles and people were taxed, with the money going into the Native Authority treasury. In this way an amazingly accurate census was kept similar to an ever-updated Doomsday Book. The villagers were invited to tell of their problems and other grievances which were not the sort that could be settled in the Tribal Court. Lastly, it was also customary for the DO to hold a surgery where he doled out a limited supply of medicines to those in need.

Saturday, 24 November 1962

On tour in Central and South Ndungu on the Luvale side

As if to make up for the night before, the rain came down in earnest accompanied by thunder and lightning galore. It very decently decided to stop just before breakfast so I was able to have that in the dry, thank heaven. The Messengers, *Kapasus* and I set out soon after 7.00 a.m. and trudged our way through dripping trees and sodden undergrowth. Most of the way was along a dambo which added to our discomfort. However, the sun soon came out and it wasn't long before we arrived at our first village picturesquely laid out on the banks of the Chinyingi. It was very attractive and clean. We crossed the Chinyingi on a low bank, which would later be used as a base for fish traps and came to our second village, which was even more attractive than the first. It was on a mound and dotted with hundreds of shady mango trees fringed with rustling banana plantations. This afternoon I called the roll in Chipopa village. It was nearly dark when I finished work and went to have my bath. It is probably because we are surrounded by water, but the mosquitoes are out in force tonight and I was very nearly eaten alive in my canvas bath. When I got back to my tent I had to fight my way through a mass of flying creatures and had an interesting time picking foreign bodies out of my soup. I eventually gave up the unequal struggle and dived under my net under the baleful eye of a large speckled creature which clung tenaciously to the mosquito netting. I had no desire to get better acquainted.

Sunday, 25 November 1962

The carriers decided to have a long, loud and very heated discussion about their sex lives right outside my tent last night, so it was some time before I managed to get some sleep. I woke next morning to a lovely day, and we set off just before 7.00 a.m. and tramped about 7 miles through some really beautiful woodland interspersed with streams. Time after time I found myself doing my tight rope act over slippery, half submerged logs and consider myself quite an expert now. We had five villages to look at, all on the banks of the Zambezi. We also dropped in on Mr Umbilici, the newly appointed UNIP candidate, at his farm. He was very pleasant and gave us cups of tea with door-step sandwiches and then showed us round his citrus plantation. This made a very pleasant and interesting break. We managed to look round all the villages and call the rolls by 2.00 p.m. I'm afraid the villages were all very sordid, which is strange considering their beautiful locations and the potential offered for growing vegetables and fruit. However, the feeling of lethargy is palpable and all questions are answered with a shrug of the shoulders. At about 5.00 p.m. I went for a stroll on my own and followed a path which brought me out onto a beautiful little stream that had hollowed itself out into a natural deep, clear pool set about with lush green grassy banks. I sat here for about half an hour and just let my mind wander. It was marvellously relaxing.

Friday, 29 March 1963

On tour in the Kahoka area

This morning we left Ngongola and splashed and sweated our way across 16 miles of soggy plain. Many was the time I wondered what dry feet felt like as I ploughed knee deep in black, sand-filled water. The trouble with this wet walking is that the sand gets washed into one's shoes and gets between the toes. As one's feet are wet and therefore soft, the sand plays merry hell with one's skin. My feet are now raw between the toes and very sore which makes walking extremely painful. When we arrived at our camp at Nyangambula we found the site under water and had to scout around for another. After washing the sand from my feet and changing into dry socks and shoes, we went to call the villagers. All went well until I asked if they had anything to speak to me about. Now the trouble started as they flatly refused to pay their dog taxes for, as they put it, 'Dogs are not men therefore should not be taxed.' After letting them have their say, I issued an ultimatum, either they license their dogs or I shoot them, the dogs I mean. This kicked off a wonderful game of bluff. I asked my Messenger to collect my gun, which was still in its case, and my cartridge bag. Whilst the villagers argued and blustered, I slowly assembled and loaded my gun and then told the Messengers and *Kapasus* to collect up all the dogs. As soon as the dogs were herded into the centre of the village, the money started pouring in. The Native Authority officials were suitably impressed and afterwards I was amused to see and hear them strutting about, patting each other on the back and saying, 'We must be firm with these people.'

Sunday, 31 March 1963

A surgery at Muyembe camp

After lunch, I called the roll outside the camp and was prepared for a violent outburst when the time came for questions because the people in this village have a reputation for being 'outspoken'. As it turned out all went very smoothly and we entered into an interesting discussion about the need for a hospital in the area. After tea I opened my 'hospital' and a long queue quickly formed containing some of the sickest looking Africans I have ever seen. They lined up before me clutching various parts of their anatomies as though they were in the last stages. I judged by the position of the 'clutch' and the look on their faces what the best medicine might be, whether cough mixture, aspirin or liniment. After some time it dawned on me that some faces were familiar and that they were coming round for a second helping. This was confirmed by my Messenger, John, who whispered in my ear that the DO's medicine was worth a lot on the black market. I had to put a stop to this charade, but it had to be done in a way which would appeal to their wonderful, school boy, banana skin sense of humour, so I asked John in a loud voice to fetch me a large chopping block and an axe. A hush fell on the assembled gathering as John came back solemnly carrying a large wooden block and an axe which he placed before me with due ceremony. I stood and equally solemnly beckoned forward the next in line, whom I recognised as having previously come to me clutching his head. This time he was limping most pathetically so I ran my hand over his foot and then stepped back and invited him to place his foot on the block. Slowly I raised the axe above my head, the crowd fell silent and the man's face turned ashen, then I dropped the axe and burst out laughing. Immediately the place erupted in laughter, none more so than my erstwhile patient and all went about their way clutching their sides, but not this time in mock pain.

Like most administrative jobs, work in the boma tended to be very repetitive, boring and interspersed with occasional amusing or interesting episodes. For the most part, however, it consisted of liaising with the Native Authority Court Clerks, checking their court records and trial balances, operating the radio for either the morning or afternoon shift or sometimes both. This radio link was very important as it was a way for the Provincial centre, Solwezi, to keep in instant touch with all the districts within the province. It needed some getting used to as the static, particularly during the afternoon sessions, could make conversation almost impossible.

A more interesting part of office life was dealing with problems and complaints which the Africans would bring to our door either in person or by letter. One such letter came from one of the political representatives, who was obviously having a hard time with the DC. He could find no way of venting his frustration until he hit upon the idea of writing a letter to the highest authority he could think of, who happened to be Jesus. The letter was addressed to 'Jesus c/o God the Father, PO Box Heaven'. I forget the exact wording of the letter but it was along the following lines: 'Dear Jesus, Why have you made me so miserable and heaped the cares of the world on my shoulders? Please call me and the DC to your court so that you can hear our case.' The African postmaster, on receiving this envelope and after a bit of head-scratching, decided the nearest thing to 'God the Father' was the DC and directed the letter to the boma.

Another more out-of-the-ordinary occasion was when we received a visit from the Chief Secretary, who visited Balovale on 15 November 1962 to carry out an investiture, bestowing medals to Chiefs Chinyama Litapi and Ishinde. It was an 'occasion', which meant the Chief Secretary was in full uniform with plumed helmet and sword. The PC was also in attendance, but the DC was thrown into a complete panic because the boma Land Rovers were very battered and he didn't consider them smart enough to transport the great man and his wife. He decided that I would have to drive them in my Ford Anglia. Now an Anglia was never designed to be an official limousine, and apart from the fact it was very small with not much headroom, it only had two doors. As everyone knows, a dignitary always has to sit in the back seat behind the chauffeur so that an assassin's bullet will hit the chauffeur first. So we were presented with the problem of loading the CS into the Anglia through the front passenger door together with his plumed helmet and sword. The loading was hard but not impossible because this was done in the privacy of the DC's drive; the problem really came when we arrived in convoy behind the DC in his battered Land Rover and the PC in his slightly smarter one and had to decant the CS and his wife with due pomp and ceremony outside the court-house with everybody watching. Luckily, the CS and his wife both had a great sense of humour, so that his wife managed to squeeze out of the back seat with a great deal of panache, keeping her hat on. But when the CS emerged he did so bottom-first with his sword tangled up between his legs, hanging on to the door frame with one hand and his plumed helmet with the other. He emerged, very red in the face, slowly straightened, removing the kinks from his back and neck, adjusted his helmet, disentangled his sword and marched resolutely into the court as though he did this sort of thing every day of his life. The investiture went off without a hitch and afterwards I was put in charge of the bar and dispensed vast quantities of whisky, lime and Fanta, all mixed together, to the Chiefs and their entourages.

Social life revolved around the club, tennis-court and the sandbank on the Zambezi where we used to organise picnics and swimming parties. We would hold regular Scottish country dances in the club and serious tennis matches, with the high spot being the 'Dimple Haig' tournament. This was a men's foursome where a bottle of Dimple Haig was placed beside the net and after every game the participants would have a tot. As the game progressed, the tennis would become more and more erratic, or spectacular, depending on whether one was watching or playing. At the end of the match, the losers would pay for the whisky, but by then it didn't really matter.

On 7 September 1963, Jane, Charles, our very young son, and I were transferred to Solwezi, the Provincial HQ, attached to the DC's office. By now we all knew that Independence was very near and the country was gearing up for the elections which would usher in the new era.

My work time in Solwezi was almost entirely spent with the Native Authority, trying to get the councillors to accept the responsibility of drawing up budgets which had a chance of balancing. Unfortunately for the councillors, the political situation was hotting up daily, with the UNIP representatives beginning to flex their muscles. This meant that the councillors were caught between the established Administration – the boma and central Government – and the would-be Government in the form of the UNIP members, who were demanding official recognition with a say in how things should be run. As a result, nothing could be resolved without endless, seemingly needless, negotiations, which was extremely frustrating for all concerned.

The other spectre forever haunting us was the situation in the Congo, which was turning very nasty indeed. Our first contact was when groups of Katangese soldiers numbering up to 3,000 would come across the border searching for pay, which never materialised, and food. When asked to move on they would meekly head for Angola, searching vainly for the same things, only to be told far more forcibly to push off. There was always the fear that sooner or later their patience would wear thin and trouble would ensue.

By the end of 1963 it was clear to me that there was no long-term future for my family and me so we booked our passage back to England for October 1964. The last day of December 1963 not only saw the beginning of the end of our African dream, but also the end of the experiment which was the Federation of Rhodesia and Nyasaland.

Monday, 20 January 1964

The alarm went off at 5 this morning and I was in the court at 6 a.m. to begin sealing the ballot-boxes and getting the room ready for polling. We opened at 6.30 and didn't draw breath until 4.30 p.m. We had 851 people through to vote and the queue stretched for about 200 yards at times. Everything went very smoothly and the crowds were cooperative. About one person in twenty knew what he or she had to do with their ballot-paper, so the procedure had to be explained very carefully to everyone. Even so there were about forty papers found under the table, between the boxes and on top of them. The DC arrived soon after 4.30 p.m. and told me there had been a bit of trouble in the morning when a crowd of people had turned up at Chovwe when they should have been voting at Chisasa, 50 miles away. At Chisasa about 200 people had stormed the school all trying to vote at once. We closed the polling-station at 5 p.m. and at about 5.30 p.m. a Land Rover came tearing up with a message from the polling officer saying that things were looking nasty at Chisasa as the crowd were demanding to be able to vote there and were getting very upset. The DC decided to return to Chisasa to try and sort things out.

We heard on the news this evening that there had been a military coup in Tanganyika and Nyerere was under house arrest.

We also heard that a local man had been beaten up by UNIP youths not far from here.

One of our tasks at this time was to promote self-help projects for building schools and dispensaries. One such project was to rebuild the old, dilapidated and dangerous school at Mapunga, which was in a very isolated part of the district. In order to help with persuading the people to rally round the project it was decided to enlist the help of the Jesuit priests.

Tuesday, 7 April 1964

This morning we loaded up two Land Rovers and at 9 a.m. we went round to the Mission House to pick up Brother Francis and Father Joseph. We made good time along the main road, but it was entirely different when we hit the Mapunga road. We crawled along at about 5 mph through towering grass, over pot holes, tree stumps and boulders, assailed all the while by swarms of tsetse flies. Brother Francis had to sit on the bonnet of my Land Rover to act as scout, warning me of impending hazards whilst Father Joseph followed close behind. Eventually at 3 p.m. we arrived at Mapunga. There was no time to snatch a meal so we called the people together and began exhorting them to build the new school. It worked like a charm and everyone was most enthusiastic. When we had finished our *indaba* we went prospecting for suitable building sand and stone and found just what we needed by the river. I was intrigued by a peculiar type of canoe they have here; not the normal hollowed out tree trunk but instead formed with a sheet of bark with turned up edges and turned up ends sewn together to form the bow and stern. We had an early supper cooked by Father Joseph and then called the school children together to put on a sing-song and dance. They were a bit shy to begin with but soon livened up and put on a very jolly, impromptu concert. Tonight I slept in the Land Rover to escape the dew.

The self-help projects which started so enthusiastically began to lose their impetus, as my diary entry shows.

157

Friday, 19 June 1964

I had to write a progress report on the schools which are being built by self-help in the district. It would seem that interest is already on the wane. At Matebo, where they have been working for a month, they have only managed to make 14,000 bricks and yet at Mushindamo, where they have been working for only four days, they have already made 8,000. The supervisor at Mapunga has almost given up in disgust as in three months they have only made 10,000 bricks. He says the people are too interested in drinking beer and not in work.

> The wind of change became more and more apparent as the date for Independence drew nearer. I had been offered a job back in England and so was granted leave to fly home before the actual day. The general air of uncertainty grew daily both for the Provincial Administration staff, including Messengers and *Kapasus*, but also for the Chiefs.

Thursday, 2 July 1964

The PC it seems is now definitely going and his replacement, the Regional Secretary, is almost certain to be a European and not an African as originally thought. The DC is also thinking of moving to make way for the new District Secretary, but nothing is certain. Suffice to say there are going to be changes and when they come they will be fast and drastic. There are moves afoot to do away with Messengers and *Kapasus* and amalgamate them with the Police, Prisons, Forestry and other departments. There are also plans to amalgamate the Native Courts and to remove judicial powers from the Chiefs. These moves will undermine the power of the Chiefs and will not be popular. This evening a statement on the radio said that the future changes would not affect the Chiefs in any way. Just what is going on?

> From 15 July 1964 when we handed over our house in Solwezi until the day we flew back to England on 24 July our lives were in a haze because Jane went down with

infective hepatitis and I followed suit a few days later. Between us we had to look after Charles whilst feeling like death warmed up. For a time it was touch and go as to whether we would be allowed to fly, but in the end permission was granted.

The final entry in my diary reads:

Friday, 24 July 1964

This we did with very mixed feelings. I was very sad to leave Northern Rhodesia as I have thoroughly enjoyed my time out here and will never regret any of it. My only regret is that I have to leave the country looking so awful with yellow skin and poached eggs for eyes.

14

FORT JAMESON AND THE KUNDA VALLEY, LUNDAZI

Tony Goddard

'I mentioned, more in hope than expectation, that I just happened to be about to start a youth scheme in the Kunda Valley and could do with the assistance of someone like him.'

The following passages are drawn from Tony Goddard's book My African Stories.

We flew up to Fort Jameson with Jim Lavender, one of the other Cadets from the Cambridge Course who had travelled out ahead of his fiancée...Fort Jameson (now renamed Chipata) was both a provincial and district capital so that it boasted not only a Provincial Commissioner and his staff but also a District Commissioner and his District Officers and staff...There were three tribes in Fort Jameson District – the Chewa, the Ngoni and, furthest from the town in the Luangwa valley, was the smallest of the three tribes, the Kunda...Our first port of call in Fort Jimmy was the boma to report to the District and Provincial Commissioners. We started with the Provincial Commissioner who...began by telling us what we already knew, namely that there were two posts on offer, one as Officer in Charge of the Kunda Valley Native Authority and the other in Chadiza, a sub-station of Fort Jimmy. He went on to enquire whether we had decided between ourselves who was to go where...We were both rather non-plussed by this and seeing our hesitation the Provincial Commissioner suggested we toss for it. We both agreed. He produced a coin which he spun for us. I got the Kunda Valley and Jim Chadiza. We were, I think, both pleased with the way things turned out...

The Luangwa Valley...for which, aged twenty three, I was to be responsible, ran from north to south between the Northern and Eastern Provinces. The Luangwa River was the boundary between the two and it was therefore the western extremity of the Eastern Province. The Valley lay several hundred feet below the rest of the province being set in a rift valley, similar to the Great Rift Valley of East Africa, so that going to and from Fort Jimmy, which lay more or less in the middle of the province, one had to ascend or descend the escarpment which lay between the Valley and the plateau on which Fort Jimmy was fortunate to be sited. There was a noticeable change in temperature as one descended into the Valley...The Kunda tribe, for whom I was to be responsible, occupied the southern end of the Valley...

We soon settled into life on tour. Peter [our cook] would bring us tea soon after dawn so that we could take full advantage of the cool of the day. An eye was obviously kept on the progress of my breakfast because as soon as it was clear that I was back on duty, [Senior Messenger] James...would draw up the Messengers, including himself as first in line and any passing *Kapasus*, for my inspection. At the same time a silent line of villagers would form. When this happened the first morning I enquired what they were waiting for and was told *mankwala* (medicine). I denied any ability to prescribe let alone provide medicines but James reassured me that the boma always provided a supply of medicines for its District Officers on tour. Sure enough he produced, for my inspection, a large wooden box full of jars and bottles containing evil-looking pills and potions. The task of uniting the appropriate medicines with the waiting patients was most satisfactorily solved by my wife, who, although possessing no formal medical training, had enough knowledge and a strong enough stomach to set up a flourishing clinic dealing with a variety of complaints...Undoubtedly her efforts were appreciated and did much to ensure our welcome in the area...

*   *   *

[Until recently] there had been no history of political activity in the Valley, and certainly no tradition of resentment against European officers, of whom, indeed, in general [the people] appeared to be rather fond. Perhaps this was because until my arrival they had seen so little of them. Unfortunately the UNIP officials who started to move into the area regarded the expatriate civil servants, and District Officer Cadet Goddard in particular, as representing a repressive foreign regime which was holding them in bondage...

The attitude of the officers who, like me, were in the front line was irritation that the politicians were creating a climate in which it was difficult to deliver the services which the local population badly needed. In the case of the Provincial Administration this meant, I suppose, ensuring that the area enjoyed an orderly and peaceful existence in which local government provided by...the Chiefs and central Government could give the local population the necessary services it required. The Chiefs were placed in a most invidious position...District Officers, such as me...pointed out that if they wanted to continue to receive a stipend from the Government and be provided with Court Clerks and *Kapasus*, they would in exchange have to uphold the law, even if this upset the local UNIP officials. These officials on the other hand put the Chiefs under considerable pressure to throw in their lot with the party which would soon be forming the new Government and who would not forget Chiefs who had been unsympathetic to their cause...

I had been warned by my predecessor...that UNIP was operating in the area and I had seen the occasional home-made UNIP sash or armband. I had even seen, but ignored, travelling in the Land Rover, the occasional UNIP wave (hands held up with fingers extended and waving to illustrate the sun coming up; in other words 'the dawn of freedom') but this had been done in a slightly embarrassed fashion...

Gradually the scale of the political activity increased with the arrival of a new and more inflammatory Constituency Chairman who came to visit me. He made no bones about his intention to have me removed and for his party under his leadership to take over the administration of the area. I explained, I trust politely, that my orders prevented my allowing this and that if he or his henchmen broke the law I would have no hesitation in arresting him and them. He obviously paid no attention to my warning and incidents of violence began to mount. There was virtually no ANC presence in the area, or if there was any they wisely kept their heads down, but gangs of youths were recruited to deter anyone who might be opposed to the party and they toured the Valley causing mayhem. Their favourite trick was to set up roadblocks and demand to see the party cards of those passing by. Those who failed to produce them were persuaded to join on payment of a fee. Those who tried to object were manhandled. The victims, although happy to tell their tale, were too frightened by the threat of reprisals (usually having their huts burned down) to want to take the matter further. The Chiefs and their *Kapasus* knew exactly what was going on but were themselves too terrified of the consequences to take action…

It was against that background that I had the bright idea of setting up a youth scheme. I would ask the Chiefs to volunteer their six naughtiest young men for three months and I would provide them with a rudimentary uniform and food and lodging and training in bricklaying, thatching and carpentry. The advantage to the young men was that it would give them trades which would enable them to earn a living and remain in the area. The advantage to the Government, as the Chiefs with whom I discussed it were quick to see, was that it would keep the young men in the villages and provide the means and incentive to the more affluent of their subjects to improve their houses. For me there was the advantage that it would keep thirty-six potential stone throwers out of my way for a while.

I chewed the practicalities of the scheme over for some time. It was comparatively easy to recruit the tradesmen to teach the skills and to pay them as Native Authority employees. The funds for this purpose and for the provision of uniforms (purchased at a huge discount from the Indian stores in Jumbe) and the provision of equipment and materials...came from the Native Authority. To disguise this expenditure and with the cooperation of the Treasurer, we [used] money allocated for the maintenance of the roads, which anyway, as I argued, would be washed away by the rains. I was, of course, spared the restraints that would even then have been imposed had the exercise been proposed in Britain, such as Planning Consent or Health and Safety approvals or insurance...

What was difficult was finding someone to undertake the day-to-day supervision and discipline of the enterprise. Obviously I could not tie myself up for the three months that was required and indeed I was not really sure exactly what kind of person or persons I needed. In the event, as so often happens, the hour produced the man in the shape, in fact, of two men. One was a Volunteer for Service Overseas, an incredibly insouciant young man, I suppose of about eighteen, just out of...school, who by some extraordinary good luck for me, had found his way to the boma apparently without any clear idea of what he was meant to be doing. How or why he was there I had and have not the slightest idea, nor in the circumstances did I care; I was only grateful that a beneficent providence had provided me with just the kind of confident young man with powers of leadership, as I assumed, who would allow himself to be deposited in the Kunda Valley to oversee the self-improvement of thirty-six of the area's most belligerent young men. He seemed perfectly happy with my proposition that he should be seconded to me for some months and live on his own in the Valley. The District Commissioner also approved the placement which relieved him, I suspect, of having to find something else for him to do.

Whatever worries I may have felt about my new recruit's safety...were calmed by the further recruit who fell into my hands. He was an African Police Inspector whom I met at the Katete Agricultural Show...While watching the Police Band putting on a display, I fell into conversation with the Inspector who was, I think, suspended from duty following an accident or illness, and he was bemoaning the fact that he was getting bored with nothing to do. I mentioned, more in hope than expectation, that I just happened to be about to start a youth scheme in the Kunda Valley and could do with the assistance of someone just like him. To my delighted amazement he immediately volunteered that it was just the kind of thing that he was looking for. Both of us agreed that it might be unfair to trouble his superiors with the matter, in case they worried about the advisability of a Policeman, and one of the few African Inspectors to boot, being attached to an unofficial scheme dreamed up by a very new Cadet.

The enormous advantage of these two volunteers was that they would be paid for by some other organisation, although I suspect that I may have been able to offer some assistance with their food. And so it was that the Kunda Valley Youth Training Scheme came into being [at Masumba]. The thirty-six young men duly appeared, at the bidding of their various Chiefs, looking rather apprehensive, as they had every right to be…

The…scheme was due to end as soon as the rains started, but I had allowed the time to pass without making the necessary arrangements for the passing-out parade, and now the rains had started with unexpected vigour. I then received word that there had been trouble…near Masumba. I had no alternative but to head for the Valley, praying that the river at Jumbe did not rise too high for me to get through. As soon as I got to Jumbe I headed straight for the ford…I groaned as I saw the foaming torrent that had replaced the usual trickle of water…I stood and pondered for some time…There was no question of James trying to swim it, and…it was clear from their expressions that the other younger Messengers were not very keen either. In the event I decided I should try. I accordingly walked at least a hundred yards up the river before wading in…No sooner had I entered the water than I was swept away…All I had to do was to swim as hard as I could across the stream, with the result that I travelled at an angle that, incredibly quickly, took me in view of ... the reception committee ... on the other side ... I only just got within reach of the hands that stretched out to catch me ... Both the Police Inspector and a Messenger and a *Kapasu* were waiting for me and insisted on saluting me as the water ran off me ...

[They reported that] the boys were all ready for my inspection and [asked] what I was proposing to do with their prisoners, who were getting hungry. 'What prisoners?' I enquired. It emerged that a gang of UNIP youths had been terrorising [the] area ... and the Chief had sent to Masumba for assistance. The Police Inspector had not hesitated to respond to the call and, with the approval of my VSO, had recruited the boys on the course (overlooking their previous records) to assist, pointing out that, as they had been eating food provided by the Government for the past six months, the least they could do was to lend the Government a hand in its hour of need. The boys had, it seemed, enthusiastically agreed and so the Kunda lorry, which had fortuitously been in the area, had been commandeered and the boys and all available Messengers and *Kapasus* loaded into it and driven to the rescue. The UNIP gang, confronted with what must have appeared over-whelming force, had immediately capitulated and been arrested with due formality by the enterprising Inspector ...

The first thing, as everybody insisted, was to hold a closing ceremony and to hand out the certificates in thatching, carpentry and bricklaying that the Kunda headquarters had supplied and to congratulate the boys, and indeed the staff, on what had been a most successful venture. I confess to having little recollection of the formalities, which is not surprising, as I was trying to work out how to convey a dozen or so prisoners over a flooded river and on to the boma. Accordingly as soon as the boys had left in groups, singing on their way back to their villages, the Kunda lorry was loaded up with the staff, and the prisoners and myself, and driven back to the river. There the staff and the prisoners were left to fend for themselves as best they could, while I recrossed the river in the same fashion as I had crossed it earlier in the day, and drove back to the boma to get transport for the prisoners and some means of transporting them across the flood ...

The next day I persuaded the District Commissioner to lend me the boma lorry and on it I loaded a number of empty 44-gallon oil drums, a rudimentary kind of metal boat that I commandeered from a road gang, some planks and a great deal of rope of various sizes and, most important, a block and tackle...The river had...dropped a little, but nothing like sufficiently to allow the lorry to cross. We accordingly set to, to build a raft out of the oil drums lashed on to some of the planks...The raft...[needed] to be attached to a rope, both to avoid [it] being washed away and to give...a means of propulsion...So once again I took to the water with a rope around my waist, despite the fact that the crowd, rather tactlessly I thought, had insisted that I should inspect the corpse of a man who had been drowned the previous day trying to cross the river at the same place as I was about to try and cross.

Anyway, I successfully crossed the river and the boat was duly attached and with many willing hands on the rope it was pulled across the river with me on it. The prisoners were interested spectators of this activity and indeed had pulled on the rope with enthusiasm but when it was suggested to them that they should allow themselves to be transported on the boat or, when it was completed, the raft, they politely but firmly declined the privilege. In vain did I point out that I had just crossed the river on the boat. That was different, they said. You are an *msungu* (a European) and can swim. Nothing that I or the Inspector could say would move them and I was in despair what to do when it occurred to me to crave the assistance of my wife, who had, fortuitously and unusually, obtained leave to come with me for the trip. I recrossed the river, explained the difficulty and suggested that, if she were prepared to cross the river on the raft, the prisoners might be shamed into doing so. She was a trifle dubious, rightly so, as she was not a strong swimmer, but in the event allowed herself to be a guinea-pig and crossed and recrossed the river. Following her example, the prisoners and the Masumba staff were safely pulled across the river and loaded on to the lorry and, in due course, transported to Fort Jameson Police Station. I made a point of going a few minutes ahead of the lorry to prepare the Police for a number of unexpected malefactors and giving credit for their capture to one of their own Inspectors. My news caused a considerable stir, and the Station Commander was called, who wanted to know which of his African Inspectors had succeeded in arresting a dozen or so malcontents, apparently single-handed. When I gave him the name of the Inspector and explained how he had been assisting with a youth training scheme in the Valley for the past few months, for which I was, I assured him, extremely grateful, he turned very red and demanded to know by what authority I had, without his permission or even knowledge, 'borrowed' one of his more senior officers and installed him on his own in the Valley. Happily he was an Irishman and soon saw the funny side of the situation – his precious Inspector, whom he thought he had lost, being stolen by a very junior officer, only to reappear with a crew of prisoners. Fortunately, he did not take the matter any further...

*   *   *

Back in Fort Jameson life went on pretty well as before...I got permission to take some local leave so as to be able to explore the country. The first place on our list was Lundazi, a District Headquarters just over a hundred miles to the north of Fort Jimmy...We decided in the first instance to do a day trip to spy out the land and then, if we liked it, to visit again and spend a day or two and visit the Nyika plateau. We talked our plans over with our friends, Bernard, who had just been transferred to Fort Jimmy to be the new District Officer Chewa, and Paddy, his wife. We decided to make a really early start, both to give us plenty of time to explore Lundazi and to be able to travel in the cool of the day.

Soon after dawn Paddy telephoned to say that the District Commissioner was away and so Bernard was acting District Commissioner and had been called out in the early hours because there was serious trouble in Lundazi...I pulled on some clothes and drove down to the boma. Bernard was looking grave, as well he might. He had received word that the Lenshinas in the Eastern Province, working in concert with their brethren across the

Luangwa, had gone on the warpath, sweeping through Lundazi, attacking and taking the police station and killing over a hundred people. He was trying to contact the District Commissioner in Lundazi but there was no reply from the boma and either the District Commissioner and his District Officer were out on tour, or he feared they had been killed in their beds. To make matters worse the interim Provincial Commissioner...had gone on leave and although his replacement was on his way he had not yet arrived. Someone from the Provincial Administration needed urgently to go up to Lundazi and find out what had happened to the District Commissioner and, if he could not be found, hold the fort until he could be found or replaced...Half an hour later, after I made a very brief stop at home to explain the situation and to collect the minimum of clothes, the Land Rover, with the Messengers looking very warlike with their rifles between their knees, was at the door to collect me.

Although I had been too much taken up with the Kunda Valley to pay attention to it, the Lenshinas, or more accurately members of the Lumpa Church, founded by Alice Lenshina in the Chinsali District of the Northern Province, had often been in trouble and in the news as a result of problems with both the authorities and UNIP, Chinsali being a hotbed of nationalist political activity. Alice Lenshina was reputed to look like, and was, a typical village woman until she had a vision, telling her to preach against witchcraft, which by all accounts was rife in Chinsali District...There was certainly no doubt as to the loyalty she inspired in her followers, as demonstrated by the 'Cathedral' that was built for her in her home village. There had been conflict, some years previously, with the local Chiefs, who resented the challenge she represented to their authority, and subsequently with the District Commissioner, who was forced to call in the Police Mobile Unit. Eventually, and with no little difficulty, some of the leaders were arrested and the disturbance was quelled but not until there had been some loss of life...More recently there had been trouble between UNIP and the Church and again the Mobile Unit had been called in and again the Lenshinas had reacted violently, succeeding in chasing off the Unit on several occasions and inflicting casualties on them. The Lenshinas were eventually defeated, with considerable loss, but not until the Army had been called in. [More information about the events in Chinsali District is set out by Mick Bond in Chapter 11. *Ed.*]

The Lumpa Church had for some time operated in the Lundazi District of the Eastern province and this attack was obviously connected with what had been happening to their brethren in Chinsali.

We covered the miles at breakneck speed and arrived in Lundazi late in the morning. I recall it as a pleasant little town with plenty of mature trees. The entire population seemed to be gathered in a large grassy area in the middle of the town. I must have been to the boma and the Police Station, the latter of which had been sacked, but I confess to having no recollection of what I found. What I do recall is the panic of the crowd. I had the difficulty that the people in Lundazi were a different tribe to those in the Fort Jimmy area, and so I could not communicate with them except through an interpreter. As we drove on to the grassy area the crowd which had gathered there surged around us and a schoolmaster attached himself to me as an unofficial interpreter. I and the Messengers tried to discover from the people exactly what had happened. There was no difficulty in finding people bursting to tell their tale, but they were badly rattled and it was difficult to extract a coherent story. The best we could piece together was that several hundred Lenshinas had swept through the township that night, stabbing and hacking to death anyone they found. It was thought that both the District Commissioner and his District Officer were out on tour and had therefore escaped the slaughter. It subsequently emerged that nearly two hundred people of various ages and sexes had been killed and another fifty or sixty had been wounded. No Europeans, they thought, had been harmed, although they were not sure about the European couple who ran the Lundazi Castle Hotel.

Rumours constantly swept the crowd, which numbered, I guess, the best part of a thousand. Suddenly from one side of the ground or the other the cry would go up, 'They are coming!' and immediately the crowd would surge across the ground away from the expected point of attack. Heart thumping I loaded the Messengers, who had got out to talk to the crowd, and drove towards the area from which it was rumoured the attack was coming. For the first time or two that this happened, when I got to the end of the grassed area nearest to where the attack was said to be imminent, I ordered the Messengers (who had already at my order loaded their rifles) to spread out and take up firing positions. After the third or fourth false alarm we simply drove the Land Rover across to the threatened area with me sitting on the bonnet of the vehicle calling out to the crowd not to panic and reassuring them, with easy mendacity, that we would protect them.

This went on for some hours during which period I was the nearest thing that the Government had to a presence on the ground. The first person to relieve me was, I believe, the District Commissioner from Fort Jameson with another load of Messengers and then the advance guard of the Northern Rhodesia Regiment arrived by air on to the little grass strip just outside the boma. After that everyone started to appear. The first demand of the army was for transport, they having arrived by air, and they were not very particular how they acquired it. As soon as I could I went to visit the hotel. The couple who ran the hotel under some kind of arrangement with the Government had had a very lucky escape. They had heard the Lenshinas prowling, like the hosts of Midian, around the hotel, and had hidden themselves in case they got in. They were a strange couple, she large and English and he small, bearded and French. He was a swimming instructor by trade. I forget by what strange circumstance they had ended up running a fantasy castle hotel in the middle of Africa. I have a recollection that she had been something of a heroine, in having insisted on going out early in the morning to discover what had happened, and had alerted the authorities to the massacre. In any event by the time I visited them they were open for business and ready to welcome the relieving forces that were starting to arrive and required accommodation. It was fortunate that, despite being so junior, I got a room as a result of being an early arrival.

Plate 9a   *Repairing a bridge after the rains, Mkushi, 1960*

Plate 9b   *Rainy season road, Mporokoso, 1964*

Plate 10a   Always a welcome sight: the grader, approaching Mkushi boma, 1960

Plate 10b   Crossing by pontoon, into W. Lunga Reserve, Mwinilunga, 1963

Plate 11a   First aeroplane to land on the airstrip, Kabompo, 1963

*Plate 11b   Probably the two most common forms of transport, Mporokoso,
1962*

Plate 12a   Signs were straightforward if not always straight!

Plate 12b   Smallpox vaccination campaign, Mkushi, 1960

Plate 13a   Election poster, Mporokoso, 1963

Plate 13b   Bottle store polling station, Mporokoso, 1963

Plate 14a Lumpa 'cathedral' at Sione, Chinsali, 1964

Plate 14b Sione, interior, after the battle, Chinsali, 1964

Plate 15a   The Governor, Sir Evelyn Hone, honouring Snr Chief Nsama, Mporokoso, 1963

Plate 15b   Being sent by the DC to the dentist in Ndola, 1964

Plate 16a   Lake Bangweulu, Samfya, 1961

Plate 16b   Lake Tanganyika, Sumbu Game Reserve, 1962

To complicate matters the interim Provincial Commissioner had left the province and, although his successor was on his way, there was no one, in the absence of the Lundazi District Commissioner, to take command of a most difficult situation, except our own District Commissioner from Fort Jimmy as acting Provincial Commissioner. His first priority, and that of the commanding officer of the Northern Rhodesia Regiment, when he arrived with the advance guard, after satisfying himself that the town was secure, was to ensure that there was no further attack by the Lenshinas, who had withdrawn to their fortified village of Chipoma, a few miles outside Lundazi, beyond the airport. As the troops flew in, it was therefore ordered that there was to be an attack made on Chipoma village as soon as it could be mounted the next day. One of the Lundazi District Officers reappeared, either during the night or early the next day, and was appointed to accompany the Colonel as the representative of the civil power in the advance on the village.

Incredibly, by the time the advance on the village was mounted late the next morning some seven or eight representatives of the world's press had arrived and were demanding to have a ringside seat for the action. They were accommodated for this purpose in a long-wheel, covered-in Land Rover. I was ordered to take charge of the gentlemen of the press and to be sure, on pain of death, to keep them out of the Colonel's way, at the rear of the convoy which formed in preparation for the advance on Chipoma. Ominously, one of the aircraft which had been flying in the troops had crashed, and although no one had been injured, it had caught fire and a pall of oily black smoke billowed over us as we passed by the end of the runway ... As we drove through the smoke, we did not know the reason for the crash and whether it might have been caused by the Lenshinas or whether or not there had been any loss of life. I and my eight Messengers brought up the rear of the long convoy with the press Land Rover immediately in front of us.

Eventually the convoy halted ... to offload the troops. When eventually the press and I got to the head of the queue, I found that the lorries which had been carrying the troops had been left unattended in a clearing in the bush. With the thought that the burning aircraft might have had something to do with the Lenshinas operating in our rear and that they might do the same kind of thing to the lorries, I took it upon myself to leave my Messengers with their rifles to guard the lorries, while I with one Messenger and [a] driver, went on with the press corps, who were already demanding to move forward to see the action. I left my Messengers calmly loading their rifles and, under the direction of the Senior Messenger, spreading out in defensive positions around the lorries.

I took care to put my Land Rover in front of the press corps vehicle and drove cautiously on to the crest of a gentle slope leading down to the village of Chipoma where, being very conscious of my orders to keep well to the rear and keep the press safe and out of the way of the Colonel, I halted. Although the slope down to the village was clear, being cultivated as gardens so that we had a clear view of all that was happening, the press were not content and demanded that they be allowed to move forward. I explained my orders, but one or two of them became belligerent and, after a fair amount of abuse, made as if to ignore my directions and walk on to catch up with the troops. I was worrying about my decision to leave the Messengers with the lorries and what would happen if I was right and the Lenshinas attacked us in the rear. They would, if in sufficient numbers, soon overrun my handful of Messengers with their rifles. With that worry on my mind I was not going to put up with the wretched pressmen agitating to go and make a nuisance of themselves amongst the troops. I accordingly seized the rifle from my remaining Messenger and, putting a bullet in the chamber, I warned them that I would put a bullet into the first of them that attempted to move past me. I must have looked fairly convincing because no further effort was made to go on past me. Instead they contented themselves with clambering up on to the top of their Land Rover to get a better view.

The troops in open order were advancing slowly on the village…Almost a small town, I would estimate it would have had a population of around a thousand. It was surrounded by some kind of stockade made of tree trunks and branches. There was clearly some kind of meeting going on in the village. There was a crowd and they were being harangued, presumably by one of their leaders. There was a great deal of shouting. The crowd was obviously being worked up for action. The recently returned District Officer, dressed in his white office uniform, to make him clearly visible, was walking among the leading troops calling out through a loud hailer for the villagers to come out quietly and unarmed to avoid the troops opening fire. This was very brave of him because there was a strong suspicion that the Lenshinas did have at least one firearm. No response was made to the District Officer's appeals. Instead the crowd erupted from the village and spread out with the obvious intention of surrounding the troops.

One of the arms of their advance was headed beyond and behind where the press and I were standing on top of our slope. The press were busy photographing this until there was an outraged yell from the top of the press Land Rover and, with one accord and considerable alacrity, the press corps vacated their grandstand seats and instead went to earth under the Land Rover. From there they demanded, with the same urgency as they had previously demanded to see more of the action, that I should protect them. Apparently one of the more belligerent of them had had a bullet go through a fold in his shirt... Certainly the man had a hole in his shirt to confirm his story and give substance to the rumour that the Lenshinas had a firearm. However, no one else other than Lenshinas was shot, and no firearm was ever found. In any event it clearly made sense to move forward to be nearer the troops, who were beginning to open fire on the Lenshinas, many of them women who, brandishing a variety of weapons, charged at the soldiers. Despite the casualties and with ridiculous bravery they kept coming on. We heard later that the leaders had promised that bullets could not hurt them. Where we were, at the rear, the Lenshinas were pretty thin on the ground, but one old lady waving a stick kept coming and a young soldier shot her in the arm. A White Father, who had somehow managed to accompany the troops, went forward to help her and I went with him. As we tried to put some kind of dressing on the wound, to our horror, one of the gentlemen of the press tried to take it off so that he could get a better picture of the wound. I fussed and worried about my Messengers and tried to get permission to drive back to them, which was very properly refused, and in the event when I was reunited with them I found them to have been in no danger.

We eventually entered the village and the press had a field day taking pictures of the horrors. The White Father made the front pages of the papers, cuddling children whom he had rescued from the shambles in the village. So also did a doctor (not English) who gave interviews to the press while operating on the wounded. I helped load the bodies of the dead (there were eighty or so of them) on to flatbed lorries which were hidden under guard for the night. I was ordered to supervise their burial in a mass grave early the next morning.

It had been an extremely unpleasant experience. It was impossible not to feel that it should have been possible to have disarmed and arrested the Lenshinas without shooting so many of them. The fit young soldier who shot the old lady, for instance, could have taken the stick she was carrying off her with one muscular arm tied behind his back. Perhaps that was an isolated example. It is true that these were the self-same people, or at least some of them were, who had massacred some two hundred innocent people in their beds the night before. Certainly the Colonel, who gave the order to open fire, was entitled, and indeed under a duty, to carry out his orders with the least risk to his men. The Lenshinas had been given more than adequate warning to throw down their weapons (however impotent they might seem in comparison to the automatic rifles of the soldiers) and it could well be argued that it did not make sense to risk trying to disarm even a female Lenshina by hand, even at minimal risk, when the soldier could do so at no risk at all by using his rifle. The Colonel was also entitled to take into account that he had just come from the Northern Province where the Lenshinas had routed a unit of the Police Mobile Unit and that they were reputed to have at least one firearm available to them.

We expatriate officers could not, however, be unaffected by the knowledge that the Lenshinas had received a great deal of harassment from UNIP, the lower echelons of which had little sympathy with the claim of the Lenshinas that they had no interest in politics and regarded membership of UNIP as conflicting with loyalty to their church. It seemed too much of a coincidence not to attribute the present trouble to the realisation by the Lenshinas that, with the coming to power of a UNIP Government, they could in future expect little mercy, whatever the efforts of Kenneth Kaunda and the hierarchy of his party to reassure them to the contrary.

Among the representatives of all kinds of strange departments and organisations who, over the next few days discovered that they had something to contribute to the situation, appeared senior representatives of the African Government in waiting. Although at pains to assure the expatriate civil servants, who were dealing with the matter, that they had no intention of wanting to take over responsibility for the decisions that had to be taken, they left them in no doubt that they expected them to clear things up before they took over and were not concerned at how drastic any solution might be ...

* * *

[Later, after helping to deal with the aftermath of this affair,] we spent ... four weeks in Ndola ... while I underwent some rudimentary training, sitting with an excellent African Resident Magistrate, prior to my formal appointment to sit on my own as a Resident Magistrate in my own right in the Balovale (now Zambezi) and Kabompo Districts in North Western Province. It was while we were in Ndola that, on 24 October 1964, Zambia became an Independent Republic within the Commonwealth and I put in my letter of resignation from the permanent and pensionable employment of the Colonial Service. It was already clear that there was to be no long-term future for expatriate officers in the Provincial Administration. Although the need for expatriate Resident Magistrates would last rather longer, I could foresee all kinds of situations in which a magistrate would be under pressure to produce the decision the Executive wanted. Much better, I thought, to leave while the new Administration and I were still on good terms and while I was still young enough to start a new career back in England.

15

BALOVALE, SOLWEZI, NCHELENGE, KAWAMBWA, BANCROFT

Jonathan Leach

*'Don't worry, Bwana, I am the senior prisoner
and I have the keys here.'*

After four years with the Oxfordshire and Buckinghamshire
Light Infantry in Germany and Cyprus I arrived in Balovale
(now Zambezi), on the banks of the Zambezi River in the North
Western Province of Northern Rhodesia, in August 1958.

One of my first duties as a District Assistant was to warn the
Senior Warder that a certain prisoner was to be brought to the
boma at 6 a.m. for transportation to Provincial Headquarters in
Solwezi, as the crime of which he had been convicted required a
more severe sentence than the maximum powers of the District
Commissioner permitted. It was dusk as I walked through the
mango-tree grove to the squash-court-shaped gaol. The trunks
of the mango trees were concealed in pitch darkness. All was still
and calm.

'Warder!' I called in my best military/colonial voice. Not a
sound. Nothing stirred. Several times I repeated my summons
with rising crescendo, with no effect. Finally a ghostlike figure in
white prison garb slowly emerged in the evening gloom from the
deepest recesses of a mango tree.

'Bwana?', the apparition spoke timidly.

'Who are you? Where are the warders?', I demanded with increasing concern.

'Don't worry, Bwana. I am the senior prisoner and I have the keys here. All the prisoners are safely locked up. The warders have gone visiting.'

Whereupon I transmitted the District Commissioner's orders to the senior prisoner, who proved worthy of his high office when the dangerous felon appeared manacled and escorted at 6 a.m. at the boma.

In March 1959 Kenneth Kaunda was restricted to Kabompo District. He was brought to Balovale by plane and could not be held in gaol pending transport to Kabompo because he had not been charged with any offence. So a District Officer, Vaughan Preece, and I entertained him for lunch, where with relaxed friendly charm he unfolded his philosophy of life. (He had no problem with white people. It was just the system he opposed.) After lunch a police vehicle arrived for him and I learnt later that Vaughan and I were reported by the Special Branch for shaking hands with him when we said goodbye. We had merely thought it was a common courtesy. The wheel turned full circle when in 1965 President Kaunda visited Bancroft, where I was the senior Government officer 'bowing and scraping' to His Excellency.

One of my treasured memories of Balovale was being placed in charge of Chinyami polling-station for the election to the Legislative Council in 1959, when a small number of African voters were able to take part for the first time. This required a trek of several hours across the Kalahari plains through the 5-foot-tall savannah grass to a small village. On arrival I sent District Messengers in all directions, summoning the entire elec-torate to report at 9 a.m. at the polling-station, which was a thatched rondavel commandeered for the occasion. Since the entire roll of qualified voters amounted to only eight souls, the task was not onerous. The roll consisted of a Sub-Chief, three headmen, two teachers, a farmer with a given number of cattle and a store keeper. Aware of the historic implications of this event I went to great lengths to follow the elaborate instructions.

It became clear to me that over 50 per cent of the electorate had no idea what was happening but were very happy to participate. A District Messenger gave assistance in the polling-booth when necessary. On 'pain-of-death' the sealed ballot-box was never to be unattended and out of sight of the polling officer until handed over under signature to an appropriate authority. The following day we struck camp and started the long walk back to the boma. Before I knew what was happening a carrier had picked up the ballot-box, placed it on his head and left at a steady trot. The long grass hid the procession from sight, and all I could see was the ballot-box, my galvanised bath and the rest of my *katundu* (luggage) sailing away sublimely on the waves of the Kalahari savannah. When I finally caught up I was relieved to find the ballot-box with the seals intact, slung unceremoniously in a corner with the rest of the camping gear.

I was transferred to Solwezi around the time that the Congo blew up and thousands of Belgians fled through the Kipushi border post and then through Solwezi on their way south. We gained the impression, which was never confirmed, that the flight was led by the administrative personnel followed by the police and only then by the settlers. At Solwezi I became friends with the Provincial Education Officer, Ken Balcomb, and his family. It was possible this friendship was partly energised by the presence during school holidays of his stunningly beautiful elder daughter Jane with her cascade of auburn hair. Providentially she was awarded a scholarship to an art college in London at the same time as I was sent to the Cambridge Course.

The boma accountant was married at Solwezi at a gala wedding attended by the whole European community as well as notable Africans. It was indeed a sumptuous occasion. The bridegroom had financed the celebration by paying a large number of ghost road labourers. The fraud was discovered while the happy couple were on honeymoon, and a Solwezi detective was sent to hunt them down, and bring the culprit back. He admitted the crime and went to prison. He was a friend of mine, so I stood surety for him before the court case so that he did not have to be remanded in prison. I was fairly sure he would not make a run for it.

One sleepy Solwezi morning a District Messenger burst into the boma to report a mass prison break. The first officer to reach the prison said he found the senior warder standing to attention, blowing his whistle and pointing across the dambo, where the entire white-clad prison contingent were rapidly fading into the distance. Suddenly they all stopped, turned around and slowly walked back towards the boma and the prison, many of them doubled up with laughter. Apparently two convicts had made a break for freedom and the rest had set off in pursuit to bring them back. It was a matter of huge entertainment for the prison population. I noted that the standard of living in boma prisons was often higher than that outside.

So Jane Balcomb arrived at the London Byam Shaw School of Drawing and Painting a little before I arrived at the Cambridge Course, where I became friends with Valentine Musakanya (Chapter 9), who came to stay at our family farm. Little did we know he would become Secretary to the Cabinet in Kaunda's Government, and later Governor of the Bank of Zambia before his catastrophic fall from grace. Our lectures were not demanding and I had plenty of opportunity to woo the auburn-haired beauty from the bush. We became engaged, Jane being not yet eighteen, during our joint year in England. Back in Northern Rhodesia, as it still was, we were married five days after Jane's twentieth birthday, at Livingstone, where Ken Balcomb was the Provincial Education Officer. My cousin David Taylor (Chapters 1 and 10), also on the Cambridge Course, was my best man and arranged some riotous activities for me on the eve of my wedding. The Livingstone elephants had crossed the road in front and behind our car when I took my parents for a drive to see the Victoria Falls. My father reported to the family back in UK that the wedding was attended by elephants both of the grey and pink variety. We spent our honeymoon at Troutbeck in the Eastern Highlands of the former Southern Rhodesia, while David Taylor took my parents on a tour.

On our return we drove back to Nchelenge in the Luapula Province, where I was stationed with John Hart, the senior District Officer. On the way through the Congo pedicle we were stopped by armed troops who wanted money. My new wife was blazing angry at this impertinence and ordered me to drive on notwithstanding the automatic weapon in my face. The leader spoke impeccable Oxford English and was most courteous. In the end we were allowed to proceed, having paid a very modest 'toll'. We later learnt that they were renegade soldiers from Moise Tshombe's army.

Jane was the only white woman in Nchelenge, which had a European population of four including us. She would come on tour with me undaunted by distance, dust and isolation. Kilwa Island on the far side of Lake Mweru was in our district. On one occasion I had unwisely decided to take the boma launch across the lake in the evening, ready for an administrative tour the next day. A fierce storm blew up, with dark clouds and heavy rain. It was very hard to keep one's bearings. I gave Jane the helm and walked forward to the prow to see if I could detect any landmarks where we might anchor for the night. Far away I saw the light of a bonfire on what I thought was the shore. Horror struck when I realised the fire was on the deck of an anchored Greek trader about 30 yards dead ahead. I yelled and waved at Jane, who could neither hear nor see me clearly. I scrambled back to the cockpit and fell on the wheel, spinning it with all my might in desperation. We missed the other vessel by a lick of paint. Just imagine the headlines. Even as I write, I shudder.

While stationed at Nchelenge I arrived at a Chief's Court where an angry mob wanted to lynch a man pointed out by a witch as being responsible for someone's death. He was locked in a cell and protected by the *Kapasus*, each with a red fez on his head. They were the Chief's constables. I had a District Messenger with me who strengthened the Government forces. My presence only inflamed the mob, so I ordered the driver to back the Land Rover up to the cell door. I handcuffed the terrified man to myself, a *Kapasu* opened the cell door and we both leapt into the back of the vehicle and the driver raced off. Stones were thrown which broke the windows but no one was injured. In due course the ringleader served six months in the Nchelenge lock-up, during which time he would work in our garden and he and Jane became good friends. When the time came for his release he refused to leave. The conversation went like this:

DO: 'You have served your sentence and are free to go home.'

Mabangu: 'No, I will not go.'

DO: 'Why not? You are no longer a prisoner.'

Mabangu: 'My bus does not leave until Tuesday. I have no relatives in Nchelenge.'

DO: 'This is a prison, not a hotel. You may not stay here.'

Mabangu: 'I have nowhere to go. I am staying here until my bus comes on Tuesday.'

Well, that was that! I have to confess that Her Imperial Britannic Majesty provided Mr Mabangu with board and lodging for several days longer than warranted by the court.

After a short time as District Commissioner Kawambwa, before Ian Breingan took over and the Union Jack was lowered and the Zambian flag was raised, we were transferred to Bancroft as the Assistant District Secretary, with Chingola being the new District Headquarters. We lived in the spacious house of the former District Commissioner with its spreading gardens, from where our first daughter Jacqueline was born. The flag-pole in the driveway flew the Zambian flag. I remember being awed by three telephones on my office desk, black, green and beige. I was never to use the green one, which indeed rang one day to my alarm. It was His Excellency the President, who had a few years earlier been under my joint care. He wanted to know about some report I had submitted recommending hiring labour to flatten anthills along the national boundary. The President later made an official visit to Bancroft (now Chililabombwe, or Croaking Frog), and I was responsible for co-ordinating his schedule. It was the conclusion of my colonial career, during which I had never witnessed any brutality, injustice or oppressive action by the administration. Yes, there was a 'Blimp' factor in some quarters but even this was not representative of the Service as a whole.

While stationed at Bancroft I experienced the most significant encounter, perhaps even more impacting than the birth of our daughter. We were visiting my in-laws at Broken Hill, where Ken Balcomb was again the Provincial Education Officer. My mother-in-law Fe bullied us into attending a Pentecostal prayer meeting on the 'other-side-of-the-railway-tracks' where the railway people lived. The venue was a school classroom. Small children were asleep on the bare floor in their pyjamas. Everyone was calling on the name of the Lord at the top of their voices. It was bedlam. I was shocked and hugely embarrassed. As I stood rigid in a line of chairs I was aware of a giant just behind me to my left. He was bald-headed and had forearms like tree trunks. Perhaps a stoker? Tears were streaming down his face as he repeated in a rough raw voice, 'I lof you Je…SUS. I lof you Je…SUS.' In a blinding flash I knew he was completely genuine and at the same time I was a fraud from top to toe. About six months later the stoker's Jesus came into my life. I studied for the ministry for four years in London, mostly informally, was ordained in July 1970 in London and inducted as pastor of a charismatic church in Durban in February 1971. I have been exercising a pastoral and preaching ministry ever since in South Africa, and occasionally in Swaziland, Mozambique, Zimbabwe, the USA and the UK. I cannot think of any denomination in which I have not had the privilege of preaching about the love of Jesus Christ.

16

KASEMPA

Paul Wigram

*'I got round all the villages on my bicycle with a perspiring
Chief in the record time of three days.'*

I arrived in Lusaka in July 1962 by air from Nairobi as I had taken
my embarkation leave in Kenya, where I lived. While in Kenya I
got engaged to Jinty. I remember being a day late as I missed my
flight, which was never called in Nairobi, as the South African rug-
ger side was leaving on the same flight and other passengers were
not considered. In Lusaka, where I must have spent a couple of
days, I bought a second-hand Volkswagen Beetle from Rhodesian
Development Motors. Credit was no problem: even Cadets were
as good as a bank. I met up with Tony Schur (Chapter 8), who
handed me a revolver and ammo, which he had brought out by
boat for me. I had no licence, nor did Tony, but again Cadets were
trustworthy and reliable, even if they drank the ship dry before the
first port was reached. Those were the days.

We stopped off in Chingola, where we arranged for a weekly supply of sausages, bacon, cheese and butter to be sent to our bomas
by CARS bus.[1] We must have reported to Hugh Bayldon, the PC
in Solwezi, and then carried on until the roads to Kasempa and
Kabompo diverged. There Tony left and I drove the last 30 miles
into Kasempa. Government strength was then the DC (Harold

Going), a DO1 (Tony Lander) and another DO, Brian Nixon. We also had a Tsetse Fly Officer (Rowley Morris and wife Anne) and someone who I think was a sort of QM. Harold was a great chap but sadly broke his Achilles tendon after a year and a half so had to be invalided out. His replacement almost immediately contracted sleeping sickness so he was off, too. We then had an African DC who saw me out. Tony Lander and Brian Nixon both left soon after I arrived and David and Di Downes came. They were good neighbours but were shunted off to Lusaka for a desk job before I left. There was also a Game Department man whose name I forget, but I think he was Polish. He spent most of his time in a camp on the Lunga River shooting crocodiles and hippo (and the odd elephant). Dried hippo and elephant meat was the only meat we had to eat on the boma as the tsetse fly meant that no domestic livestock could survive. At one time I was able to borrow a .303 or some such light rifle and shoot an antelope for fresh meat.

I took my local leave after a year and flew back to England to get married. Jinty and I returned after a honeymoon on the Kenya coast and settled into a newish boma house and started a garden from scratch. Our son Tom was born at the Mukinge Hill mission hospital a year later. This mission had been started during World War I by an American couple called Foster, who had walked to the hill from Lusaka. They were both still alive, though retired, when we were there. The missionaries were all American and lived what we considered a life of luxury. There was electricity on the mission and so fridges and freezers abounded and they had an airstrip and a plane or two. They were very hospitable. The hospital was first class and seemed to be able to cope with anything and everything. The British NHS would have been most envious.

I remember my first tour with umpteen porters, the number being stipulated in 'the book'. Looking back, I think I must have done it really badly. The job was primarily to count heads for tax purposes and see who was still alive and where they were. Most young males were on the Copperbelt. Every family was due to pay their tax and most hadn't. This all went into the book. I got round all the villages on my bicycle with a perspiring Chief in the record time of three days. What I failed to do was to establish any sort of rapport with anybody. Brian Nixon some time before had toured Chizera, a larger area, taking three weeks. I feel his report would have been worth reading; mine was not.

Once self-government was announced leading to Independence the number of DOs on the boma decreased and touring diminished very quickly. After that first one most of my trips to the periphery of the district were for a specific purpose. Kasempa District was 24,000 square miles in area and recorded as having 24,000 people so we were pretty thin on the ground. I was amazed at the competence and energy of the Messengers. One young fellow in his late twenties was sent to Chizera on his bicycle for an important task demanding an instant answer to something. Chizera is 100 miles from Kasempa. He left at dawn one day and was reporting back to the DC at 7 the same evening. He had taken a short cut along the village paths, but even so it was an outstanding feat.

Kasempa District boasted one commercial enterprise: the Kaimbwe salt works situated half-way between Kasempa and the main road to Balovale. It was a great favourite of Harold's, in fact his *raison d'être*. Kaimbwe salt was said to have magical qualities and be the favourite of everyone for hundreds of miles. Its development could only be a good thing. But it required almost daily visits by Harold and much labour – the prisoners! Of these we had many, as the gaol was full of tax defaulters. Regardless of the official prison budget for the district, the Provincial Accountant, with whom we were not popular, had to pay for prisoners to be fed despite their huge numbers. Maize meal was sold at a Government fixed price and the ration was 2 lb per head per day. So the money had to be sent to us. By good luck Kasempa grew much sorghum, which the prisoners preferred and was half the price of maize. So there was some spare funding available for worthwhile enterprises! Once Harold left, Kaimbwe slowly faded, his successors finding it very difficult to market the salt and justify the running expenses.

While I was at Kasempa it was suggested by the Provincial Agricultural Officer that we should grow Burley tobacco; so we did, with yours truly in charge. It grew well that year and I had the pleasure of a few days in Lusaka selling it at auction. We did quite well. I was glad to stop off in Mumbwa on the way and see John Theakstone (Chapter 19).

The large area between the Lunga and Kafue rivers was in our district and was almost uninhabited and full of game. It is now the Kafue National Park. Naturally there were poachers, as the law prohibited the killing of wild animals without a licence. One of the senior game wardens (I'm not sure where he came from) called Johnny Uys was determined to reduce the level of poaching so a joint Game Department, Tsetse Department and PA expedition was mounted. It lasted three days and was great fun. We caught some poachers on our side of the Kafue whom we had ambushed at dawn, and returned to Kasempa in triumph, where they were duly prosecuted and became another burden for the Provincial Accountant. I felt sorry for the poachers; they had lived on the banks of the Kafue for ever and what else was there to eat? Johnny Uys was a very likeable and knowledgeable person and I wished he had stayed around for longer.

On 1 January 1963 I took out an elephant licence, valid for a year, costing £10, which was a large proportion of my monthly salary. At some stage in the year I had an excuse to visit good elephant country on the Mankoya road, about 50 miles from Kasempa. I set out at 6 a.m. with the boma .375 magnum, which was said by some to be big enough to kill an elephant and by many others not. I had a couple of guides and we accumulated a few more on the way, hoping for meat. We walked all day and at about lunch-time sat down for a rest by a dambo – what did we see but a herd of elephant walking up the middle of the dambo. My guides smiled and pointed them out and said the tusks were huge and expected me to walk to the middle of the dambo, hold up my hand like a traffic policeman and shoot one. I said the tusks were too small and we should wait. This we did until, at about 6 p.m., just as it was beginning to get dark and we were returning to camp knowing we had failed, both guides trudging on either side of me suddenly turned around and shot off backwards. I looked up and there about 30 yards away was a lone bull with tusks of about 60 lb. My almost instant decision was that a .375 magnum was not the ideal weapon for this job, so seconds later I joined my companions in flight. That day we must have walked about 40 miles and I lost my £10.

Early in 1964 a group of HM Overseas Survey people arrived from Lusaka and spent about three weeks surveying part of the district. They had all the best equipment, were full of learning and extremely conscientious. I spent a day with one of them measuring altitudes with an aneroid barometer. At every measuring position the barometer had to be left under a hat for a minimum of ten minutes before the reading was taken. On a hill nearby the boss had a similar instrument and every thirty minutes he took a reading of his control instrument. He had to sit in this one position all day. In the evening they never opened the whisky bottle until all readings had been adjusted. Jinty and I soon learned at what time to call for a chat. Anyone living in Zambia can rest assured that the maps of the Kasempa area are one hundred per cent accurate. (Anyone living in today's Portugal, where I have been based until recently, may be assured that the maps are graphic fiction.)

One occasion I recall with some amusement. We had had a report that the driver's mate from a lorry had been killed in a very obscure part of the district near our border with Mwinilunga. I was sent to investigate and after many hours' driving found that an Angolan-registered lorry had turned over, tipping its load of drums of pitch on to the ground, regrettably on top of the driver's mate, who had jumped the wrong way. He was very dead, of which there was no possible doubt. I ordered him to be buried and returned to Kasempa. Harold heard the story and said, 'Where is the body?'

'Buried six feet under,' I said.

'What if the Angolans suggest suspicious circumstances? Go back and dig up the body and take it to the mission hospital for autopsy.'

'Are you serious, Harold?'

'Yes, but...wait a minute, as the chap is an Angolan this could be said to be a Special Branch case – let's send our SB chap, who never has anything to do.'

Recently we had had a Special Branch expatriate posted to the boma and for some reason he did not fit in with the rest of us very easily, so it was a brilliant move. Next day at dawn the SB man was off in his Land Rover, armed to the teeth with rifle and revolver, and returned in the evening with the body strapped to the roof. Mission accomplished.

Towards Independence in 1964 politics began to rear its ugly head around the boma. Gangs of youths started misbehaving and on a couple of occasions we had to issue firearms to some of the Messengers. Just the sight of a rifle was enough to cool things off, and I cannot say that at any time were we worried that the situation would get out of hand. I remember sitting as a Magistrate and finding that even in my junior position I was able to send a man down for a year. This was effective, and gang leaders convicted and given a sentence of over a certain time were removed from the boma.

More annoying than local gangs was the rubbish being fed to the people in the villages by the politicians. In late 1963 the inhabitants of the area where I did not shoot my elephant were told not to bother to plant for the rains as the new Government would provide food for everyone after Independence. In June 1964 I had to do an emergency visit to that area to assess how much maize the 'old' Government would have to, and did, provide for the hungry ones foolish enough to believe.

Socially we led a fairly quiet life. There was a club in the centre of the park-like boma compound, with a tennis-court attached. I don't remember playing much tennis but we all used to congregate at weekends for drinks and curry lunches which the wives produced. I was in charge of the bar. The most important side of that was to ensure that we never ran out of Lion beer. There were Castle and Lion beers, and though Castle is still, it seems, the beer of South Africa, Kasempa was a Lion stronghold. Harold was a large man and in the hot weather required a carton of twenty-four dumpies to keep him going. The club bought it in bulk from the wholesalers. Jinty and I used to go for weekends occasionally to the camp the Game Department had set up on the Lunga. There after a good dinner we would all go hunting crocodiles by boat after dark. We also visited Kabompo, Balovale and Solwezi. When Jinty was pregnant she had to go to the dentist twice, which meant trips to the Copperbelt. We stayed with friends in Kitwe, which helped.

Twice while I was there we had major visits, once by the Governor and also by Kenneth Kaunda. On each occasion the DC had a reception at his house, to which Senior Chief Kasempa had to be invited. SCK was the only man to whom Harold had to bow out when it came to alcohol consumption. The Chief did not consider it polite to leave until all the bottles of hooch on show had been emptied. As the senior DO by that time I was informed it was my duty to think of a ruse to get the Chief out of the DC's house before midnight. It was an arduous task.

We had a swimming pool fed by a spring at the bottom of the boma vegetable garden. We spent a lot of time there in the hot weather. Near the pool, living in the rushes, was a leguvon, a sort of giant lizard about 4 feet long. We did not disturb each other. Two black mambas took up residence for a while, so we liked to establish their whereabouts before relaxing too much. In fact snakes were quite a major part of life. I have never seen so many. Twice we had spitting cobras on the veranda and cobras killed our chickens. The man who looked after the two milk cows on the boma died of snake bite, only discovered when the milk didn't turn up one morning. A missionary at Chizera, soon after I left, was bitten by a mamba, but survived as a plane was summoned by radio from the mission at Mukinge Hill, but he was a sick man for many months.

I made one observation on mambas. Some readers may have come across Richard Meinertzhagen's book *Kenya Diary 1902–1906*, in which he tried an experiment to prove or otherwise that a black mamba could move as fast as a galloping horse, as was claimed. He obtained a mamba and managed to get it extremely angry and was able to time its subsequent dash for freedom at about 8 mph. He concluded that this was about as fast as a mamba could go. I was walking in the bush on one occasion and about 10 yards to my right I saw a flash of black moving in the same direction as me towards a termite mound just ahead of us. The snake seemed to cover the distance in an incredibly short time and its centre of gravity seemed to be about a foot off the ground. I could not time it but I am very much of the opinion that I would need to have been on a galloping horse to escape it rather than use my own sprinting ability.

Jinty was in charge of the Government guest house for most of the time she was there. We had some interesting visitors; in particular I remember the Overseas Survey trio. I think she was paid a few pounds every month for this. She earned it, as she redecorated it with fresh curtains and chair covers.

We had some house guests, mostly visiting DOs, but also the dean of my Cambridge college. In his youth he had bicycled from Cambridge to Jerusalem in 1936, so hiring a car to the North West Province was a doddle. His chief destination was Kabompo, where the DC had gone to the same college, and got a 'First', I think. He knew much of Africa from previous visits to old college graduates and was a keen collector of stones and most observant.

During the final few months before Independence I had decided that I would not carry on in the new Zambia, but return to my native Kenya. I passed my General Orders and surprisingly ciBemba, too. We spoke kiKaonde in the district but I'm not sure anyone was qualified to examine in it. My Bemba was bad, my Kaonde no better, but I spoke Swahili and by mixing all three together I left no blanks on the questionnaire and with the help of two very relaxed examining missionaries managed to stumble through the spoken section as well. I was then qualified to become a District Officer! After leaving Zambia I was paid a pension of £64 per annum for the next thirty-five years, until I reached the age of sixty-five, when it went up quite a bit. But we didn't join the Administration for the money!

Note

1 Central African Road Services (CARS) buses connected the rural areas with the Copperbelt and Lusaka. In North Western Province there were two buses a week. As well as bringing provisions to the more distant bomas, they also carried the mail and consignments of cash. During the rainy season the roads could become impassable and their journeys delayed.

17

MPOROKOSO, CHINSALI, BANCROFT, MONGU, LUSAKA, KITWE

Wendy Bond

'Harvesting millet is extremely hard work, tasking the wrist and fingers, but the contents of the teapots and the company made for a very jolly day.'

My memory is hard to control and usually functions in vivid recollections of incidents or places rather than useful sequences. For example, I can still see myself standing quivering on the bed in the Government rest-house in Lusaka in 1962, just arrived from the UK for the first time, while Mick bravely tried to demolish the big flat spider crossing the wall. This always brings with it a sense of deep shame. I don't know who it was who told me in no uncertain terms that these spiders were in hot pursuit of mosquitoes, not me. I have never knowingly destroyed a spider since then and did much enjoy photographing one beauty in close-up as she silk-wrapped her victims in her web for later consumption (eventually published in *Orbit* – of which more later).

Mporokoso

Many practical details of domestic life elude me. I know I became utterly at ease with wood stoves – they seemed so odd at first as they made the kitchen really hot, but they were so versatile for so many jobs – drying clothes in the rains, boiling buckets of nappies, heating the flat irons, with constant hot water in the kettle and perfect for making Christmas puddings, as all you had to do was put on another log every hour, all day. I still miss a wood stove in the kitchen! On the other hand, I never got used to powdered milk!

I remember cycling off to the mission at Kashinda from Mporokoso, where the water came in a trickle, thick and brown, with the nappy bucket on the handlebars and babe tied on my back. Kathie Cruchley at Kashinda had a good supply of clean water in which I could rinse out the soap. Relieved of so much of the housework, I had determined to deal with all the children's laundry myself. One evening as I returned – I had probably stayed talking until nearly dusk – I was suddenly aware of the huge overhanging trees as I negotiated the sandy road, and remembered that no one had as yet managed to locate the owner of the very large cat footprints near the patch of ancient forest (known as *mushitu*) at the boma, and leopards can climb trees!

Those trees have disappeared now, along with most of the bush on the approach roads to Mporokoso, replaced by endless maize fields, as the population has grown so much. I grew quickly to love the trees of the bush, though rarely knowing their names, as I pottered around the township.

Interestingly, I have no recollection of how I dealt with terry nappies when living in the Copperbelt towns of Bancroft (now Chililabombwe) or Kitwe. I do, though, remember how hard it was for us all to adjust to things like electricity. On our first night in Bancroft, Lamecki, whose evening job in Chinsali was to put a lighted pixie lamp in the bathroom and get the tilley lamps going for the rest of the house, solemnly went around switching on every light in the house.

Another vivid snapshot – the first rain. I was at the Women's Welfare, the spare house in the Messengers' Lines where we met every weekday in the afternoon. There was a clatter on the roof and we all gathered in the doorway as the children dashed outside. The big drops of rain fell, creating shining paths down through the dust on the delighted faces of the dancing children. The smell of the wet earth was one of the most exciting sensations I have ever experienced. It was something to look forward to every year.

The Women's Welfare was the task allocated to me by the DC's wife (even though I never met her: she left on the plane that brought us to Kasama from Lusaka with her children, who were going away to school) and I grew to love it. It was an entirely inappropriate duty for me, as I had been bottom of every needlework class in my life, but 'Mrs Collingwood does the Girl Guides so you will do the Women's Welfare.' Unlike Maggie, I had been a guide for six years (without ever even attempting my Needlewoman badge!). But I had fortunately purchased a copy of *Every Girl's Book of Needlecraft* in Lusaka in anticipation of a do-it-yourself lifestyle in the bush, and we started together at Chapter 1. I got the Guides, too, when Maggie left. One outstanding Girl Guide that I remember from the Mporokoso company was the young Violet Sampa – still a major personality and voice in the country, and internationally, today.[1]

Once I got my eye in at the Welfare, I refined things a bit – samples of knitting wools from Bulawayo in lovely colours went to everyone's heads, and we sent off an order which actually came. Some lovely jumpers were knitted. And one day when we had absolutely no materials, I commandeered rolls of brown paper from the boma, made charcoal sticks in the wood stove and we drew – the results were so wild and such fun that I turned many of them into motifs which I traced onto plain fabric to make into curtains and everyone came to tea at our house and embroidered them in wools. Most of the women were very accomplished already, particularly good at crochet, which I couldn't master at all. This astonished them as there was a lingering belief that European women were perfectly skilled at everything. Membership eventually reached over sixty and we held a huge Christmas party.

I remember some of the group with great affection: Christina, Victoria, Bulandina, Esther Malama ... They taught me so much! Especially about babies. I was definitely not one of those girls who knew things about babies. But it was our servant, James Mwaba Bowa Nonde, who introduced me to the *impapa*. I remember that we were walking across the airstrip and into the tall grass on the other side as he explained the word – it means skin. In the old days the women carried their babies in animal skins, but the word also conveys how a baby carried in a cloth is somehow still inside the mother's skin and this is a good thing, for both mother and baby.

My *impapa* was the same as everyone else's – bright-blue ones were the rule then – and made by the tailor who worked on the veranda outside the store. For ages, it seemed, I didn't dare put Alastair on my back unless next to a bed – just in case! And I found it really hard to keep my bundle from slipping too far to one side or the other. But the theory was so sound – and we couldn't afford a pram even if there had been a single surface in Mporokoso on which to push one! I persevered. Eventually I got the hang of swinging him through the air, and tucking his arm under my chin while I spread both arms to bring the cloth into position. A bounce or two, a bit of tightening here and there, and tie the knot – job done!

While the technique was still rather shaky, we went to Mukupa Kaoma for the monthly audit of the accounts, staying in the little brick rest-house above the waterfall. Mick had gone off to the *musumba* (Chief's headquarters) and I was standing outside in the early sun with babe in my arms, when a procession of ladies with hoes and so forth appeared on the path below on their way to their gardens. One very old lady peeled off from the others, climbed up over the rocks to where I stood and proceeded to harangue me with much shaking of a warning finger and pointing at the child in my arms. With a final toss of her head, she rejoined the others. Considerably shaken, I asked Black Mpundu, our cook, what she had said. I imagined a curse at least.

He translated: 'You are not holding him properly! If you let him fall, I will take you to court and give evidence against you!' From that moment I knew that my children were completely safe in that country – and so it proved. Later that day, with the baby somehow tied to my back – it was still very early days – I walked past the houses to join Mick. Every woman I passed, after greeting, pulled me close and proceeded to undo the *impapa* and retie it properly! So I knew I had a lot to learn.

The *impapa*, however, did not go down so well in Kasama, where I was sent for our post-natal examinations. The DC had dispatched me to the provincial capital, 120 miles away, six weeks before the birth so there would be no emergency trip along roads wrecked by the rains to get me to hospital in time. Much of my waiting time had been kindly filled for me by various European ladies holding coffee mornings – I lost count of how many. But when I set off on the path from the Kasama rest-house to the hospital for the check-ups, with babe tied firmly on my back, I was cut dead by each of those ladies that saw me. A great relief, as I'm sure I wouldn't have remembered names.

Hospitals were segregated in the old days. Kasama's European hospital was small and old. There were two of us in there when I had my first child, the other being a White Father drying out, I was told. But it was an African policeman who donated a pint of his blood for me – he came to see whether I really deserved it afterwards! They were always short of breast milk at the African hospitals – both in Kasama and Kitwe, my surplus was sent along to help out. Children in the African hospital were at least two to a cot, which did not help recovery. The doctors were legends. Derek Braithwaite was the Scout Commissioner as well as Provincial Medical Officer. He drove a Land Rover around Kasama but flew his own Cessna plane when he visited the other districts. Completely unflappable and utterly selfless. The diminutive, hilarious, very elderly, Irish Dr Hope Trant was unique. Our son had the privilege of being delivered by her. She kept a series of pet monkeys, of which Audrey was the last and most infamous. In the Lumpa troubles (see below) she worked without pause, not only dealing with injured patients but organising the rural hospital at Isoka so that a vast medical emergency could run smoothly there. It is impossible to do her justice here. At a different level, but very important, was our medical orderly at Mporokoso, Herbert Nondo, who vaccinated everyone on every bus passing through against smallpox, and every football team before every match.

Thus was that dreadful disease eradicated. The newspaper in 1963 was publishing the weekly figures for smallpox deaths on its front page. By 1968 the disease had been conquered in Zambia.

Eventually I acquired a set of pram wheels onto which we tied one of those huge bamboo fish baskets. In due course, babies 2 and 3 lay in this for many of our longer journeys, the whole thing covered in mosquito net, a perfect airy place they could see out of. But I still used the *impapa*. The baby faces forwards, is part of every conversation – and the mother has two hands free! It's really practical as well as comforting for both. But unlike everybody else, I rarely sat down with the baby tied on, preferring to place them on the floor on their cloth when visiting or at the Welfare so they could kick their legs or sleep.

I became fascinated by the work of various local craftsmen – it was of a very high quality – and soon began what became a large collection. An amiable gentle giant, Peter Mukupo, made my first drum, from hardwood, with the monitor-lizard-skin membrane fastened on with thorns and topped with small lumps of beeswax to protect the drummer's fingers during a long night's drumming. He also made us a *kalimba* (also called a thumb piano) – his fingers were huge as bananas but played it with great delicacy – and a stool. The drum later became an essential ingredient of Bemba weddings in Lusaka. From a Tabwa basket-maker I ordered the cradle and other baskets for my babies. They were superb, much admired and actually were sent for from Lusaka for the craft exhibition held there to mark Independence (so that Ruth had to lie in a fish basket for a month or so). Many people wanted one for themselves, but as he had enough money now for shoes, he was not interested! There was remarkably little appetite for economic activity – the only shops were at the boma or in towns, apart from the occasional bottle store. There might be a market built at a *musumba* or mission but there was very little to buy there. That's why we had to grow our own vegetables. So different now.

There was drama in those early days in Mporokoso, like the boma leopard, and excitement when a plane landed, to see who it might be, and we were royally entertained to concerts at the school for the blind which were a delight.

The White Fathers had just completed the buildings when we arrived and went off around the villages collecting children to fill them, finding them hidden away in dark huts by disappointed parents. The school's attitude was cheerfully bracing – in a matter of days a crocodile of children was taken to swim in the gravel pits and very soon the football-with-a-bell-in-it was rejected by the boys in favour of 'a proper one'. Their first musical instruments were devised from used tins – flattened as percussion rattles, beaten as drums, filled with dried peas and suchlike – and how they could sing! By the time the Governor came to do the formal opening, they were adept at rearranging themselves into giant pyramids and dancing, and already reading Braille. Father Carrière roped us in to learn this too so that we could transcribe more material for reading. It was not easy.

We renewed Father Carrière's acquaintance in Lusaka many years later when he ran the Rising Stars band, a lively group of young boys who eventually played at State House and even toured Europe. He'd collected them by playing the piano at the mission in one of the townships, inviting in those who stayed at the window to listen, then training them to play by tonic sol-fa, standing them in a line to represent the notes on the piano. The boys, most of whom could not read or write, took turns in assuming responsibility for the band's food, uniforms, accounts and so on, and most learnt several instruments. When Father Carrière went to the parents, inviting them to come for their first concert, each one assumed he'd come with a tale of wrongdoing and punishment. There were tears as they watched their children perform immaculately.

Evening classes got going at the primary school (no secondary school then), as most people needed Form 2 qualifications to move on in their careers and few had been to secondary school. I took my tilley lamp to light the path across the airstrip and for illumination in the classroom. I also much enjoyed doing the clerking for the midwives at the Kashinda maternity clinic in exchange for regular ante-natal check-ups after Mildred Francis, the missionary's wife who had run it for thirty years, went on leave. The new babies looked so sweet lying tucked up in brightly coloured blankets in green plastic bowls covered with mosquito netting.

Even harder to remember is the instruction we were given in how to work the police radio and its generator, in case we wives had to operate it if all the men were away dealing with some emergency, for in our first months it was still the aftermath of the 'cha-cha-cha' campaign. Trouble was constantly expected by those who had had to deal with the unrest. But Mick and I were soon exchanging '*Kwacha*!' greetings (the slogan of those campaigning for independence, meaning 'dawn') and the special wave with people beside the road, and the customary joviality of the Bemba people reasserted itself. Independence was clearly on its way. We had the first elections – this was an opportunity for me to visit various villages, where we played the election calypso, 'O listen to me, O listen to me, I have a song for this territoree: In October, we have election, Yes, we are going in the right direction!' and showed everyone how to cast a vote.

So, what did I understand as my role in this tail-end of the colonial era in Africa? When I arrived, I was already dubbed, and apparently dreaded, as a 'Girton bluestocking' – so clearly a colonial wife should not be in any way intellectual! Presentable, yes. Able to entertain unexpected visitors, bake a cake, put people up at a moment's notice and turn a hand to whatever task the DC gave one. I was dispatched at one stage across to the prison in Mporokoso when a lorry load of women (the first ever in the prison) had arrived after a revolt at a distant village, to keep them occupied with needlework. While we were busy – doing what, I have no recollection – my disgraceful toddler helped himself to the tinful of fried caterpillars that were being saved as a special treat. We were expected to create gardens yet be able to move stations at the drop of a hat, and take over any poultry and suchlike that our predecessors had left. Above all, I suspect, we were not supposed to rock the boat in any way. So it was perhaps as well that Independence was just around the corner!

There was no doubt that we were expected to be able to IMPROVISE whenever required. This had, of course, always been the case and was part of the fun. When the only protein available in Chinsali during the Lumpa troubles was in tins of corned beef, we just had to find ways of making it palatable day after day. When UDI in Rhodesia meant a similar shortage of goods in the shops in the city, the cookery programme on ZTV mimicked what was happening in every kitchen – 'This is the recipe, but as you won't have any *x*, then *y* might do instead – or just leave it out!' My mother's wartime recipes came in very useful – the eggless, fatless cakes, and so on! I even created and hand-sewed a pair of trousers for my way-over-6-foot husband, complete with pockets and zip, as well as endless clothes, toys and games for the children together with curtains, and clothes for myself, and actually enjoyed it.

Chinsali

Being catapulted to Chinsali, where the Lumpa troubles were hotting up, at twelve hours' notice, was something one was expected to take in one's stride, just as one was expected to stay calm and useful, however fraught the situation. My priorities there in the first couple of weeks must have been my two menfolk: Mick out in the bush every day, and sixteen-month-old Alastair, providing sustenance to both and entertainment to the latter. The first was difficult, as nothing was being delivered to the shops in Chinsali, which in those days were across the stream and quite a walk away. I do remember the number of people who greeted me as we walked there, and being glad that I was still in Bemba-land and could reply properly! It was also difficult because I never knew when/if Mick would be there, but do recall preparing many packages of sandwiches. I suppose James was trying his hand at unfamiliar tasks such as baking bread. Supplies eventually dwindled to those tins of corned beef. I have rarely been able to face it since. The shelves in the store never really filled up again during our whole time in Chinsali. Certainly, when we spent two days in July, before departing on leave, in Lusaka with Maggie Collingwood, our stomachs were unable to tolerate all the goodies she tried to feed us up with; and when faced, in London, with groaning supermarket shelves full of dozens of varieties of each commodity to choose from, I found shopping a nightmare. I've never really grown out of this feeling of awe at the profligacy of the Western economy.

To keep myself from thinking about what might be going on wherever Mick was, I read *The Lord of the Rings* (how did that come to be there?). Unfortunately, there were parallels: as Bilbo Baggins encountered the hazards of Mirkwood, so Mick was somewhere out there, deep in the forest that rolled as far as the eye could see from the ridge on which we lived, also facing unknown dangers! I was heavily pregnant with Ruth by now so I had an excuse to read while Alastair had his sleep. We had taken his cot but probably few or no toys, yet he and I were always able to find things to amuse us in the bush, such as seeds, bugs, and so forth. I was lucky that my response to keeping company with a small child was to share his interests with enthusiasm and on his level.

I shall always be immensely grateful to James for his quick reaction when the news of a casualty was buzzing round the boma: 'Bwana Mutali is dead!' He found out that Mick was safe even before I knew anything at all. Then he made sure that I received the facts in the best possible order. I realised then that he was looking after me and that made a real difference.

James was recommended to us in Mporokoso. He was a 'local lad', born and bred in Lupungu's village a few miles away. He and BaDaviness still live there now. His football nickname, Bowa, is still the one everyone knows him by – though if I am right and it means those huge mushrooms that appear in the rains, it doesn't say much for his swiftness on the pitch! But he was always quick-witted and particularly well tuned-in to the bush telegraph – we were always up to date with what was going on! He took over our lives, totally reliable and caring for the family, enjoying cooking, noting down recipes in ciBemba though his English was good, and full of stories and useful information, like which tree produces twigs to use for toothbrushes. He was young and dashing when we first met him, and grew more resourceful and wise every day, never fazed.

The strong feeling of fear among the people was palpable and there was desperate poverty: people had lost their homes and possessions, their crops and their work. One day, very early on, a man came to my door with a leopard skin to sell. I knew all the reasons why one should never buy such things as this would encourage poaching, but this was his prized possession. He didn't want to sell it, but was desperate for money. Normal rules didn't apply in Chinsali then and I bought it, for £2. Every day since, it has reminded me of the straits people can be brought to, so very quickly.

What pleased me enormously when things settled down in Chinsali after the Lumpa troubles there, was that the women started their own Women's Welfare and turned up at the house to see if I'd like to become a member. This was a very much better arrangement! To raise money, they arranged to go and harvest millet for a well-off man with several gardens. It was to be a daylong affair, and Alastair and I went along. We carried enormous empty baskets and knives. Many of the women had teapots on their heads, not necessarily full of tea, it transpired. Harvesting millet is extremely hard work, tasking the wrist and fingers, but the contents of the teapots and the company made for a very jolly day, and we trudged back with the baskets full of millet heads – they must have weighed an awful lot. I seem to remember the group was paid a shilling for each basket.

By Independence Day on 24 October, Ruth had been born in Kasama and we'd both been flown home in Derek Braithwaite's Cessna and we were no longer camping in an empty house but stationed firmly in Chinsali. I have two clear memories of my feelings at that significant time: one is that with Independence I was no longer thought of as a European but had become simply another human being. All resentment of past unkindness and injustices that people had suffered seemed to melt away and vanish. It was amazing, because I knew I would not have been able to feel so magnanimous had I been in that position. People had been treated appallingly in the silliest ways – for instance, at the butcher's in Kasama there was a separate window – not even a door – for Africans to purchase 'boys' meat' as the bonier cuts were called, bundled up roughly in paper and with no choice. I hope we two had been more civilised in our ways.

The other memory is of the 'cage', the temporary prison where the Lumpa survivors of the fighting at Sione were housed in tiny brick huts on a steep slope. The women were each sitting on their doorstep with their children, all in the total silence of shock, it seemed for weeks, unable to communicate. They were terrified that their end would come with Independence. But on the night, no one seemed to remember their existence at all and they were left alone. My body still goes tense with sadness when I picture them there.

With our own things around us once again, though several boxes remained unpacked (something I came to realise always happened, at every transfer from station to station) and settled in to the DC's house, Alastair was absorbed into the crowd of little boys who played in the garden with their wire cars, and he would go off with them down to the mango trees on the edge of the golf-course, where the Mobile Unit had camped. The bigger boys could knock the far-from-ripe mangoes down with sticks (no child could ever wait for them to ripen, ours, too, preferring them green and tasting of turpentine!). The other children looked after him very well, as all larger children looked after the smaller ones. Our children never saw bullying until they went to school in the UK. I remember a row of kids sitting on the draining-board in our kitchen in Chinsali, singing in perfect harmony, one afternoon. If he wandered too far, a District Messenger would be seen in the distance walking along with a golden head about the level of his knee, bringing him back home. Meanwhile I was busy with our delightful daughter! I also learnt how to make a clay pot, at the knee of one tiny, expert, toothless old lady.

In retrospect, I realise that I was a complete failure in the role of the 'DC's wife' – perhaps because I had never known a role model. We had been looked after so well by our bachelor DCs. I should probably have taken this on in Chinsali in a more conscious and conscientious way, especially as Zambian officers were often arriving in the bush for the first time. I'm sorry about that. On the other hand, I discover from a cache of letters that not only did we host the President and his family for their Christmas visit home to see Mama Helen Kaunda, but we also gave a Christmas dinner for twelve, and counted up that we had entertained under our roof in the first two months of 1965 all but five members of the Cabinet, plus Permanent Secretaries and countless other visiting officials, and had a DO and his dog billeted on us permanently! And we were both teaching night school classes. So I was busy.

By the end of our first tour, spent at two bomas, Mporokoso and Chinsali, I was so thoroughly adjusted to rural life, dirt roads, a sparse diet, miombo woodland and black skins that I found Lusaka hard to adjust to as we passed through, let alone the UK.

Nothing can equal the impact of a happy posting to the back of beyond, and much as we enjoyed the next eight years, the intense feeling of nostalgia for those two places remains as strong as ever.

'Leave' meant a chance to return to the UK for two months every three years – originally I expect this was in order to recover one's health after exposure to tropical diseases and heat. It always seemed to be arranged in the summer months, for obvious reasons, but this was very disorienting: in Zambia I worked by the sun rather than a clock as it rose at 6 a.m. and set at 6 p.m. every day, but it was still light at 11 p.m. in the UK, and the evening meal was still to prepare! While it was good to be with our families again and to enable them to meet the children, we found, as so often happens, that after the first few hours, no one was really wanting to listen to our tales – it was too different a way of life to comprehend. We were delighted to get back 'home' again to Zambia and see how the new country was getting on.

After Independence

The next eight years were certainly very different from the first 'tour', but not initially because of the new status of the country. The Civil Service structure continued to control our lives even if designations changed, and we went first to the Copperbelt and then to Mongu and Lusaka. We were no longer remote from facilities and our range of acquaintances increased enormously. Because the country was buzzing with optimism and opportunity, it was easy to find yourself getting involved with a dozen new activities you'd never tried before. We were in a play on the radio, on various committees, produced another baby; I joined the YWCA and then found I was running their craft shop; there was the International Playgroup, the Wildlife Conservation Society, which led on to *Chongololo* magazine and clubs; the Mindolo Ecumenical Foundation, where there was a swimming pool where I tried to keep up with the children's skills; a teaching job at the Evelyn Hone college; I qualified as a teacher at the brand-new University of Zambia; the children started school; I started *Orbit* magazine...It was all very exciting because everyone was determined to make a success of the new nation after the restrained and measured progress of colonial days, and to do it fast! Doors were opening for everyone. All this while external events were far from dull: UDI, Biafra, Angola, the Congo and the miniskirt. Zambia became international, with 'experts' from all over the world arriving with promises and bribes; there were new projects and new cars and new buildings going up and new roads.

The main threat to wildlife in those days was seen as poaching, but it was a far-sighted decision of the Wildlife Conservation Society to devote resources to enthusing the children to care for the creatures and plants of the country. Chongololo clubs continue to this day and remain very important if Zambia's natural resources are to survive and remain as an asset. The *Chongololo* magazine I helped to start is still going, too, and they've added a Saturday-morning radio broadcast. Then, every garden was full of lizards, snakes, birds and butterflies. The reason there were so many spears to do harm during the Lumpa troubles was that every villager carried one necessarily as there were always animals nearby. While the game parks were great places to visit, they were far from the only places to enjoy seeing wildlife in those days. The increase in the population and the vanishing of the bush nowadays mean that most people are no longer familiar with their own wild creatures as we and they once were.

Orbit deserves space for its story. Valentine Musakanya (see Chapter 9) had shared a house with us in Cambridge and become a good friend. When he became Minister of State for Technical Education, the man who as a boy had endless curiosity about how things worked and experimented constantly, seized the opportunity to develop technology in Zambia for everyone, beginning by learning to fly an aeroplane himself. The Zambia Institute of Technology was set up to train young Zambians for an industrial future. But he wanted to lay a really secure technical foundation for every child. I was summoned to recommend a good science magazine to circulate in the schools. It very quickly became clear to me that no one in Europe was producing such a thing, at least not one that could make sense to every Zambian child, including those in villages, whose only experience of electricity, for example, was at most in a torch.

Valentine said, 'When science and technology replace witchcraft, as they must, here, everyone should have the knowledge to understand them and not blindly believe, changing one superstition for another.' This, then, became my brief for the new Zambian science magazine for children that we decided to do ourselves. Valentine negotiated with Geminiscan in London and Peter Clark became the third member of the team. We wanted to raise the expectations and ambitions of our young readers, so the front cover had a space adventure serial starring two young Zambians. No one was left in any doubt that this was *the* magazine to be reading, because it was so exciting.

To begin with, I sent text and photos to Geminiscan and they did all the artwork and layout. I collected from the airport the transparencies from which Monterey printed the magazine and then picked up the magazines from the printers. One priority was to keep the vocabulary I used small enough for most people to manage – English as the means of instruction had only just been introduced into schools. Reading would improve quickly if readers were excited by the appearance of the magazine, as they were, and if new technical words were introduced carefully.

There had been a lot of research in East and Central Africa into the most effective style of illustrations. On the whole, people's experience was thought to be 2D rather than 3D – the explanation for village women in busy town streets rushing across the road into the traffic was that they did not appreciate that a car that looked small was further away than one that looked large. We have some copper pictures of landscapes that bear this out. So for posters and suchlike the preferred option was to show figures with no background. We chose to do the opposite and flood our readers' minds with really good and exciting pictures using perspective, to realign their vision. Remarkably soon we were offered not only excellent stories but strip cartoons from our readers, good enough to publish. Valentine and Peter must have done a lot of work in the background as we acquired an energetic VSO, Chris Buckley, who took over distribution, and a HiAce van for him. They would also have arranged the details when we sent two young people over to the UK, and when we went to various pan-African education conferences where I tried in vain to persuade other countries to use our material for magazines of their own – Zambia remained unique in having *Orbit*. And somewhere there must remain a store of reusable material that today's young people would enjoy reading.

The Ackson stories, contributed by Robert Baptie, were about a very believable and highly enterprising young Zambian boy and made us laugh. We had puzzles, science experiments, a detective story, wildlife articles, a competition, and so on. The quality was very high, with a standard of colour illustration rarely seen in Africa and there were no advertisements in the thirty-two pages. Soon we were asked by other ministries to add in the Young Farmers' page and a series on African history as there was a new syllabus in the schools but, as yet, no materials. The middle-page spread on the waterborne disease, bilharzia, was notorious but effective.

The greatest success was the page where we answered readers' questions, which arrived literally by the sack-load at the tiny *Orbit* office. Young people all over the country were eager to get answers to all sorts of questions.

Of all the competitions, my favourite was the wire car competition. There were ten bus depots in the country and the manager of each was asked to choose the ten best wire cars that were brought to him. These then arrived by bus in Lusaka and we exhibited these '100 Best in the Country' at the national Art Gallery. Suddenly, something that adults thought of as child's play was seen for the highly skilled achievement that it was. There were Land Rovers, Mercedes, VWs, lorries... The winner was a precise replica of a bus imported from Yugoslavia only six weeks before, perfect right down to the folding door for the luggage compartment! We auctioned them when the exhibition closed and sent the money to the young makers.

No job could have been more satisfying or such fun. I was very lucky and privileged to do it. After six issues, calamity struck – the price paid for copper fell from £600 per ton to £40, thanks to the behaviour of world markets. That was the sort of roller-coaster ride that everything was then. We were told to close. Fortunately, somehow, Valentine managed to find the resources to keep it going and we eventually became a Civil Service department, which meant longevity, if poorer-quality paper. We had to stop posting the magazine 'On Government Service' to all the schools in the country unless they managed to pay for their copies, but under one umbrella or another, *Orbit* continued for forty years. Most of those original copies were passed around and read until they fell apart, but there are a few in the National Archives in Lusaka today. Originally a copy cost 5 ngwee. By 1996 the price was 250 kwacha. I have met people in the UK who had copied *Orbit* science material for their textbooks for other African countries.

Zambia was undoubtedly a wonderful place to raise children – fresh, clean air, no need to wear shoes, or indeed much clothing at all, and trees to climb and lots of friends. Ours learnt good manners and fear of snakes from Daviness, James' wife, and developed their curiosity and love of nature. They never saw sweets, but loved to eat fruit. They learnt to swim early and kept an eye open for crocs and water-snakes. They had the usual quota of accidents and diseases but were very healthy.

Looking back, things took time to change, but eventually, pounds did become kwacha, and the metric system came in (with very little fuss), the airport, the Parliament building, Mulungishi conference centre, the University became familiar parts of the Lusaka landscape, joining the old landmarks like the Showground, the Secretariat and the Cathedral. Our son started school at Northmead, where nearly thirty different mother tongues were spoken. Every primary classroom had fifty desks and fifty pupils – and our children found that they were way ahead of their English contemporaries when they reached the UK. It was a terrible wrench for them to leave, as it was for us. They remain both colour-blind and avid travellers. We set out in 1962, to help bring about Independence in as smooth a way as possible. We left an energetic and positive country in 1973.

Note

1 Violet Sampa is a Member of Parliament in Zambia and an ordained minister of the United Church of Zambia.

18

SINAZONGWE

John Edwards

*'A mature king cobra raised its head and started
to move it back and forth.'*

A Surprising First Day on the Job

In June 1962, having arrived in Livingstone the day before, I
was driven in a Land Rover for many hours eastwards across
a plain and then southwards down a long escarpment to the
shore of Lake Kariba at Sinazongwe, where I was to be stationed
and where I was to meet the District Officer-in-Charge, my boss.
Unbeknownst to me, he had been away on his honeymoon,
somehow managed to slip his disc on a camp bed and was under
medical treatment somewhere. This I learnt from a radio telephone conversation with the District Commissioner. Hence this
twenty-one-year-old became instantly the senior administrator
in that part of the district.

Within hours, I was off in a motorboat with a couple of
Messengers to find a body that had been seen floating in the lake.
We found it very soon, pulled it into the boat and returned to
shore. The body had been in the water so long that the pigmentation had been leached out; it had been chewed in places, partially
wrapped in Nile weed and it stank. The first dead body I had

ever seen and to my embarrassment I was very sick. It was clear that we had to send it up the escarpment to Choma, where an autopsy could be conducted, a journey of three hours or more. It was now becoming dark and the driver refused to go because he feared that the spirit of the dead man might appear. His fear was assuaged by sending a less superstitious Messenger with him. I eventually learnt that the dead man was a local fisherman who had been assumed drowned.

Crime and Punishment

My subsequent public-service career in Canada ended with several years as Commissioner of Corrections responsible for federal prisons and parole; during that time I would often recall my experiences in Northern Rhodesia.

In the Zambezi Valley, we did not have prisons and generally not many prisoners since those facing homicide or other very serious charges were sent quickly up the escarpment to be remanded in prison until their trial. Small work-gangs of those with short sentences would maintain the grounds of the boma or nearby roads under the supervision of Messengers. In the hot weather, they worked from 7 a.m. to 2 p.m., then we would put them on a 5-ton truck and take them to the harbour, where they would strip and play in the water. At night their arms would be handcuffed around trees: far more pleasant than being locked up in concrete block houses without air-conditioning.

One of the most fascinating days began very early when I arrived at my office having inspected the parade of Messengers on duty. I was informed that a very old man and his granddaughter, having walked many hours, were waiting to talk to me. They came in with a Messenger as interpreter. The old man alleged that his twelve-year-old granddaughter had been raped by a young man in the same village and he should be punished. The old man told the child to describe what happened, how she had been washing clothes in a stream. Her calm, almost matter-of-fact detailing of the rape was to me astonishing. I then asked what they wanted to happen. The old man was very insistent that the assailant be locked up for many years. I then asked if he also expected compensation. He replied in the affirmative, even indicating how many livestock would be acceptable. I had to explain to him that at that moment in history there were two legal systems – the Chief's court which sought to compensate for harm done and the British courts that punished those guilty of crimes, often through imprisonment – and asked him which would be preferable from his perspective. After more discussion, he chose to take his case to the Chief and the two left.

I would love to know how the lives of the young girl and the young man developed over the years that followed, particularly as we in many Western countries try to find better ways of meeting the needs of victims, offenders and their communities by such means as community sentencing circles and restorative justice. Had the young man been convicted and sent for several years to a tough prison, would he have come out of that experience a better person? I doubt it.

Snakes

Snakes account for many of my memories of the Southern Province along Lake Kariba. I was surprised to learn how anxious most snakes, even the most dangerous, were to get out of the way of humans (and other large creatures). Coming back on foot in the dark from hunting, one would hear them slithering away from the trail, which to begin with left me terrified.

From time to time, I would be supervising gangs of workers clearing bush along the edge of Lake Kariba before the water level of what was then the world's largest manmade lake submerged it. These lightly clothed workers, swinging machetes or more often their traditional small axes, would occasionally corner dangerous snakes and, when this happened, they would slash them to death. This deeply concerned me, since I had the anti-toxin and the needle with the responsibility to give any injection needed – a distressing prospect given my sensitivities at the time. Fortunately, I was never put to the test.

One day I was out on Lake Kariba in a small boat with an outboard engine with the District Officer-in-Charge to see how it was rising and expanding. Late in the day we saw the top of a tree sticking out of the water with a large python wrapped around its top, having presumably retreated up the tree to escape the water. We decided to try to save it, managing to lasso it with a rope and pull it into the boat. The python was, luckily, very listless, having been out in the baking sun for hours. We reached the fish camp where our Land Rover was, carried the python ashore and measured it at 14 feet before putting it into a large sack and weighing it on the fish scale at 44 lb. We brought it back to the boma with a vague plan to send it to a zoo and decided to lock it up in the spare room of my cook's concrete block home, though the cook was not too happy about that. Later that evening, we brought some dinner guests to see it and found the room empty and my cook convinced it had escaped by changing into a spirit.

Very early one morning, entering the living-room my wife heard a strange rustling sound near the sofa and called to me. I moved the sofa and a mature king cobra raised its head and started to move it back and forth in a somewhat hypnotic manner. We opened a nearby door to the outside, armed ourselves with brooms and gently encouraged it to back away until it retreated into a corner of our veranda. At that point my cook arrived, saw the situation, disappeared for a few moments, then returned with a bucket and, from a distance, threw the contents over the snake, over the veranda and up the wall to the roof; it was petrol. He had intended to burn the snake but this was no longer an option. At that moment, my Alsatian got out to join the fun, barking madly and charging towards the snake only to back off prudently before being in range of its frenzied lunges. The snake would have struck the dog but the petrol seemed to have temporarily blinded him. A Messenger came running with a group of prisoners armed with machetes who quickly killed the cobra. Ironically and sadly, the Alsatian died some months later from an unrelated snake bite.

Political Tensions

From the time we arrived in Northern Rhodesia, we knew that we were into a period of transition towards Independence. One step towards that goal was the need to register voters, which took place in September/October 1963. The manner of registration was spelt out in considerable detail and it worked well in areas where the population was generally stable, even if illiterate, or in areas where the people had good documentary evidence of who they were. It didn't work so smoothly when many of those seeking registration were not known in the community and did not have relevant documentation proving they were Northern Rhodesians, as I was to discover.

I was in charge of registering applicants and this took place in Chief Simamba's court-house, a brick building with large unglazed windows along both sides. In accordance with the guide registering officers received, I set up a panel of local people including the Chief, plus a Messenger who knew well the population of the one urban area at Siavonga. These panellists could generally, through questioning, determine who the applicant was. The first week's progress was steady and a thousand registrations were completed. However, a serious problem was beginning to emerge.

The registration activity was only a few miles from the commercial establishments of Kariba Township just across the border with Southern Rhodesia so that quite a number came claiming to be Northern Rhodesians but rarely had papers to prove this; moreover even Northern Rhodesians that had not normally been resident in Northern Rhodesia in the previous two years were not eligible. Whenever we had an applicant who could not prove their eligibility, we invited them to go home and find relevant papers and stressed their right to appeal the decision. Nevertheless, a growing number became quite agitated; it was not helped by the known fact that this area of Northern Rhodesia was a bastion of support for the African National Congress, while many of the strangers claimed to be from areas dominated by the United National Independence Party (UNIP). Nor was it helped by rumours that those who did not get registered would have lost for ever their chance to become citizens.

In the second week, it became evident that some people had arrived who were not seeking to apply for registration, but were in animated discussion with those who had been rejected.

Eventually the leader of this group, a woman, who turned out to be a UNIP representative not from the Kariba Valley but from a town on the plateau, demanded the right to be on the panel. Since I could not see how this would help in the registration process and was more likely to cause clashes with the existing members of the panel, I refused to permit this. At this she refused to leave the court-house even when Messengers attempted to lead her out, and some of her followers started to get involved in shouting and threatening motions. I warned her and them that if registration was going to be disrupted I would exercise my authority to close down registration until such time as order had been re-established. Soon afterwards I did just that and left with a Messenger and a couple of the Chief's *Kapasus*. The Chief and other panellists disappeared.

This strategy did not work out too well. The woman raced after me, got ahead and then stood in front of me on the path and refused to let me pass, demanding that I return and register all those whose applications had been rejected. I told her if she did not let me pass, I would have no alternative but to have her arrested. When this warning achieved nothing, I ordered her arrest and two of the *Kapasus* managed to handcuff one wrist, but then she managed to break away, swinging the loose part of the handcuff and hitting a *Kapasu* and slitting open his forehead. This momentary diversion gave me the chance to walk quickly, if somewhat stiffly, to my tent, where my cook and my wife were.

We were now at the hottest time of the day. I stood outside my tent, my wife was inside and a group of perhaps fifty people were milling around in front of me, sometimes running forward waving makeshift clubs, one or two with the traditional small axes, before going back. The only thing they hurled was insults, one often repeated and I recall with some bemusement was, 'Your wife smells just as bad as ours do.' It was a standoff but could have got very ugly, and I can remember responding sharply to my wife when she suggested she take some photographs.

After an hour or so, I was delighted to hear the sound of a Land Rover coming, thinking it was from the boma. It wasn't, but instead it was the boss of the UNIP representative, a man

whom I had met on one earlier occasion and found very reasonable. I explained to him what had happened. He was surprised to
hear the particulars of the policy I was following, so we sat down
side by side at a table and I showed him the official documentation. He asked me what I wanted in order to get the registration
process restarted. We struck a compromise: the woman was not
to come near the court-house and he would be permitted to sit
in the court-house to observe the process but not to participate.
The registration process then proceeded as before.

There were other tensions through the remaining period of
registration. After it was all over, I had nightmares for some
months, imagining what might have happened had someone
thrown a rock or some other missile. To my knowledge, none
of those who were rejected in the end availed themselves of the
right of appeal.

19

MUMBWA, BROKEN HILL, MKUSHI

John Theakstone

'Regular payments were made to mine pensioners which were acknowledged in the main by a thumbprint; the scope for misappropriation of funds was there but it never arose.'

My own recollections of my service in Northern Rhodesia would not be complete without some reference to the Overseas Services Course. When studying Geography at Oxford University in the 1950s, I chose as a special subject the social and political geography of the colonies. This was largely instrumental in my decision to apply to join the Overseas Civil Service. However, National Service still existed and I chose to take a three-year short-service commission in the Royal Air Force. That period saw Harold Macmillan's wind of change speech, reflecting the changes which were occurring and about to take effect in Africa. I arrived at Cambridge when my twin brother was completing his research there, and we shared a flat. For this and other reasons I was rather an outsider on the course. I had to take early release from the RAF to start the course but was unable to be discharged as I was regarded as medically unfit, having recently undergone major surgery. I had to take time off from the course in order to attend a medical examination and so achieve my discharge in November.

I had become a qualified track and field official and so spent time at the University Athletics Club.

What of the course itself? I'm sure that in earlier days it was most apposite. However, for my generation – destined not to remain in the service for a career – much (on reflection) was not fully appropriate. I much enjoyed the lectures in law and the attachment to a London court – but my only magisterial duties in Zambia were in the last few months: I married a (white) couple and I served as visiting magistrate on death row. (I am a lifelong opponent of capital punishment.) As to language, the efforts of a Welsh cleric to teach ciBemba remain memorable for their ineffectiveness; in any event it was a language quite inapposite for Mumbwa in the 1960s. Three other aspects of the course at Cambridge are ingrained in my memory. One is that terms of service were changed for the worse whilst we were on the course. A second is that we were advised of our postings before taking the end-of-course examinations. The other is that pressure was put upon me not to take my Oxford MA until after completion of the course; had I done so I would not have been subject to restrictions imposed on junior members of the University.

I was posted to Mumbwa in Central Province. A few days after arrival at Lusaka I was collected by the District Commissioner and his wife. Philip Rees was the only person I have ever known whose standard tipple was pink gin. He adopted a relaxed stance to his office, delegating freely and allowing very casual dress to work. The limited number of houses on the Mumbwa boma meant that I had to share a house with the District Officer, John Haddow. Just five days after my arrival I was on tour, accompanying John on a routine visit to part of the district. I was destined to remain in my first posting rather longer than was the norm: I did not leave Mumbwa until September 1964.

My duties at Mumbwa were spelled out early by Philip Rees; I was put in charge of finances, African housing, stores and the prison. The first of these brought me into regular contact with the provincial accountant, Urban Vermuelen – one of the more impressive members of the service with whom I became acquainted. One thought occurs in retrospect of an aspect of financial duties at Mumbwa: regular payments were made to mine pensioners which were acknowledged in the main by a thumbprint; the scope for misappropriation of funds was there but it never arose. Money for all purposes was collected from Broken Hill (now Kabwe) and transported to Mumbwa by Land Rover with me, a District Messenger and a driver: little thought was given to security – though the Messenger had a rifle. Responsibility for the prison (where hard labour was anything but) was routine until near the time of my departure from Mumbwa.

I had relatively little to do with the Native Authority as that was John Haddow's responsibility. I met local Chiefs on tour and occasionally on other occasions, including the installation of a new Chief Moono following the death of the district's most impressive Chief. Touring took me to most parts of the district but there were areas I never visited. (Fifty years on, the lack of surfaced roads and motorised transport then would perhaps surprise many.)

Touring was the most frequent disruption of my book-keeping duties. I do not recall Philip Rees going on tour. After my initial tour with John Haddow I undertook three solo ones within the next four months. Sometimes a Land Rover would be brought into use but the usual arrangement was to use bicycles. As I had no cycle of my own one would be borrowed and its owner remunerated as a carrier. A routine was followed which must have been the norm for many years: a stockade was built around one's nightly campsite and the Union flag was hoisted. Checking on tax featured prominently in the daily round. I made a point of writing my report before returning to the boma in the knowledge that a huge in-tray would be awaiting my return. Looking back fifty years on I realise how limited was the communication, given that a District Messenger was my interpreter in my touring duties.

In order to be confirmed in post one had to pass a language examination. My first attempt was a fiasco. It was in ciBemba – a language not spoken in Mumbwa and which was to be associated with the political parties in opposition to the African National

Congress of Harry Nkumbula, which had overwhelming support in Mumbwa. I duly made my way to Broken Hill, where, after a couple of minutes, I suggested to the examiner that I was wasting everybody's time. In due course I did pass, thanks to the efforts of our water affairs technician (and club barman), who spent hours walking around the boma with me, teaching me ciBemba more efficiently than had the Revd Mr Quick at Cambridge.

In the early days of John Haddow and I house-sharing, we achieved some popularity when an avocado tree bore fruit for the first time. John did not like the fruit and we gave much away. The local mango trees never yielded edible fruit as it was removed unripe by local children. Lemons at the boma were so numerous that one drove over them as they lay on the road. A boma speciality was grapefruit; Philip Rees had planted many varieties behind the Administration building. One learned to distinguish between varieties, and I have wondered since why it is that we label apples and pears but not citrus. By now I had a battery-operated radiogram on which I played records regularly bought from Henry Stave of Dean Street, Soho. Although some supplies of food were bought or ordered locally through one of Mumbwa's Asian-owned and -run stores, there were day trips to Lusaka for other purchases. The round trip took most of the day and involved dealing with dust and corrugations in the dry season and unstable laterite surfaces when wet. (On my first visit to the capital the Land Rover broke down and I walked the last 3 miles of the journey.)

In January 1963 I had an attachment to the resident magistrate's court in Broken Hill. I recall little of this save for the case of Beauty Myunda, which remained unresolved when my attachment ended: was she mute of malice or mute by the visitation of God? The following month saw us don best bib and tucker for a visit by the acting Governor, and in March I dislocated a finger playing my first- and last-ever match of volleyball. In July 1963 I made my first visit to the Chombwa site: under this scheme local farmers were to be given 20 acres of land, of which 12 acres would be cleared for the farmer. On these were to be planted 4 acres each of cotton, groundnuts and maize. The remaining area was to be cleared by the farmer for personal use. Somewhere in the archives must be copies of reports I made on this ill-fated mechanised farming scheme. I was tasked with recruiting farmers into the scheme. I paid frequent visits and remained unimpressed. Failure of the rains in the first season resulted in poor yields, and much harvesting was done by hand. A local view was that the cleared land was on a traditional burial site, hence its failure. In that part of the district the most entrepreneurial farmers were migrants from south of the country's border. They had the most use of tractors, bought on loans. When loans were not repaid a writ for seizure would be issued but invariably the bush telegraph worked more speedily than the bailiff, who arrived to find no sign of a tractor.

Philip Rees was posted to the Secretariat and John Haddow was promoted District Commissioner in August 1963; together we moved into the District Commissioner's house. It was the only one with electric light, powered by a generator really destined (I believe) for the prison. (We promoted the gardener to indoor servant but he drank our alcohol and was dismissed.) In August, too, Dick Grimshaw arrived as Agricultural Officer: he was a member of the 1961 Cambridge agriculture course. A month later we had a visit from the Governor. When an election was held in October I was dispatched to the area of Chief Kaindu near the Kafue River: my recollections of this are less ingrained than those relating to the pre-Independence election of January 1964, although I recall vividly the earlier voter registration. I was sent to the furthest corner of the district to supervise the poll of January 1964. At the close of voting the ballot-boxes had to be sealed, for which purpose I was issued with a small heater, sealing-wax and a boot-polish tin. As the wax melted the District Messenger decided to remove the tin, burned his fingers and dropped the tin. The result was that hot wax splashed onto my feet. I have the scars to this day.

John Haddow left Mumbwa in June 1964 and for the first time I was given a house of my own. I inherited Nyeleti, who had served us well as cook since my arrival. He knew our ways and had a sense of humour in addition to being very good as cook.

I was sorry that when I left Mumbwa he did not feel able to move away. He coped remarkably with the primitive arrangements of domestic life at Mumbwa, where water was heated outside in half barrels, lighting was by means of tilley lamps (which generated heat) and food was kept cool in paraffin-operated refrigerators. In July I was chosen to help instruct on an Outward Bound course run by D'Arcy Payne (Chapter 2) near Abercorn (now Mbala). I leave him to describe it. I returned to Mumbwa to find the prison no longer that. It was a fully-fledged detention centre under the control of a Police Superintendent; the District Commissioner had lost his generator. It housed Alice Lenshina (Chapters 11 and 14).

Mumbwa had a small resident white population: I do not think that those resident on the boma ever exceeded a score. There was relatively little social life: what there was centred on the small club and the hotel run by Jukes and Sue Curtis. The boma's white population was mixed: the District Commissioner and District Officers were British, as were the two Agricultural Officers at the time of my arrival (one of whom had a white Trinidadian wife), the tsetse control officer and the officer in charge of buildings; the last two and the second agricultural officer were unmarried. The police officer was a married former member of the Royal Ulster Constabulary and there was a married Liverpudlian whose specific duties I no longer recall. The veterinary officer was a married English-speaking South African. Roads, mechanical services, water affairs and paramedical matters were in the hands of married Afrikaans speakers. The club had a small pool and a couple of laterite tennis-courts. The bar served no food but was popular generally. A number of residents ate Saturday dinner at the bar of the hotel, keeping an eye on the bush-baby which had a tendency to urinate from above. (The hotel's other pet was a cheetah. It would occasionally escape, and local African children never learned that it could outstrip them for pace; it was, however, in poor condition.) Life at the club was disrupted when I nominated the barman for membership; he was of mixed race, and those Afrikaans-speaking members who had previously attended resigned upon his selection.

Tsetse fly was a major problem at Mumbwa. Three tsetse control officers covered the district. One, a former would-be golf professional, lived on the boma, and I looked after his bullterrier whilst he was on home leave. The others lived in isolation in the district. Bert Hewson reputedly had been a junior tennis champion in South Africa. Eric and Tups Mingard were to become my closest friends in the country. Both were children of missionary migrants to South Africa. Eric served as a game warden in the Kruger Park until the Verwoerd Government's decision to make Afrikaans the official language drove him north. I was early taken under their wing and travelled often to their home at Kambulwe. After Independence they moved back to South Africa, where Eric initially took a post looking after the grounds of Rhodes University. He died some years ago but I remain in touch with Tups (so named because of her short stature), now in her eighties and living in Kwazulu-Natal.

Parts of Mumbwa had seen better days. The Matala gold mine was long closed (though I learn that a concession to mine it again has recently been agreed). The Big Concession had been set up for farming between the wars but in the mid-1960s only one resident remained. Jack Ferguson combined farming with working on the roads for Government. The sole white farmer resident in Mumbwa was Geoff Wedekind, a South African former stockbroker, who lived with his wife near the Kafue River. There, they collected butterflies and had a small menagerie.[1]

There were two missions in Mumbwa, and the contrast between them was striking. The Methodist mission at Namwala was of long standing. Despite this the family then there seemed preoccupied with keeping body and soul together and to feel isolated. In contrast the White Fathers appeared to have ensured that those at the Karenda mission were able to live in relative comfort. In truth, the Administration at Mumbwa had little contact with either. I was then a confirmed member of the Church of England but there were no Anglican facilities. On 18 April 1964 (my birthday) the Archbishop of Central Africa visited Mumbwa and conducted a service. This was held in the District Commissioner's house, then occupied by John Haddow and

227

myself. As John was Nonconformist it fell to me to arrange matters. I think that I now can claim to be the only atheist to have received Holy Communion in his/her own house at the hands of an archbishop.

Even Mumbwa's firmest friends could not claim it to be the most attractive part of the country: miles of brachystegia and mopane woodland, few hills and many dambos. The Blue Lagoon on the Kafue Flats was not easy of access: I visited it only once. The Kafue Park lay partly in the district but that, too, was not immediately accessible. A visit certainly brought its rewards in the wildlife seen – though I saw my first elephant when on tour much nearer the boma. Mumbwa seemed to me to have more venomous snakes per acre than it ought to have. Bertie Johnson, the ex-RUC police officer, did not believe in investigating a murder for the first twenty-four hours; his theory was that in most cases the person responsible would take his own life within that time. At one session of the High Court all the capital charges involved Mumbwa residents.

In September 1964, after more than two years at Mumbwa I was posted to Broken Hill. Although my posting in theory was to the district administration I found myself straddling two worlds as the pace of life quickened. Provincial and district offices shared a location. Not being of the shorts and long socks brigade I exchanged my Mumbwa casual wear for long trousers. The principal provincial officers were in marked contrast: Mark Heathcote was a somewhat retiring Provincial Commissioner whereas his deputy Roger Pawle was said not to need the use of a telephone as he could be heard at the other end of town. Independence came in October, and I attended the ceremonies at Lusaka. I moved house in November; five days later the house was burgled and most of my worldly goods and chattels were taken. Soon I was responsible for ascertaining the wishes of District Messengers throughout Central Province as to their future employment. This involved visiting all the districts. I especially recall a flight to Feira and sitting on the banks of the Zambezi. I had already met Neil Morris (Chapter 3) at Broken Hill and now renewed friendship with David Alexander

(Chapter 21) at Serenje. Urban Vermuelen left for Bethlehem in the Orange Free State and I inherited his aged dog. In due course it was put on the railway to rejoin its old master. In April I took the only local leave I had in my three years, visiting the Wankie Park, Victoria Falls, the Matopas and Zimbabwe with Bob Abell, a geologist. I had a long weekend at the Falls with other friends in the following month.

On 28 May I was transferred temporarily to Mkushi to fill the gap between the departure of the last European District Secretary and the arrival of his African successor. I had a lively time. On 1 June there was a murder, a fatal accident and a marauding hippo. The accident victims were placed, for want of a morgue, in the boma store. The bodies were collected for transport to Broken Hill some days later; by then rigor mortis had set in, and they travelled in a police car with a pair of legs protruding from a window on either side of the vehicle. When I accompanied the new District Secretary to the white farming area, one farmer refused to shake his hand. I did not join the club from which David Alexander had been thrown out for his political views. By the beginning of July I was back at Broken Hill. On 29 July I embarked on a five-month around-the-world journey home. The generous baggage allowance allowed David Alexander to transport both his own luggage and mine.

I began by reflecting on how little an impact the Cambridge Course had on my brief life as a District Officer. I conclude, however, by stating that my service in Africa was the major influence on my later life. The Overseas Resettlement Bureau has been criticised by some but it quickly found me a post with City and Guilds of London Institute, then seemingly a haven of rest for former members of the Overseas Civil Service. The lure of Africa remained, however, and I was soon to join the Inter-University Council for Higher Education Overseas, the start of a life devoted to improving higher education in Africa, with frequent visits to many parts of the continent. I was a Vice-President of the Royal African Society for a number of years and served as a member of the Council between 1989 and 2007.

Note

1   Some time ago I came across a report by an entomologist, Tim Dening, who wrote that on 24 January 1965 he visited his friend Geoff Wedekind, who had discovered a sub-species subsequently named after his wife. Mr Dening went up to the house but the Wedekinds were away. The house was open and Mr Dening walked in. Standing behind the bar in the living-room was a hartebeest. He asked it for a gin and tonic, but they are not very intelligent-looking animals. The otters were cavorting around in a boisterous manner. Mr Dening felt it wise to withdraw.

20

BANCROFT, CHINGOLA, MONGU, LUSAKA, KITWE

Mick Bond

'We had to crash our way through these road-blocks and
at one of them a man fired his muzzle-loader as we left.'

Much of Zambia's post-Independence period was seriously affected by Rhodesia's UDI (Unilateral Declaration of
Independence) on 11 November 1965. While on leave in the
UK, Wendy and I were (wrongly) convinced that the Wilson
Government would not allow this to happen. When it did, I was
sorely tempted to take out Zambian citizenship and renounce
British. UDI of course affected our work and lives to some extent
(increasing food shortages as anti-Rhodesian sanctions bit, petrol rationing, and so forth), but only to a tolerable degree. It was
much more serious for the country's economy and communica-
tions. First there had to be an airlift of oil by Britannia aircraft
from Dar es Salaam to a refinery at Ndola, an arrangement later
replaced by the 1,200 mile TAZAMA pipeline; copper had to
be exported in ingots on lorries up the Great North Road to
Dar, and the road was soon dubbed, with reason, the 'Hell Run';
from 1966 to 1969 this vital road was upgraded and tarred; in
1969 the copper mines were nationalised; from 1970 to 1975
the Chinese built the TAZARA railway from Kapiri Mposhi to

Dar. Meanwhile Zambia was harbouring east of Lusaka the freedom fighters who would eventually, through an avoidable war which cost thousands of lives (for which I blamed Britain), bring about the downfall of Smith's racist regime.

Bancroft and Chingola,
September 1965 to October 1966

On our return in November 1965 for our second tour of duty we were posted to Bancroft. I took over from Jonathan Leach (Chapter 15), one of our Cambridge Course colleagues, as District Secretary; I was the only officer of the Provincial and District Government there, in what was the smallest and perhaps most insignificant of the Copperbelt districts.

The posting to an urban station was quite a shock, after three delightful years in the Northern Province. There were tarred roads, electricity and telephones, and of course a large European and expatriate population. We had bought our first car. On the work side, too, things were very different from a rural station. For instance, what on earth did I do here with the smart District Messengers, when there were no Chiefs to communicate with or roads and bridges to repair? A new experience, too, was the number of fairly frequent weddings I had to perform as, ex officio, the Registrar of Births, Deaths and Marriages.

Bancroft, like the larger Copperbelt towns, was in some ways two adjacent towns. The major part was the mine township, situated around the bottom of the prominent hill. Famously, the houses on the one road winding up this hill were occupied by senior mine staff in strict order of status, with the General Manager living at the top next to the mine's central offices. Only occasionally did I visit those offices.

The other part of Bancroft was the smaller civic township: the Government offices, the Town Council, the primary school and the shopping area. Round the corner from the boma were the offices of the Bancroft Town Council with which, as an ex-officio member, I had a lot of dealings. The town and District were renamed Chililabombwe in 1968, after we left. Previously this name had applied only to the high-density township to the north of the centre, and meant 'croaking frogs'. (In 2012 we were amused to see that a statue of a frog was now set on a pillar outside the present Municipal Council Chamber and offices, and a frog was the emblem on the town's flag!)

At the top of the main street was the UCZ church (United Church of Zambia) which we regularly attended. When the minister was on leave I was one of those lay members who filled in and ran a few services, preaching on topics relevant to the prevailing immorality of the new 'permissive society' of the time!

Some 12 miles north of Bancroft was Konkola Mine, reputed to be the deepest copper mine in the world. Nearby was the Congolese border at Kasumbalesa. I used to go there quite often to visit the Immigration Officer, Bill Hayes, and his wife. Intelligence work was the main reason for my visits, as in 1966 we were to experience the build-up to, and then the reality of, a rush of Belgians (and other Europeans) fleeing from Elisabethville. Sese Mobutu had come to power in the Congo; in May 1966 he had changed that city's name to Lubumbashi and in December of that year he nationalised the highly profitable mining company of Union Minière du Haut Katanga. Bill kept his ear very close to the ground during 1966, and I gratefully used his tales to inform my weekly intelligence reports to the Provincial Secretary in Ndola – the awesome Colonel Middleton (ex-Indian Army).

In February 1966 I was told to be District Secretary of Chingola District, in addition to Bancroft. From then onwards I would commute daily to Chingola to work there, usually in the afternoons only. Of course, I also became ex officio a member of the Chingola Municipal Council.

Two main issues dominated, for me, the early part of 1966, and I had to deal with them in both districts. Firstly, I had to open and run offices to deal with petrol rationing, recently introduced as a direct result of Rhodesia's UDI. In Chingola boma I had two ladies working full-time on this, but every so often I had to arbitrate when they were confronted by irate European locals who needed more fuel to keep their businesses afloat, especially those running transport companies with dozens of vehicles. It was all very time-consuming, and of course unpopular – if necessary.

Secondly, mine strikes occurred in both towns (I think only the white mining unions) and these involved me in a lot of hard work in close collaboration with Special Branch and the local Labour Officers. I recall that at one stage we worked solidly for seventy-two hours without sleep, checking and acting on lists of the miners.

In early October 1966 we were suddenly posted to Mongu. I have no recollection of handing over either station to anybody.

The Mongu Episode, October 1966 to October 1967

This was, with hindsight, a strange year and not the happiest for either Wendy or myself, though Barotse (now Western) Province was fascinating and very different from what we had become accustomed to, in that it was dominated by the Zambezi River, which flooded dramatically across a huge area every year, rendering many roads impassable and river transport vital. The soil was white and very sandy, unlike the red soil of much of the rest of the country, and the vegetation was different, too. The majority of the people were Lozi, who were cattle owners and different from the Bemba in many respects. Mongu itself was perched on a ridge overlooking the flood plain and was joined to the main river by a channel.

I was to be District Secretary in Mongu. At the same time I was told that I was to take over as Acting Resident Secretary of the Province in November, for a temporary but unspecified period.

The District's official title was Mongu-Lealui. This, like so much else, reflected the different way in which Barotse Province was regarded. In colonial times it had been a separate Protectorate within the Protectorate of Northern Rhodesia. The Litunga, the Paramount Chief of the Lozi, lived at Lealui and under the old colonial Indirect Rule system had evidently enjoyed more prestige in the Government's eyes than other Paramount or Senior Chiefs. In my first month Mr Nyumbu, my Lozi District Officer, took me to meet the Litunga at his palace in Lealui. The palace was set in a large grove of trees on a slight rise, with views in all directions across the flood plain. A high reed stockade enclosed an outer court containing a dozen or so thatched houses of normal size, and from this one went through a lower stockade into an inner court where his closest family members had their various houses. Mr Nyumbu in traditional manner lay on his back on the ground, clapping in humble greeting to his monarch.

The Resident Secretary when I arrived was Mr Mwale, a delightful old-world Zambian from Eastern Province – in his fifties, pipe-smoking, very laid-back and jovial, and if he hadn't been very sincere in all he did I might have thought he was trying to ape the caricature of an old colonial officer. He was to go off to the UK for some 'refresher' course, and sadly I was never to hear of him again.

The Resident Minister of the Province, Mr Monga, was quiet, gentlemanly and dignified, very different from many senior politicians of my previous experience. He was a Tonga from Southern Province, and I suspected that he had been given the status of Minister because he was one of the few senior politicians from that Province who had not been supporters of Harry Nkumbula's rival ANC party. He was a charming man, and if I'd reported to him more often and made a point of getting to know him better I'm sure we could have had a more productive relationship.

My main preoccupation while Acting Resident Secretary was to organise the movement of a large group of refugees who had recently fled across the border into our western Kalabo District from the fighting in Angola. Fortunately for me the main responsibility lay with UNHCR (the United Nations High Commission for Refugees), which had already set up a large temporary camp in the south of Balovale District, just north of the Barotse Province boundary. But I had to liaise with the UNHCR representatives and to give them guarantees that we could as a team move the refugees there. The team I assembled comprised the obvious: primarily the Provincial Public Works Officer for transport, the Provincial Marketing Officer for sacks of food, the Provincial Roads Engineer, the Provincial Medical Officer, the Provincial Commissioner of Police and the Special Branch Officer. But nature gave us a time limit. We *had* to transport them by road from Kalabo through Mongu and Lukulu into the corner of North Western Province before the Zambezi's annual flood covered the roads. This was expected to be by early December in that year. I 'assumed' authority, as if it were a declared state of emergency, to commandeer every available Government vehicle in Mongu and Kalabo, and I don't recall any departmental officer being uncooperative in this. We made it in time, just.

In November I went by motor boat to Kalabo to see how the collection of refugees from its western border was going, what transit accommodation they had been given and what logistical problems there were in loading them all on to vehicles for the bumpy ride across the flood plain to Mongu. I also paid a visit, in early December, to the refugee camp in Balovale District to see how the inmates were settling down. The UNHCR staff had initially arranged tents plus camp kitchens and ablution blocks. By the time of my visit they were getting the refugees to build their own pole-and-dagga huts and to construct proper brick latrine blocks and a meeting hall. The latter was intended for some teaching – adult literacy classes to begin with, doubtless to be followed by the equivalent of primary school classes.

When that refugee episode was over a new permanent Resident Secretary arrived. He didn't appear to have much of a Civil Service background or ethos, and he might have been a political appointee. He was very full of his own importance and, try as I might, I didn't get on well with him. I obviously reverted to my substantive position of District Secretary. My DO, Mr Nyumbu, was an elderly and hard-working Lozi. I was more than content to leave to him the more mundane and time-consuming work of handling all the *milandu* (problems/issues) of local individuals: trading and fishing licences, taxes, liaising with local Chiefs and village headmen, deceased estates, and so forth. He had more dealings than I with the local politicians and particularly the recently formed local District Council. To give him his due, he also organised a very successful Annual Agricultural Show on the town's show-ground, with a band, craft stalls, children's sports, *makishi* dancing and many other forms of entertainment.

My transport as District Secretary consisted of two Land Rovers, a motor boat and four horses; I was not accustomed to the last items. Many of the other senior officers used their departmental boats for trips with their families at weekends, motoring along the canal from the little harbour to the Zambezi. I took the high moral stance that my boat was for business, not for leisure, although I knew that I was thereby depriving the family of some fun. I used it mainly for work trips to Kalabo or up the Zambezi to Lukulu, a delightful spot on a bluff above the river with a mission, a small hospital and a Government rest-house.

As for the horses, I never rode them. Their presence reflected the way the old colonial officers had had to get around the District, before the advent of 4×4s for tackling the Barotse sand. The Local Government Officer, and his lively partner who opened the one small hotel in the town (the 'Lyambai'), were keen to exercise the horses and I was happy that they should. There was one amusing incident. The oldest horse died. Shortly afterwards, Government auditors came to do a check on the boma holdings and I received a peremptory letter asking me to explain why I was 'deficient in one vehicle' and how/why I had disposed of it 'without it being properly written off by the authority of a Board of Survey'. I replied that the said vehicle had been buried with full equestrian honours under a Veterinary Officer's supervision, and asked them how they would account for an unauthorised increase in my transport fleet – by the imminent birth of a foal. I heard no more.

Mongu's main social life centred on the Club. The Club was supposed to be open to all residents but was in effect a 'Europeans-only' bar, social and sports club. There was certainly an undercurrent of racist attitudes among many of the expatriates, even if not overtly expressed. I did try to encourage some Zambian officers to join the Club, but none was keen and they clearly considered it was for expatriates only. I called in often to keep abreast of the gossip but Wendy rarely went there.

At the beginning of 1967 the First National Development Plan was published, after two years of preparation since Independence. The main architect of this five-year plan was a Mr Heseltine, an expatriate who'd previously worked in Madagascar and who was now the Director of the Office of the NDP. We all read the parts of the Plan affecting Barotse Province (the rest was a strato-spheric form of jargon-ridden economics). In the time-honoured British way of facing the challenge of implementing the Plan, we formed committees. Then all District Secretaries were sum-moned to a conference in Kitwe to discuss Plan implementation; there I boldly proposed that the Government should set up sepa-rate posts of Provincial Development Officers since, from my brief personal experience, a Provincial/Resident Secretary would be too busy on other duties to co-ordinate the work involved. Before the end of May 1967 I had been appointed as the new PDO for Barotse Province and handed over the District Secretary position to Mr Nyumbu – who felt due recognition at last.

I was grateful that Aaron Milner as Minister of State for the Civil Service had taken on board my proviso at the Kitwe confer-ence that PDOs should be answerable through their Provincial Secretaries to the Permanent Secretary, Office of the President, in Lusaka.

I soon established a reporting system from every District Secretary, with agendas and minutes of their District Development Committees to keep me up to date. Next, I set up a Provincial Development Committee, whose membership included all the Provincial Heads of Departments plus a select group of local UNIP politicians, and asked the Minister (Mr Monga) to chair it. We had our first monthly meeting of this committee in June 1967.

For the September meeting of our Provincial Development Committee, we had some heavyweight visitors from Lusaka: Simon Kapwepwe (Vice-President) and Mr Heseltine. Kapwepwe took the chair at the meeting, totally dismissed my agenda and thereby took several officers completely by surprise by asking for detailed facts and figures for which they were not prepared. It was a deliberate political manoeuvre by Kapwepwe and Heseltine to blame expatriate officers for the relative lack of progress on the Plan in Barotse compared with other provinces. I was not permitted to speak. I would have wished to point out that this province suffered from extensive flood plains and a sandy soil and therefore from communication/transport problems.

After all my preparations, the meeting was a disaster. The invitations to me and several expatriate Heads of Departments to a sun-downer at the Minister's that evening were revoked and, instead, four of us were told by Heseltine to report at the airport the following morning to accompany the visitors back to Lusaka 'for further talks'. The Provincial PWD, Agriculture and Water Affairs Officers and I duly presented ourselves at the airport in the morning. Here, to his intense embarrassment, my friend the Special Branch Officer was instructed to frisk us for any possible weapons before we boarded the plane with Kapwepwe and Heseltine (I never recovered my nice little penknife). At Lusaka we were taken to Special Branch HQ and effectively kept there under open arrest, with no explanations being given. SBOs took us under guard down to the Lusaka Hotel in Cairo Road for lunch, where, by very good luck, I saw the national Director of Water Affairs, who had also attended our meeting in Mongu, and quickly whispered to him what seemed to be going on. I heard later that within the hour four Permanent Secretaries including my own corpulent Michael Bwalya were thumping the table in the office of the Cabinet Secretary and Head of the Civil Service (our friend Valentine Musakanya) demanding chastisement of those who had treated their Provincial Officers so abominably.

The President, Kaunda, was apparently woken from his siesta to be told by Valentine what had gone on, and this led to not the first big row involving me between Kaunda and Kapwepwe. Michael Bwalya came personally to rescue the four of us from Special Branch HQ, and early the next morning he accompanied us by plane back to Mongu; he told me he wanted to calm the probable apprehensions other expatriates there might have had after our sudden departure under escort. He also admitted that in Lusaka they had seen the likelihood of some trouble brewing for me and apologised for not moving me in time. Now, within a matter of days, he arranged a transfer for me, on promotion, to my next job as Senior Principal (Housing) in the Ministry of Local Government and Housing in the capital.

I was not sorry to leave Mongu, although much of my time had been a valuable experience and 'interesting'.

How, by 1967, were things in the provinces different since Independence? On the whole I had not found any cataclysmic changes in the Civil Service itself: the obvious process of Zambianisation seemed to go steadily and smoothly. At a Copperbelt provincial meeting in early 1966 to discuss petrol rationing, I noticed that all that province's District Secretaries were still expatriates. But in Barotse Province I was the sole expatriate DS and, at the 1967 Kitwe conference on the National Development Plan, I think expatriate DSs numbered no more than four. As I have described in my Chinsali chapter, the transfer after Independence of many responsibilities of former DCs to other departments had led to a decrease in junior officers such as DOs in the Provincial and District Government. Resident Ministers (politicians) were introduced into each province at Independence in 1964, but it was later that District Governors, local politicians, were appointed (in 1967, I think). Above all, we generally noticed no anti-expatriate feelings or actions.

Ministry of Local Government and Housing, November 1967 to August 1968

I was now Senior Principal (Housing) in the Ministry of Local Government and Housing. This promotion put me on the bottom of the Civil Service upper salary grade, 'superscale 6'. The offices were a short way down Church Road beyond the Cathedral. My main tasks covered the partial funding of all the city and town councils in the country for their development of various housing schemes. I effectively controlled a budget equivalent in those days to around £3 million (some £45 million in today's terms), which seemed an enormous amount to somebody of my innocence. Most of the work, so far as I can recall, was in encouraging a particular town council to do more, or by correspondence to discuss plans and township sites and funding. I liaised closely with a friend, Jim Robertson of the Zambia Housing Association. We worked together on the new 'site and service' schemes, in which the city/town council laid out the roads, water and sewage for an estate and then provided building materials on loans, so that the individual could then build his own house according to an approved design.

In about July 1968 I was approached by a senior colleague (I cannot remember who) with a hush-hush proposition. How would I like a new, exciting job, with plenty of travelling? 'It might have political dangers attached; your name has been put forward to the President [Kaunda], who would approve your appointment if you were willing.' I was doing my best in the housing job, but it was not the most interesting or challenging that I'd had. I said 'Yes' to a move.

Cabinet Office: Elections Office, August 1968 to 22 July 1969

I was appointed Assistant Director of Elections (Senior Principal grade) in the new sub-department set up in the Cabinet Office to run the first national elections in independent Zambia. The elections were to be held on 19 December 1968. The Elections Office consisted of a Director and Deputy Director, my old friend Angus McDonald, myself, two young Zambians of 'executive' grade and two miniskirted expatriate secretaries. Angus was Secretary to the Electoral Commission set up to oversee the operations and ensure they met international standards in fairness; the Commission was chaired by Judge Pickles (with whom Angus had worked on the Commission of Inquiry into the Lumpa Church, and who knew me from my testimony to that body); one member was a distinguished local barrister, Eddie Shamwana.

Our offices were in an annexe of the Secretariat, the grand 1932 building in the most prominent position on Ridgeway. Before Independence this had housed all the important departments of Government, as well as the chamber of the Legislative Council. Now it housed the Cabinet Office, the Office of the President (which included the Provincial and District Government, in which I had served for five years), the Establishments Division and the Audit Office. Various 'experts' and special advisers also wandered around, much as I imagine they do in Downing Street.

Once we had as a team worked out precisely how the elections would be run, the Deputy Director spent much of his time with a Parliamentary Draftsman in the long process of preparing the necessary Bill and Statutory Instruments. My main jobs, helped by the two executive officers, were: to select, appoint and train all the Returning Officers and Election Officers throughout the country; to write an Election Officers' Handbook which told them precisely what to do and covered every foreseeable problem; and to assemble and distribute all the equipment and small items needed for every polling-station – and, at the last stage, the ballot-papers themselves. It was a massive job to be completed in four months. We had the trust of the Electoral Commission, and of Kaunda himself, who was obviously keen to enhance his international reputation by ensuring these would be the best-run and fairest national elections in Africa.

Each District Secretary was ex officio appointed as the Election Officer for all the constituencies in his district; the number of constituencies in a single district might vary, from one to six. That job entailed choosing premises for all the polling-stations, appointing all the election staff to man these on polling day, later dividing up and locally distributing all the equipment and supplies I would deliver to them for their district, collecting it all back afterwards, and dealing with all the travel/subsistence claims for payments by those involved. The logistics of all this in a rural district were considerable. A Returning Officer's duties were less onerous, but absolute integrity was required both on Nomination Day and at the close of the poll. All the Election and Returning Officers were summoned to Lusaka, where I trained them in their duties, going carefully through the contents of the Handbook. I like to think my Handbook was a success; it was published by the Government Printer – my only publication to date.

By November and early December I was dashing madly round the country, visiting every District Headquarters including those (Eastern, Southern and North Western) which I had not previously seen, first to check progress on the preparations being made by Election Officers, later, along with the executive officers, delivering election materials. It was all challenging but great fun and I met many interesting District Secretaries (all Zambian by this date).

For Nomination Day we foresaw the likelihood of political troubles, especially in Eastern Province. So I flew there, picking up a 'pool' Land Rover for driving around the Province. Rob Molteno, a researcher in political science at the University of Zambia, came there too but under his own steam. Come Nomination Day itself, I set off with a driver for Lundazi, which embraced three constituencies. On the road we were confronted by three road-blocks, set up by local UNIP activists clearly to prevent any candidate from the other parties getting to lodge their nomination papers at Lundazi boma. We had to crash our way through these barriers, and a man at one of them fired his muzzle-loader at our rear as we left – he missed. I was furious: I don't like being shot at! Rob Molteno had meanwhile gone the shorter distances to Chadiza and Katete bomas and experienced similar road-blocks.

I flew back to Lusaka, grabbed a secretary and dictated a 'strictly confidential' report immediately. By the evening this had been read by the Judge and passed at once to the President. The outcome was that the 'unopposed election' of MPs in seven constituencies where there had been such road-blocks 'be declared null and void'. Kaunda, even without any pressure from the Electoral Commission, had no choice if he wished the elections to be seen to be fair. It was all so unnecessary of UNIP, as they were bound to win all the Eastern Province seats anyway. The seven seats included those of three Cabinet Ministers. By-elections had to be mounted.

Despite that incident, the management of these first national elections was regarded as a great success. For the record, the political results were:

Presidential election:

Kenneth Kaunda	UNIP	1,079,970 votes	81.8%
Harry Nkumbula	ANC	240,017 votes	18.2%

National Assembly elections:

UNIP	657,764 votes	73.2%	81 seats
ANC	228,277 votes	25.4%	23 seats
Independents	12,619 votes	1.4%	1 seat

Voter turnout was 82.5 per cent in the parliamentary election, but 87.1 per cent in the presidential election. The Mpika Returning Officer (the DS) was the last to get his polling results, poor man: it took three days for District Messengers to carry the ballot-boxes up from a polling-station down by the Luangwa River and for others to come by canoe across the Bangweulu Wetlands to the boma!

But I was aware that in due course my name might be associated with the report which had triggered the need for seven by-elections. Action came fairly fast. In January 1967 Kaunda went off to a Commonwealth Prime Ministers' Conference, leaving Simon Kapwepwe as Acting President. I received a letter dated 23 January from the Establishment Division saying that 'in six months you are required to retire in the public interest'. Sacked! – And, I quickly discovered, on Kapwepwe's instructions.

I had previously crossed swords with Kapwepwe twice: over the ex-Lumpas at Mulanga Mission in August 1964 and over the 'open arrest' following the Provincial Development Committee meeting in Mongu. The report on the Eastern Province road-blocks for Kapwepwe was the last straw. Bond must go. The Judge and the rest of the Electoral Commission rushed to my defence, as did the Expatriate Civil Servants' Association. I understood that when Kaunda returned he would have supported me (and the Electoral Commission), but to overturn Kapwepwe's decision would create for him a massive political row.

While others fought on my behalf, I considered my next career step. Without my asking, the British Foreign and Commonwealth Office (the Colonial Office was by now dead) wrote to offer me a post in the Solomon Islands – after experiencing independent Zambia that would really be putting the clock back! Neither

I nor Wendy wanted to leave Zambia. Then Eddie Shamwana of the Electoral Commission invited me to take the position of Company Secretary in his furniture firm and, as this was a means of staying put, I accepted.

Meanwhile, I was seeing out my six months in the Elections Office. Our next task was to prepare, similarly, for a national constitutional referendum. This was held on 17 June 1969, on a proposal to remove the requirement for future amendments of clauses in the Constitution protecting fundamental rights to go to a public referendum, and instead to require only a two-thirds majority in the National Assembly. The referendum was passed with 85 per cent in favour of the change. Voter turnout was 69.5 per cent.

Willykit (Zambia) Ltd,
2 October 1969 to 13 March 1971

We went on 'leave pending retirement' in July 1969 and returned to Lusaka in the October. We moved into a house provided by Willykit for its senior staff, just off the Great East Road.

The company produced wooden and upholstered furniture and prefabricated housing panels. My main task was to oversee the accounts and to bring these up to trial balance stage. A qualified accountant came in every month to deal with the higher levels of company accounts; he was a refugee from Biafra, where the war with Nigeria had recently finished. I quickly saw that Bond and the 'profit motive' are incompatible. But I felt a loyalty to Eddie Shamwana and, having put my hand to the plough, I knew I must do all I could to help him. I was so grateful to him: he had helped us to stay in Zambia as we had wished, and had given me a salary commensurate with my Civil Service level – plus a free house.

Then fortunes changed. Kapwepwe fell from grace, and was imprisoned on Chilubi Island in the middle of Lake Bangweulu for a short time. Out of the blue I received a call from an expatriate colleague in the Establishments Division: 'Mick, should you wish to come back into the Civil Service, now Kapwepwe's gone, I think we have the ideal position for you, in the new Zambia

Institute of Technology (ZIT) in Kitwe.' This came under the Ministry of Technical and Vocational Education, of which our friend Valentine was now Minister of State; so it was fairly clear from where the suggestion for my appointment had come. After seventeen months at Willykit I felt I could resign without dishonour, and Eddie understood.

Zambia Institute of Technology, March 1971 to April 1973

Technical Education was Canada's form of aid to a developing Commonwealth country; the senior staff at the Department's HQ in Lusaka, ZIT's Principal and all its heads of department were Canadian, while most of the lecturers were British.

My position was as Registrar and Administrative Vice-Principal of ZIT. I seemed to work a seven-day week of some eighty to a hundred hours usually, but it was enjoyable even in the details: controlling the accounts, all the personnel work, smoothing relationships between the overpaid Canadian staff and their relatively underpaid British counterparts, staff and student numbers planning, and (through a former Bancroft friend I recruited) overseeing all student affairs including catering, accommodation and social/sports activities. I used to visit the other campuses regularly, at Luanshimba and Luanshya, where the main courses in various technologies were delivered, and at Kitwe centre (the Secretarial College).

Our administrative offices were in a former Baptist church on the outskirts of Kitwe. Behind these offices the new Institute was being built while I was there, and of course I was much involved in its planning and made frequent visits to watch its construction. (Later, well after I left, this became the Copperbelt University, ZIT's successor establishment.)

This was the time when Wendy, from a room in our house, continued to develop her great *Orbit* magazine, which she had started in Lusaka at the request of our friend Valentine Musakanya. With her conspicuous little blue van she used to travel a lot, both to Lusaka and around schools, and developed all her practical skills in composing, editing, publishing and distributing this incredibly successful children's educational magazine. The whole family went along when she attended the All-Africa Education Conference in Nairobi to promote the magazine for science education. Our (now three) children were all happy at Kitwe Primary School, led very busy lives and had many friends.

In April 1973 my initial contract with ZIT was coming to an end, and I was now thirty-five and, conscious of our original recognition of a 'suicide career', felt I should postpone no longer the hassle of finding employment for the first time back in the UK. Alastair, our oldest child, was now ten and we had to think of a secondary school for him. A ZIT colleague drew my attention to a suitable advertised post at Newcastle University (she had been an undergraduate there) and, while on leave, I applied for it and was successful.

We were all very sad to be leaving Zambia but we could honestly say we left with the happiest memories of the country.

21

MKUSHI, SERENJE

David Alexander

'Zambia has a vast potential for increased agricultural production...through rural regeneration involving subsistence and small-scale farmers.'

David Alexander was a DO in Mkushi and Serenje between 1962 and 1965. After completing his MA in the UK he worked at the University of Zambia until 1975. He then taught at the University of Edinburgh until 1995. He died in 2011. The following is an extract from a paper he presented to a conference in 1982, during a difficult period in Zambia's economic development. The country had been badly affected by the need to find alternative routes for the export of its copper and the import of essential supplies following the imposition of sanctions against Southern Rhodesia, after the latter made its Unilateral Declaration of Independence in 1965. The large oil-price increases in 1973 and 1979 had also caused difficulties through raising the cost of imports and reducing the price at which the country's copper could be sold. Politically the country had also undergone change with the introduction of a one-party state in 1972 and the part nationalisation of the copper mines and other businesses. Later multi-party democracy was restored and different economic policies, including the privatisation of the mines, were adopted.

Underdevelopment in Zambia

Zambia is undergoing a period of deep economic and social crisis characterised by increasing urban and rural poverty; hunger and malnutrition; unemployment and underemployment; rural immiseration; continuing urban migration; and a large gap in incomes between 'haves' and 'have-nots'. The agricultural sector has been neglected so that sustained self-sufficiency in food for the whole population has not been achieved. Due to the decline in the world-market price, Government revenue from the dominant copper-mining industry is low. There is a chronic shortage of foreign exchange, not assisted by the poor overall performance of secondary and import substitute industries. The national ideology 'Zambian Humanism'[1] is ambiguous in that it may provide legitimation for either the continuation of the colonial and capitalist structure in the form of a mixed economy together with more egalitarian provision of schooling, health and welfare services, or, with the publication of *Humanism in Zambia Part II* in 1974[2] and *The Watershed Speech* in 1975,[3] a lurch towards a socialist interpretation based on control by the state of the major means of production, decentralisation of power and participatory democracy in industry.[4] The exploitative potential of state capitalism in the interests of elite groups is insufficiently recognised and moves towards industrial democracy may be part of an attempt by the ruling party, the United National Independence Party, to decapitate the Zambia Congress of Trade Unions and its member unions and integrate or co-opt labour leadership into the party bureaucracy. A one-party state was established in 1972.

The political process in Zambia may be seen as an intra-elite and factional conflict for spoils controlled by the state between the political leadership and an emerging bourgeois elite rather than a broader class conflict in which the interests of villagers, for example, are consciously and effectively articulated.[5] Evidence since 1975, including the fate of the 1976 *Draft Statement on*

Educational Reform,[6] does not demonstrate movement in a socialist direction.

Zambia has relied heavily on the copper-mining industry both before and after the achievement of Independence from the British in 1964. The copper industry provided export earnings, a relatively high average per capita income, purchasing power for the employed urban population and civil servants and the capacity to import food and consumer goods. However, the vast majority of the population (now an estimated 5.6 million) have benefited little from the income generated in the mining industry and if benefits were to be more widely distributed major changes in the structure of the economy and a reallocation of resources to the agricultural and rural sectors were required. These changes and reallocations have not occurred. Since 1975, low Government revenue from copper has revealed, despite stated objectives in the *First*, *Second* and *Third National Development Plans*, the failure to diversify the economy and the lack of a serious attempt to regenerate the rural economy. Western economic development theories in the 1960s, including the human capital and manpower planning approaches to educational policies and investment, influenced Government thinking and decisions. These emphasised that economic development on a broad front could be achieved by developing the 'modern' sector which would generate 'spread' effects ultimately benefiting the whole economy and population in terms of income and employment. The inadequacy of such theories in terms of the needs and interests of the vast majority of the population is exposed by the Zambian experience and the fact of increasing poverty. The *Third National Development Plan* admits that past experience in Zambia demonstrates that substantial rates of growth in the GDP has led neither to significant increases in employment nor to a 'trickle-down' of benefits to the poorest and that performance in these areas has been 'pathetic'.[7] It also demonstrates the dysfunctional and inegalitarian nature of an expanded educational system tied to the selection requirements of the modern sector of the economy. The nature of development and educational theory adopted reflects the interests of dominant urban minority groups wishing to maintain their social and economic positions and political influence. These groups include the political leadership, the Civil Service, the small but emergent bourgeoisie and elements in the trade unions.

Due to the major structural imbalances in the economy, an estimated 40 per cent of the population now live in the urban areas, on the Line of Rail and the Copperbelt. Urban migration continues but there is no possibility that either the modern sector of the economy or the urban informal sector,[8] which is in my view approaching saturation point, can productively absorb more than a small proportion of the current labour force or the annual output of primary school leavers who cannot gain a place in secondary school, which is now approaching 130,000 per annum. Approximately half of the labour force is now in the urban areas and there is employment for perhaps a quarter of them in the modern sector. Despite forecasts in the *Third National Development Plan* (1979) that 14,000 more wage jobs would be created annually it is likely that at least another 100,000 people will be added to the urban unemployed by the end of the plan period in December 1983.

Zambia has a vast potential for increased agricultural production and in the foreseeable future it is only through rural regeneration involving subsistence and small-scale farmers that productive employment and self-employment and increased standards of living for the majority of the people may be achieved.

There has been continuity in state policy on agriculture since the 1920s.[9] That policy has been to provide a cheap and consistent food supply to the towns and mine-workers at the expense of rural incomes. Cheaper food enables the mines to pay lower wages than would otherwise be possible. The rural–urban terms of trade[10] have shifted against rural producers so that, for example, a rural producer had to produce and market three times more in 1979 than he did in 1965 to obtain the same urban goods. Rural impoverishment demonstrates that the Zambian economy has to be analysed as a whole and not as if the rural sector were independent of the 'modern' sector.

Despite stated Government intentions, expenditure in the agricultural sector has seldom exceeded 10 per cent of total Government expenditure annually. It has now been recognised that the economic crisis has 'brought to the fore the basic fact that the country's economic malaise is far deeper than what can be attributed to the collapse of copper prices',[11] and that the country's entire development strategy and social and economic priorities required reorientation. There is little evidence that this is now taking place.

Notes

1 K. D. Kaunda, *Humanism in Zambia*, Lusaka: Zambia Information Services, Government Printer, 1967; *Humanism in Zambia, Part 2*, Lusaka: Government Printer, 1974.

2 K. D. Kaunda, *Humanism in Zambia, Part 2*.

3 K. D. Kaunda, *The 'Watershed Speech'. Address by His Excellency the President to the UNIP National Council, 30 June–3 July 1975*, Lusaka: Zambia Information Services, 1975.

4 R. Clarke, 'Policy and Ideology in Educational Reform in Zambia 1974–78', unpublished MA dissertation, University of Lancaster, 1978, pp. 79–86.

5 Szeftel, 1980, pp. 64–95.

6 Ministry of Education, Education for Development, *Draft Statement on Educational Reform*, Lusaka, 1976.

7 Office of the President, *Third National Development Plan 1979–83*, Lusaka: National Commission for Development Planning, 1979, p. 25.

8 M. E. Seath, 'Education and the Economy: Primary School Leavers, the Labour Market and Non-formal Education in Zambia', unpublished MA dissertation, University of London, 1981, pp. 44–112.

9 Ben Turok, *Development in Zambia*, London: Zed Books, 1979; Klepper, 1980, pp. 120–45; Elling, 1981, pp. 1–22.

10 Young, 1971, p. 94; Elling, 1981, p. 15.

11 Office of the President, *Third National Development Plan*, p. 18.

Appendix 1

ZAMBIA AND ITS PEOPLE

Zambia, which was known as Northern Rhodesia before it gained independence in 1964, lies in the middle of the southern half of Africa. It is completely landlocked, and surrounded by eight other countries: the Democratic Republic of the Congo and Tanzania to the north, Malawi and Mozambique to the east, Zimbabwe, Botswana and Namibia to the south and Angola to the west. It is situated between 10° and 18° south of the Equator, and covers an area of 290,000 square miles, which makes it about three times the size of the United Kingdom.

Most of the country lies on a plateau ranging in height from about 1,100 to 1,400 m above sea level with a few higher mountains, mainly in the east. The land is well watered with a number of significant rivers flowing through it. Notable are the Zambezi and its main tributaries, the Kafue and the Luangwa. The Zambezi, which rises in the northwest of the country, flows south through the western provinces before turning east to form part of Zambia's southern boundary. On its journey it passes through vast flood plains and then over the Victoria Falls before it makes its way through Lake Kariba, the second largest man-made lake in the world, and on to the sea through Mozambique.

In the north of the country there are three large natural lakes: Bangweulu, which is wholly within Zambia, and Mweru and Tanganyika, which both lie partly within the borders of other countries. The Luapula River, which flows from Lake Bangweulu to Lake Mweru along the boundary with the DRC, is part of the Congo River system. Much of the country is covered by woodland, which is denser in the north than in the drier south. The trees are of hardwood varieties and keep their leaves for most of the year. Interestingly the new growth starts each year before the rainy season begins.

Because of its height above sea level the climate of Zambia is cooler than in many other parts of the tropics. There are three seasons: cool and dry from May to August, hot and dry from September to November and warm and wet from December to April. Mean maximum temperatures in the hottest time of the year range from 28°C to 35°C.

These conditions enable a good variety of crops to be grown including maize, wheat, rice, sugarcane, vegetables and fruit. While there are some large-scale commercial producers, who are mostly to be found along the main north–south railway line and in the Eastern Province, most of the cultivation is carried out by small-scale and traditional subsistence farmers. In order to increase the contribution of agriculture to the economy, and to feed the growing population, efforts are being made to improve the productivity and sustainability of the farming sector.

Zambia also possesses a wide range of other natural resources, including copper, other minerals and gems, good sources of hydro-electric power and a great variety of wildlife, especially in the renowned national parks. The country is the world's fourth largest producer of copper, and has been able to increase output of this valuable commodity as a result of new investment following the privatisation of the mines in the 1990s and rising demand. However, its large dependence on the export of copper does make the Zambian economy vulnerable to fluctuations in the world price of copper. New mining also threatens the environment.

It seems likely that copper began to be mined and processed around AD 350, but the human history of Zambia began long before that. Recent discoveries have suggested that basic stone tools were being used in the Zambezi Valley over 2 million years ago, and in 1921 a skull found at Kabwe (formerly Broken Hill) was reckoned to date from about 70,000 years ago. There are good collections of early tools and other artefacts in the Livingstone Museum and many interesting sites to visit.

The early inhabitants of what is now Zambia were Khoisan people who used stone tools and lived by hunting and foraging. They were gradually superseded by groups of Bantu-speaking people, who entered the territory from about 500 BC onwards by a number of different routes, having originally been based in west Africa. These newcomers brought with them skills in cultivation, working with iron, house-building and the keeping of domestic animals. Migration continued over the centuries with different groups, some from the south, settling in different parts of the country and establishing their own organisational and legal systems. Today there are over seventy tribes in total, with the main ones being the Bemba, the Lunda, the Ngoni, the Tonga, the Lozi, the Luvale and the Kaonde.

The other inhabitants of Zambia are mainly of European stock. So far as is known the first Europeans to visit the territory in the late eighteenth and early nineteenth centuries were Portuguese explorers from Mozambique and Angola. They were followed by the Scottish missionary and explorer David Livingstone, who undertook a number of expeditions including attempts to establish trade routes from central Africa to the Atlantic coast in the west and the Indian Ocean in the east. His aim was to defeat the slave trade by bringing legitimate commerce and Christianity to the area. He eventually died on an expedition in northern Zambia in 1873.

Towards the end of the nineteenth century, Cecil Rhodes, an Englishman who had made a fortune from diamond and gold mines in South Africa, set his sights on extending British influence into central Africa. His British South Africa Company, which entered into treaties with local rulers, sometimes by force, was granted a British Royal Charter in 1889, giving it authority over areas covered by the treaties. The company continued to administer what had become Northern Rhodesia until 1923, after which the country became a British Protectorate under the Colonial Office. Forty years later, in 1964, the country became independent as Zambia.

Today the population, which reached an estimated total of 13.8 million in 2012, of whom 99.5 per cent are African, is one of the fastest growing in the world. Nearly 40 per cent of the people now live in urban areas, particularly in the mining centres of the Copperbelt and in Lusaka, the capital. Although the economy has grown at a good rate in recent years, the rapid rise in the population has meant that poverty remains a serious concern. Life expectancy is low and there is a high incidence of HIV/AIDS, which the Government is taking steps to deal with. In spite of the difficulties it faces, Zambia is generally a peaceful and open society with very little friction between the different peoples. After a period of one-party rule between 1972 and 1991 the country is once again a multi-party parliamentary democracy, and experienced a successful change of power in 2011, when the current President, Michael Sata, defeated Rupiah Banda, who had been President since 2008. Further information about the years when Zambia was a British dependency and the period since Independence is contained in Appendix 2.

Appendix 2

COLONIAL RULE AND INDEPENDENCE

On 29 October 1889, an event took place in London which was to have a significant effect on the future of central Africa. It was the date when Queen Victoria signed the charter of the British South Africa Company, an organisation established and controlled by Cecil Rhodes, who wanted to use it to take over the land that is now occupied by the independent nations of Zambia and Zimbabwe. His interests were in exploiting the mineral wealth he believed to lie there and in taking possession of the territory for the United Kingdom. This was at the time when the so-called Scramble for Africa was at its height, and there were fears that the Germans, the Portuguese or even the South African Boers would move into the area if Britain did not act. The Government in London supported Rhodes' proposals because they enabled Britain to gain control over a large part of central Africa at no expense to the British taxpayer.

The charter gave the company authority to make agreements with local Chiefs to acquire a range of rights and powers, including those that would enable it to govern the territory and maintain law and order. It noted that the aims of those behind the company were to promote trade, commerce, civilisation and good government, and that Rhodes and his colleagues hoped to be able to suppress the slave trade in the territory as well as opening it up to European immigration. Importantly, the charter also specified that the company should not interfere with the religion of the local people, unless it was necessary to do so in the interests of humanity, and that in the administration of justice regard should be paid to existing customs and laws.

It seems that right from the start the company thought of the area north of the Zambezi, which was to become Northern Rhodesia, as being quite different from the southern territory, which became known as Southern Rhodesia. The latter was considered to be particularly suitable for European settlement, and within a year of the signing of the charter the Pioneer Column of white settlers from South Africa had arrived in the country. By contrast Northern Rhodesia was seen as an African dependency and a source of labour for the company's mines.

The company soon set about entering into agreements with local Chiefs. The first to be made in what was to become Northern Rhodesia was with Lewanika, the leader of the Lozi people, who gave the company mineral and other rights in exchange for protection from the Ndebele, who lived across the Zambezi in Southern Rhodesia. Some of the other tribes, including the Bemba and Lunda, were reluctant to surrender rights, and only did so when they realised they had little choice. The Ngoni resisted for a long time but were eventually overcome by force.

Although the company soon discovered copper in the area of what was to become the Copperbelt, it did not succeed in exploiting this resource during its time in charge of the country. Instead, as a means of raising income, it introduced a hut tax which required each household to pay a levy in the form of cash. This unpopular form of tax was favoured by the company, because it also meant that African men had to seek paid work, usually in the company's mines, in order to earn money. Much of this income was used by the company to build the railway line which runs from Southern Rhodesia in the south to the border with the Democratic Republic of the Congo in the north, passing through Lusaka and the Copperbelt on the way.

Large numbers of people of European origin moved into Southern Rhodesia during the years when the company was responsible for its administration. Initially it was in the hope of profiting from mining developments, but as these failed to materialise to the extent expected, people turned instead to farming. Over time the white population became so well established that the possibility of the country joining South Africa as its fifth province was discussed. The settlers, however, turned down this proposal in a referendum, seeking instead to be responsible for their own affairs. This was granted when the British Government decided in 1923 not to renew the company's charter and established Southern Rhodesia as a self-governing colony.

Northern Rhodesia, which at that time had only a relatively small number of white settlers, most of whom were farmers, also changed its status, and in 1924 it became a British Protectorate. The Government of the country was placed in the hands of a Governor, who was responsible to the British Colonial Office, and who was assisted by an Executive Council responsible for implementing policy and a Legislative Council to advise the Governor and pass laws.

At first the only members of the Executive Council were the Governor and five senior civil servants appointed by him, while the Legislative Council was made up of the members of the Executive Council and a small number of other Europeans nominated by the Governor. Changes were gradually introduced to the membership of both the Executive and Legislative Councils, but it was not until 1938 that the interests of Africans were formally represented when a European member was nominated to the Legislative Council for this purpose. This representation was increased in 1945 when three Europeans were appointed to fulfil this role. The first two Africans became members of the Legislative Council in 1948, their number increasing to four in 1954.

From then on developments moved at a faster pace. In 1959 under revised arrangements eight Africans and fourteen Europeans were elected to the Legislative Council to join eight nominated members in a total of thirty. An election in 1962 under a new constitution saw the two African political parties win fourteen and seven seats respectively, while the sole European party gained sixteen. There continued to be eight nominated members. The final election before Independence in 1964 was held on a one person-one vote basis for the first time, but with separate rolls for African and European voters. The result was a large majority for the African parties, with the United National Independence Party (UNIP) winning fifty-five seats, the African National Congress (ANC) ten and the European National Progressive Party (NPP) ten. Further information about these two elections is given below.

Under colonial rule the day-to-day administration of the country and responsibility for law and order were delegated to the Provincial Administration, which was organised on the basis of provinces and districts. A Provincial Commissioner (PC) was appointed to be in charge of each province, with a District Commissioner (DC) responsible for each district in the province. Depending on the size and complexity of the district the DC would have under his control one or more District Officers (DOs) and Cadets, who were probationary DOs. The work of the Provincial Administration was supported by the services of specialists such as Agriculture and Education Officers. In carrying out their work colonial civil servants were conscious that they were acting as trustees for the local people with a responsibility to help them to advance, so that at some stage in the future the country could become self-governing.

The system of administration used in Northern Rhodesia was known as Indirect Rule. This was an approach pioneered by Lord Lugard, one of the most influential of Britain's past colonial administrators. Between 1914 and 1919 he was Governor-General of Nigeria, having previously served in Uganda and Hong Kong as well as in different parts of Nigeria itself. In both Uganda and Nigeria there were well-established African monarchies and local Civil Services, which Lugard utilised as channels of government. Unlike other colonial powers, which tended to sweep aside the local systems and engage in direct rule, Britain made use of Lugard's ideas and adopted the concept of Indirect Rule in Northern Rhodesia and other African dependencies.

One of the most concise and understandable accounts to be found of how Indirect Rule was applied in Northern Rhodesia, and how it still operated there sixty years after Lugard, is given in *A Time to Mourn,* a book written by John Hudson, who was DC Isoka in Northern Rhodesia in 1963–4. Below are some extracts:

All over British colonial Africa people typically, unless they were nomads, lived in small settlements of related families under the guidance of their headmen. These villages came under Chiefs who in turn were associated with others sharing a common ancestry, speaking the same language and with the same customary system, to form tribes.

Administratively, the basic units of government were unpaid village headmen, grouped as described above under Chiefs. The latter, who received small salaries, were officially recognised as the local government bodies known as Native Authorities, which were empowered to make regulations, to raise revenue, and to spend it on local services. Chiefs also retained their pre-colonial rights, to a limited degree, to administer customary law (both civil and criminal) as presidents of local courts Both the Native Authorities and the Chiefs' courts were supervised by central Government officers of the Provincial Administration at district level. These were members of the Colonial Service, later known as HM Overseas Civil Service.

Normally recruited by formidable interview at the Colonial Office in London from university graduates, they came out as Cadets, becoming District Officers after a probationary period. A District Officer (DO) put in charge of a district was gazetted as its District Commissioner (DC).

Initially Native Authorities, which were each responsible for a defined geographical area, comprised the Chief and his traditional councillors. As time passed younger, more educated people were brought in as councillors with some being given full-time responsibilities for such matters as the authority's schools and roads. These authorities also became responsible for managing their financial affairs and employed treasurers for this purpose.

The aim was that they should evolve into local government authorities.

In the urban areas of Northern Rhodesia, where members of different tribes lived in the same townships, there were no traditional Native Authorities. Instead, Urban Advisory Councils were set up. These did not have the powers of the rural Native Authorities, but acted largely as channels of communication between the DC and the African population. They did, however, join the Native Authorities in having representatives on the Provincial Councils, which in turn appointed delegates to the national African Representative Council. It was this council which elected the first two African members of the Legislative Council in 1948.

This was the same year that the African National Congress (ANC) political party was formed out of the Federation of African Welfare Societies. Its stated purpose was to promote the educational, political, economic and social advancement of all Africans. Three years later Harry Nkumbula became its President. The colonial Government must have been worried by the growth of the party for in 1952 the Secretary of Native Affairs tried, unsuccessfully, to persuade the Chiefs not to support it.

The urban areas which served the copper mines were very much a distinguishing feature of Northern Rhodesia, and marked the country out as different from Britain's other colonial territories in Africa. The realisation in the 1920s that the country possessed large deposits of copper ore, which could be mined and processed commercially, resulted in the movement of many thousands of Africans from rural villages into the new townships on the Copperbelt to work in the mines. Large numbers of Europeans from the United Kingdom and South Africa also came into the country, attracted by the availability of well-paid jobs and the promise of a high standard of living. It was inevitable that from the start the skilled jobs went to the Europeans, while the basic labouring work was carried out by the African employees.

This state of affairs was complicated in 1940, when, empowered by the growth in demand for copper for war purposes, the white miners went on strike for a pay increase and a commitment to reserve certain jobs for white employees. This latter demand was conceded, with the result that Africans, whose knowledge and experience had developed since the early years, were denied access to all skilled and semi-skilled jobs. It was not until the 1950s that this barrier to African advancement began to be broken down. In 1959 apprenticeships were opened to all races and in 1963 the European closed shop was formally ended.

There were also other barriers to equality between the races. The Europeans who settled on the Copperbelt were keen to protect their privileged way of life and keep themselves separate from the African population as far as possible. Such was the influence of the practices in South Africa at the time, that Africans were excluded from European restaurants, hotels and cinemas; they had to use separate entrances to post offices; and in some instances could only make purchases from European shops through a separate hatch. These forms of discrimination were finally proscribed by law in 1960.

The growth in the number of European settlers in both Northern and Southern Rhodesia led to suggestions being made from an early stage that the two countries should be amalgamated under a system of self-government, similar to that which was already in force in Southern Rhodesia. Although the white inhabitants of the two countries had failed to persuade the British Government to implement their ideas in the 1930s, they raised the matter again after the end of World War II.

The two sets of settlers felt that they would be better able to develop the economic potential of the two countries by bringing together the Northern Rhodesian copper industry and Southern Rhodesia's coal and agricultural production, and that united they would be in a stronger position to influence policy relating to the African peoples. The British authorities, who were keen to reduce the risk of Southern Rhodesia coming under the influence of South Africa with its repressive racial policies, considered that, in spite of the views of most of the settlers, they would be able to ensure that a process of racial partnership continued in the territories. They, therefore, decided that the best way forward was to establish the Federation of Rhodesia and Nyasaland, which came into existence in 1953, and comprised Nyasaland (now Malawi), Northern Rhodesia and Southern Rhodesia. The Federal Government took over responsibility for a number of issues, including economic development and European education, while the individual territories continued to deal with others. The British Government retained overall control.

This decision to set up the Federation was against the wishes of the African populations, who believed that it would be dominated by the Europeans and act against their interests. Their opposition was not surprising. The policy of the British Government relating to African interests had changed over the years. The early declaration of the 'paramountcy of native interests' had been watered down, and in 1948 the British Government confirmed that 'the doctrine of paramountcy means no more than that the interests of the overwhelming majority of the indigenous population should not be subordinated to those of a minority belonging to another race, however important in itself'. And the remark by the first Prime Minister of the Federation that partnership between the races could be compared to the partnership between a horse and its rider would only have exacerbated their fears.

It soon became clear that the benefits of federation were not being shared fairly, with a disproportionate amount of income being spent in Southern Rhodesia even though much of it was being generated by the mines in Northern Rhodesia. The Federal Government, which was dominated by Southern Rhodesian interests, ensured, for example, that a new hydro-electricity scheme was constructed at Kariba on the Zambezi, with the power station on the Southern Rhodesia side, rather than on the Kafue River in Northern Rhodesia. The economy of Northern Rhodesia was also adversely affected by the need to pay 80 per cent of the mining royalties to the British South Africa Company. African education, which was a responsibility of the Northern Rhodesia Government, also suffered from inadequate funding. Most of the expenditure was devoted to primary education, with only a small proportion of students going on to secondary school.

In 1960 there was only one institution in Northern Rhodesia offering a sixth-form course.

African resistance to the Federation came to a head in 1959. In Northern Rhodesia the Zambia African National Congress (ZANC), which had been formed the previous year as a radical alternative to the existing African National Congress (ANC), was banned and its leader, Kenneth Kaunda, who was to become the first President of the independent Zambia, was detained. Released in 1960 he became leader of the newly formed United National Independence Party (UNIP). In Nyasaland a state of emergency was declared and African leaders including Dr Hastings Banda, who became the country's President after Independence, were arrested. These troubles led to the appointment of the Monckton Commission, which reported in late 1960.

Amongst the report's proposals was a recommendation that the territories should be given the right to secede from the Federation. In Northern Rhodesia a new constitution, which increased African voting power, was adopted in 1962 following a further period of unrest known as 'cha-cha-cha'. The subsequent election saw the African parties gain a majority of the elected seats with the result that Northern Rhodesia succeeded in withdrawing from the Federation, which was then dissolved at the end of 1963.[1]

In early 1964 another election was held under full adult suffrage but with a separate roll for European voters. The result was an overall majority for UNIP led by Kenneth Kaunda, which won fifty-five seats against ten for Harry Nkumbula's ANC and ten for the white National Progressive Party.[2] The situation was then complicated by an uprising in the north and east of the country by members of the Lumpa Church, led by Alice Lenshina, in which many lives were lost. Finally, on 24 October 1964 Northern Rhodesia became independent as the Republic of Zambia with Kaunda as its first President.

The new state began its life in what at first appeared to be benign circumstances. The price of copper, which was the country's main source of income, was at high levels largely because of the demand created by the war in Vietnam. The Government also benefited from having recovered the outstanding mineral rights from the British South Africa Company, and from no longer needing to contribute to the costs of the Federation. There were, however, difficulties. The number of educated Zambians was small: in 1963 there were fewer than 100 graduates and fewer than 1,000 school leavers had secondary certificates. Steps were taken, therefore, to expand primary and secondary education, and in 1965 the University of Zambia was founded. By 1971 there were 54,000 students in secondary schools and 2,000 at the university.

Unfortunately it was not long before the new Government, led by Kenneth Kaunda, faced a serious challenge. In 1965 Southern Rhodesia, which had begun to describe itself simply as Rhodesia, declared independence with the intention of perpetuating white rule in the country. This Unilateral Declaration of Independence (UDI) was not recognised by other states, and the United Nations imposed a set of sanctions on the country. Zambia, which was keen to see an end to white minority rule in southern Africa, applied the sanctions to its own detriment. With the closing of its border with Southern Rhodesia the main route for the export of its copper was cut off, as was the country's main source of oil and other imported goods such as coal and coke and foodstuffs. It thus had to find alternative routes for the export of its copper and other sources for essential supplies. New export routes through Angola and Tanzania, including the Tazama oil pipeline and, later, the Chinese-built Tazara railway, were developed and the Great North Road was tarred.

After elections in 1968, when Kaunda was re-elected President and UNIP won 81 of the 105 seats in the National Assembly, the political situation began to change. Differences began to emerge between Kaunda and Simon Kapwepwe, who was Vice-President and a long-standing senior member of UNIP. In 1971 Kapwepwe resigned from the Government admitting that he was the leader of the newly formed United Progressive Party (UPP). The following year all parties other than UNIP were banned and Kapwepwe and others were detained. Power was consolidated in the hands of Kaunda in 1973, when a new constitution brought in 'one-party participatory democracy' with UNIP as the only recognised party. Kaunda was duly re-elected President in 1973, while the newly elected National Assembly consisted entirely of UNIP members.

Meanwhile the Government had been working to acquire more control over the economy in order to make the country more self-sufficient. In the early 1970s majority holdings were acquired in the major mining companies and in other privately owned businesses. But again external influences intervened. The huge oil-price increases of 1973 and 1979 reduced the demand for copper and the income it generated. At the same time the costs of imports and transport rose. In the hope that the situation would improve, the Government borrowed large sums of money to keep the economy going. But matters continued to deteriorate and in the late 1980s the International Monetary Fund (IMF) became involved, seeking changes to the way the economy was managed. The people of Zambia, who had been struggling with higher living costs and unemployment, had also begun to protest against the way the country was being governed.

As a result Kaunda, who had been re-elected unopposed in 1978, 1983 and 1988 and had thus been continually in power since 1964, removed the ban on other political parties. A new constitution was introduced in 1991. In the election which followed, Frederick Chiluba became President with 76 per cent of the vote against 24 per cent for Kaunda, while the new President's Movement for Multiparty Democracy (MMD) won 125 of the 150 seats in the National Assembly. The new Government set about tackling the country's economic problems by following the prescriptions of the IMF, which involved lowering tariffs on imports, ending price controls and privatising publicly owned enterprises, including the mines. The measures resulted in much higher unemployment, reductions in agricultural production and manufacturing and a significant increase in poverty. National income per head, for example, was over 30 per cent lower in 2000 than it had been in 1976.

A change in the constitution, which required presidential candidates to have both parents born in Zambia and which established that Presidents could serve for only two terms, pre-vented Kaunda from standing in the 1996 election. With UNIP boycotting the polls, Chiluba was elected President for a second term, with his MMD party winning 131 National Assembly seats. As the next election approached Chiluba expressed an interest in standing for a third term as President, but was barred by the constitution from doing so. He was, therefore, replaced in the 2001 election by Levy Mwanawasa, who had been his Vice-President, and who beat ten other candidates to become President with 29 per cent of the votes. Mwanawasa then began a campaign against corruption in public life, and as a result Chiluba was prosecuted for embezzlement. He was convicted of fraud in London, but acquitted in a trial held in Zambia.

Re-elected in 2006, Levy Mwanawasa died two years later. The resulting presidential election in 2008 was won by Rupiah Banda of the MMD, who had been Vice-President. Michael Sata, representing the Patriotic Front (PF), came second. The tables were turned in 2011, when Sata defeated Banda to become President, and the PF became the largest party in the National Assembly with 60 of the 150 seats.

Having restructured its economy along the lines required by the IMF, Zambia qualified in 2005 for the Highly Indebted Poor Countries debt relief agreed by the G8 group of leading indus-trial nations at the Gleneagles Summit. The effect of this initia-tive was to reduce Zambia's crippling debt burden by around 90 per cent. Since then the economy has grown at more than 6 per cent a year, largely as a result of an increase in the demand for copper. The country nevertheless remains very poor, with its wealth unevenly distributed and many people living in poverty, especially in the rural areas. In spite of this Zambia has a proud record of democratic governance, with power having changed through the ballot-box twice in the last twenty years.

Notes

1 Under the 1962 constitution there were two electoral rolls defined by income and property, with race also being taken into account. The upper and lower rolls each elected fifteen members from single-member

constituencies. In addition there were seven two-member national constituencies in which electors on both rolls could vote. A further single-member national constituency was reserved for Asian and mixed-race electors. The outcome of the election was UNIP fourteen seats, ANC seven and the mainly European United Federal Party sixteen. The remaining eight seats were unfilled, as none of the candidates concerned gained the necessary 10 per cent of both African and European voters, as required in the national constituencies.

2 The 1964 election was held under a new constitution on a one person, one vote basis for the first time. A main roll for African voters elected sixty-five members, while a reserved roll for Europeans elected ten. Asian and mixed-race voters could choose which roll to join. The result was UNIP fifty-five seats, ANC ten and the National Progressive Party ten.

Appendix 3

CAMBRIDGE OVERSEAS SERVICES COURSE

Although training for new recruits to the Colonial Service had been introduced before World War I, it was not until 1926 that courses were established at the universities of Oxford and Cambridge. In 1946, after a break during World War II, the training was resumed in a revised format known as the Devonshire Courses.[1]

The purpose of the courses was set out in a 1954 circular issued by Alan Lennox-Boyd, then Secretary of State for the Colonies, which stated:

The essential aim of the Courses should be to give the Cadet a practical basis to his work in the territory which would be of immediate use to him on his arrival.

At the same time it is a university course and its aim, therefore, is to stimulate Cadets by giving them an intelligent introduction to subjects which they are then expected to continue to develop for themselves in action and for the rest of their careers.

In recognition of the political and constitutional developments which had been taking place the name was changed in 1958 to the Overseas Services Courses. Three different types of training were provided, with Course 'A' (Administration) being for administrative officers starting their careers, Course 'A' (Agriculture) for new agricultural officers and Course 'B' for people who had already been in the Service for several years.

Whether the new recruit to the administrative service attended Course 'A' in Oxford or in Cambridge depended on the local language he (and the course was open only to men at the time) would have to learn. Thus it was that in October 1961 those who have contributed to this book arrived in Cambridge, where they would be taught ciBemba, while those who would be going to Swaziland went to Oxford.

There were twenty-three people on the Cambridge 1961/2 'A' Course, of whom twenty-two went on to serve in Northern Rhodesia. The odd man out was Prince Stephen Karamagi from Toro in Uganda, who subsequently joined the Ugandan diplomatic service. The others comprised two African graduates from Northern Rhodesia, eight non-graduates who had been recruited under a different scheme and who had already worked in Northern Rhodesia for a few years and twelve graduates newly recruited in the UK. Taking place at the same time were a 'B' Course and an agriculture course. All those attending the courses who were new to Cambridge were admitted to the university and became members of colleges, thus enabling them to participate in a range of activities outside the course.

The 'A' Course included a number of academic subjects such as criminal law and evidence, economics, colonial history and the government of dependent territories, but even these had practical applications, for members of the course would before too long become magistrates (albeit with limited powers), as well as being concerned with economic development and constitutional change. Remarkably, some of the instruction was provided by leading practitioners in their field such as Professor Austin Robinson, an influential economist who had worked with John Maynard Keynes. Other well-known tutors included the historians John Gallagher and Ronald Robinson.

A good deal of time was devoted to the teaching of ciBemba, one of the main languages of Northern Rhodesia. Because of its structure and complexity it was regarded as providing a good basis for the study of other languages which people posted to non-Bemba districts would have to learn. The course language tutor was the Revd Griffith Quick, a Welshman who had been a missionary in Northern Rhodesia. His training, which in the summer was often given in a punt on the River Cam, helped several generations of Cadets to develop their language skills to a high level after arriving in the territory.

Other topics covered were tropical agriculture and forestry, social anthropology and field engineering, which included practical sessions on surveying, engine maintenance and even mixing concrete. Small amounts of time were also spent on tropical hygiene and dealing with civil disorder. During the university vacations secondments were arranged to local government bodies and magistrates' courts. One significant omission from the syllabus, however, was accounting, which became clear when course members later found themselves having to check Native Authority accounts. Those who had not been to the territory before were fortunate in being able to draw on the experience of those who had already worked there, and on the knowledge of the two African members of the course, who came from Northern Rhodesia.

The courses were based in the Overseas Services Club in the centre of Cambridge, where the course director, Hugh McCleery, previously a Provincial Commissioner in Tanganyika, had his office. The club premises were spacious and incorporated a bar, where sandwiches could be purchased at lunch-time, two full-size billiard tables, a library and a large sitting area. There were also one or two smaller rooms, which were used for ciBemba and law tutorials, although most of the instruction took place in other locations around the university.

The club was also a centre for social activities, especially for those members who did not have wives and families. Activities ranged from a black-tie dance to home-and-away darts matches against a favourite pub, the Ancient Shepherds at Fen Ditton. One particularly memorable event was a visit to the club by Jomo Kenyatta and Tom Mboya, leaders of the African political movement in Kenya, who were in the UK for constitutional talks with the British Government. The visit had been arranged by Princess Elizabeth Bagaaya of Toro, sister of Stephen. She was a student at Girton. Jomo Kenyatta became President of Kenya when the country became independent in 1963. Tom Mboya, who had been seen as President Kenyatta's likely successor, was assassinated in 1969.

On another occasion a group of course members made a trip to Conway Hall in London to hear an address by Kenneth Kaunda, leader of Northern Rhodesia's United National Independence Party, who became the first President of the newly indepen-dent Zambia in 1964. There were also a visit by members of the Oxford course to Cambridge, when a Cambridge team won a lively hockey match, and a return visit to Oxford, when Cambridge were defeated at cricket.

Course members were issued with small books on first aid with covers treated with insecticide. Wives and wives-to-be attended a session at the Corona Society in London, where prac-tical advice included the use of Dettol to disinfect lavatory seats, and the good news that hats were no longer required to be worn to cocktail parties!

The Cambridge 'A' (Administration) Course was held for one more year, 1962/3, after which it was merged with the 'B' Course and became known as the Cambridge Course on Development. In 1969 it moved to what is now Wolfson College. Government funding ended in 1981, after which parts of the syllabus were merged into what became an M.Phil. course in Development.

Note

1 The Devonshire Courses took their name from a committee established in 1944 to consider the future of training for the Colonial Service under the Chairmanship of the 10th Duke of Devonshire. The committee decided in favour of a training scheme to be run at the universities rather than at a Colonial Staff College.

Members of the Cambridge 1961/2 'A' Course

	Initial postings in Northern Rhodesia	
	District	*Province*
David Alexander	Mkushi	Central
Mick Bond	Mporokoso	Northern
Jeremy Burnham	Kasama	Northern
John Edwards	Sinazongwe	Southern
Tony Goddard	Fort Jameson	Eastern
Robert Humphreys	Balovale	North Western
Max Keyzar	Abercorn	Northern
Jim Lavender	Chadiza	Eastern
Jonathan Leach	Kawambwa	Luapula
Malcolm Mitchell	Choma	Southern
Neil Morris	Luwingu	Northern
Peter Moss	Mkushi	Central
Valentine Musakanya	Isoka	Northern
Lazarus Mwanza	Lusaka	Central
D'Arcy Payne	Livingstone	Southern
Richard Pelly	Kalomo	Southern
Tony Schur	Kabompo	North Western
John Shaw	Solwezi	North Western
David Taylor	Sesheke	Barotseland (now Western)
John Theakstone	Mumbwa	Central
Paul Wigram	Kasempa	North Western
John Woodmansey	Ndola Rural	Western (now Copperbelt)

BIOGRAPHICAL NOTES

David Alexander

After school in England David spent a year at Portland High School in Oregon before studying politics and economics at Keele University. On graduating he entered the Cambridge Course. He was posted to Mkushi and later to Serenje. His time at Mkushi brought challenges on account of racist attitudes he encountered amongst some of the settler community there.

In 1965 he returned to Keele University to complete his MA. Three years later he was appointed to a post as lecturer and resident tutor at the University of Zambia, teaching in Lusaka and Chipata. During his second period in the country he fought hard to ensure that all Zambians had the right of access to education.

He left Zambia in 1975 on being appointed to a lectureship in adult education at Edinburgh University. He retired as senior lecturer in the Department of Education in 1995, having had a particular interest in adult and workers' education – an interest which took him as far afield as India, Papua New Guinea and Thailand in addition to various countries in Africa. His love of Africa was manifest and he was respected for his opinions by many who met him in Zambia and elsewhere.

David was married twice, collaborating with his second wife Cathie in their shared concern with workers' education in both Africa and the United Kingdom. He died in 2011.

Mick Bond

Mick joined the Cambridge Course after National Service and having read Classics at Cambridge. He was posted first to Mporokoso, where he spent two years before moving to Chinsali to help deal with the challenges presented by the Lumpa Church. He was confirmed as District Commissioner there shortly before Independence. In 1965 he became District Secretary firstly in Chingola and Chililabombwe (formerly Bancroft) on the Copperbelt and then in Mongu, where he was Acting Resident Secretary for a while and then Provincial Development Officer.

He then transferred in 1968 to the Ministry of Local Government and Housing in Lusaka as a Senior Principal, and in 1969 to the Cabinet Office as Assistant Director of Elections. Forced to leave the Civil Service he spent two years as Company Secretary of a furniture company, before being reinstated in the Civil Service as Administrative Vice-Principal in the Zambia Institute of Technology in Kitwe.

Returning to the UK in 1973 Mick joined Newcastle University as Assistant Registrar, later becoming Deputy Registrar. In 1982 he enjoyed a six-month secondment through the British Council to Botswana to prepare its University College for full university status. Since retiring he has been Chair of the Newcastle and North of England region of the Multiple Sclerosis Society and a volunteer representative for patients and carers in a neuro-rehabilitation centre.

With his wife, Wendy, he spent a month in Zambia in 2012 to celebrate their fiftieth wedding anniversary.

Wendy Bond

Wendy read English at Cambridge, at the state's expense, before marrying Mick while he was on the Overseas Services Course. Their service in Northern Rhodesia and Zambia lasted for eleven years and took them to Mporokoso, Chinsali, Bancroft, Mongu, Lusaka and Kitwe.

Back in the UK they chose a rural home near Hadrian's Wall in the north of England as their children were used to the sense of space in Zambia. This enabled the children to be given respon-sibilities for their own goats and chickens to help them to settle in an alien land.

After a spell as secretary of the local Sheep Show, Wendy switched to supply teaching and marking exam papers before committing to teaching English at an inner-city secondary school. There she felt that she perhaps achieved rather more in after-school activities, such as the Latin Club, the Debating Society and the school's outdoor-pursuits centre, than in the classroom.

Since retiring she has helped to revitalise the local village through establishing a lively village hall and now runs the monthly farm-ers' market. Having obtained grants for the work in their small community, Wendy has served on two LEADER programmes pro-viding economic stimulus to isolated communities and is now part of the team hoping to reopen a much-needed railway station.

Jeremy Burnham

Following a tour in Mumbwa as an LDA Jeremy attended the Cambridge Course before working as a DO in Lundazi and Kasama. After a short stint in Lusaka writing speeches for the new Minister of Environment, he left Northern Rhodesia shortly before Independence to attend university in the USA. He then returned to the new Zambia to start and run the small industries section of the para-statal INDECO.

Then followed a decade of exploration into farming, sustain-able living and alternative healing in several countries, leading him eventually to South Africa as a consultant and trainer in a range of personal and environmental healing technologies. He established South African New Economics, an NGO, wrote and published the book *Your Heart – Your Planet* and project-man-aged the IUCN World Summit on Sustainable Development. He was eventually drawn into the hugely rewarding work of conflict resolution, which included facilitating conversations between combatants in the xenophobic clashes around 2007–8 and more recently in a range of corporate interventions.

Jeremy returned briefly to Zambia around 2008 to visit Peter Moss, who has contributed to Mick Bond's description of events relating to the Lumpa Church (Chapter 11), when his initial impression was one of dismay at the radical deforestation that had taken place, followed by some heart-warming reconnections with old friends, saddened only by the realisation of how many had succumbed to AIDS. He quickly realised that to ask the old question 'Was colonisation a gift or a burden?' was to invite so many opposing perspectives as to be meaningless.

John Edwards

Having obtained a first degree at the University of British Columbia, John attended the 1961/2 Overseas Services Course in Cambridge. Posted to Northern Rhodesia he worked as a Cadet in Sinazongwe, Gwembe, Siavonga and Monze.

From 1964 to 1967 he studied economics at the University of Manchester, gaining an MA (Econ.). He then returned to Canada and worked until 1997 for the federal public service. Amongst the posts he held during this period were Secretary-General, National Museums and Commissioner, Correctional Service of Canada. He was also President of the Association of Federal Public Service Executives and a commentator/adviser on Civil Service reform in Australia, Philippines, Egypt and Russia.

Since retiring John has been a commentator/adviser/consultant on Civil Service matters within Canada, with InterAmerican Development Bank and in Nepal, Peru, Bolivia and Russia. He is also President of the Ottawa John Howard Society, which provides support to offenders and youth at risk.

John is married with three stepchildren and eight grandchildren. He and his wife live in Ottawa but spend much of the time at their rural property 45 miles north of the city. They travel to other countries frequently, remaining fascinated by their history and how these societies have evolved to the present.

Tony Goddard

Tony's first posting was as a Cadet to Fort Jameson, where he was put in charge of the Kunda Valley, which included the Nsefu Game Camp. After two years he was transferred to the neighbouring district of Lundazi, where he was closely involved in dealing with the aftermath of the Lumpa Church uprising in that district. A few months later, having undergone some initial training on the Copperbelt, he moved to North Western Province as the Resident Magistrate for Balovale (now Zambezi) and Kabompo.

Having read Law at Oxford before being selected for the Cambridge Course he joined a firm of solicitors on his return to the UK, becoming qualified in 1969. A year later he became a partner with a small practice in South Devon, specialising in litigation and advocacy, before setting up on his own in 1978. After twenty years he amalgamated his practice with another firm, and has since been working as consultant to this firm and others.

Tony has a son and two grandchildren, whom he sees regularly. He recently travelled to Zambia with his second wife to celebrate his seventieth birthday, and was able to visit some of the places he worked in nearly fifty years before. His book *My African Stories* was published in 2005.

Robert Humphreys

Robert began his service with the Northern Rhodesia Government in 1958 as an LDA in Mazabuka. His time there was interrupted by four and a half months' basic military training with the Royal Rhodesia Regiment in Bulawayo in Southern Rhodesia. After a short stint in the Secretariat in Lusaka he attended the course in Cambridge, during which he married. On his return to Northern Rhodesia with his wife, Jane, he was posted as a DO to Balovale and then to Solwezi.

Moving back to the UK in 1964, he joined a firm of Chartered Surveyors in Exeter and took a correspondence course to qualify as a Land Agent. He became a partner of the firm in 1970, where he remained until he took early retirement in 1995. He also served as a magistrate from 1976 to 1995.

In 1996 Robert and Jane moved to Nevis in the West Indies, with Robert taking up a new and third career as a sculptor in bronze and silver. They returned to the UK in 2013 to be nearer to their two sons and six grandchildren.

Max Keyzar

Max was selected for the course in Cambridge after serving as an LDA in the Broken Hill (now Kabwe) Rural District. He subsequently worked in Abercorn, Mkushi, Mporokoso, Samfya and Kasama. Returning to the UK he joined the head office of the Milk Marketing Board on the personnel side.

After twelve years he went back to Africa to work as Manpower Development Officer for Triangle Ltd, the largest sugar producer in Rhodesia (Zimbabwe). This was an eventful time, with a war going on in the country. He later returned to the UK, joining a food-manufacturing organisation in the West Country and becoming its Personnel Director. Following a takeover and a subsequent management buyout Max joined Shaw Trust, a national charity placing people with disabilities into work, later working as an independent personnel consultant. His final job until 2009 was managing the Personnel Department of Kenneth Copeland Ministries, an American Christian teaching organisation with its UK/European office in Bath.

Following his retirement Max says he has been busier than ever. He is one of the leaders of a lively charismatic church of about 150 people in his home town of Bradford on Avon, and enjoys life with his family, which includes four delightfully exhausting and challenging grandchildren.

Jonathan Leach

After four years in the British Army Jonathan worked as a DA in Balovale and Solwezi. He then attended the Cambridge Course before being posted to Nchelenge, Kawambwa and finally Bancroft.

Retiring from the Overseas Civil Service in 1966 he undertook four years of theological training in London, where he was ordained. In February 1971 he was inducted as the pastor of a newly formed charismatic church congregation in Botha's Hill, 15 miles from Durban. Three years later he and Jane were transferred to Queenstown in the Eastern Cape, where they exercised a largely interdenominational ministry visiting thirty-five farms while based with the Assemblies of God.

1976 saw them return to Botha's Hill, where they developed close relationships with African and Indian pastors, which attracted the attention of the security police. Since then the church has grown and has become multi-cultural, with English-speaking Zulus and Shona refugees from Zimbabwe, as well as Indians. Services take place in a magnificent building which seats 350 and is used by other churches and organisations.

Jonathan's ministry has included preaching across most denominational boundaries and occasionally in Swaziland, Zimbabwe, Mozambique, the UK and the USA. Having retired in 2000 he is currently chairman of Tabitha Ministries in Pietermaritzburg, founded by a former member of his church, which cares for 2,000 orphans in child-headed households and runs an in-house orphanage and a school. He is also the KwaZulu-Natal co-ordinator of Contemplative Outreach, a Catholic-based international and interdenominational prayer movement focusing on listening to God in silence. Over the years Jane has developed a reputation as an artist of note.

Kate McRae (formerly Fiona Morris)

Nowadays Kate lives in Gloucester near her Cambridge-born daughter. She paints in oils, does filing for a charity shop and repackages documents in the County Archives. She tries to live quietly because of her blood pressure, but two school-age grand-children make this difficult.

After Zambia Kate produced a third baby, taking him to Hong Kong two and a half weeks later. She found an *amah* and started work as a schoolteacher, then a journalist and finally a Government Training Officer. When her husband, Neil, began working in Japan, she stayed behind with their children, only returning to the UK, now remarried, in 1985.

Unhappy in her homeland, Kate then taught adults in Turkey, Ghana (with VSO) and Mongolia. She brought her third husband to England to meet her family. Once he had requalified in English they moved to Amsterdam, where Kate learned Dutch, recorded textbooks for the blind, assisted robbed tourists and edited academic papers. When this marriage ended VSO sent her to China.

Eventually Kate retired to Somerset, volunteering at a museum, the CAB and Wells Cathedral. Cancer persuaded her to move nearer her relatives in Gloucestershire. Her Kasama-born son still lives in Hong Kong; her younger son is a musician in London.

Judy Mitchell

Judy, who was born in Southern Rhodesia, met Malcolm in Oxford, where she was working as a secretary and he was reading Classics at Balliol. They married at Easter during Malcolm's year on the course in Cambridge. Their twelve years in Northern Rhodesia and Zambia included spells in Choma, at the Chalimbana local government training centre and in Lusaka.

On their return to England in 1974, they chose to live in Shrewsbury because it was half-way between their respective parents and also so that their two sons could follow their father, uncles and grandfather to Shrewsbury School. With Malcolm beginning a new career as an articled clerk with a firm of solicitors, Judy decided she would have to be a wage-earner. After some temporary work she was appointed as assistant secretary to the Headmaster at Shrewsbury School, changing after five or six years to become Practice Manager of a doctors' practice in the town, and staying there for about fourteen years until retirement.

Malcolm became a partner of his firm in 1977, finally retiring in 2008. He was also Secretary to the local Commissioners of Taxes, as well as being Under Sheriff for about fifteen years and a governor of Shrewsbury School and two other schools.

Amongst her other activities since retiring Judy has worked in a League of Friends shop at the local hospital, helped in a variety of ways at the local hospice and co-ordinated a weekly session of a Contact Centre (a safe place where an absent parent can spend time with his or her child). All of which have stood her in good stead since Malcolm died in 2010.

Neil Morris

After National Service Neil attended Edinburgh University, where he took an honours degree in Modern Languages (German and French). While at Edinburgh he married Fiona, now known as Kate McRae, whose reminiscences are included as Chapter 12. After attending the course in Cambridge he was posted to Northern Province, firstly to Luwingu and then to Samfya, where he was gazetted acting DC for one week. After Independence he spent some time in Broken Hill (Kabwe), where he was promoted to Acting Senior Local Government Officer.

Following his return to the UK in 1965 he took up a position in the Finance branch of the Hong Kong Government, resigning to join the Hong Kong Trade Development Council in 1968. During his fifteen years with the council he enjoyed postings to Tokyo, Paris and Panama.

Taking early retirement, Neil returned to the UK with his second wife, Christine, who is French, and together they started a horticultural business, specialising in flowers for drying and the sale of fresh culinary herbs to hotels and restaurants. In 1989 they moved to south-west France, where they continued in horticulture and opened two holiday gîtes. After a spell near Saint-Emilion they retired in 2003 and now live 30 miles south of Paris.

Valentine Musakanya

Valentine Musakanya was born in a village in the Northern Province of Northern Rhodesia in 1932. After initial schooling near his home village and on the Copperbelt he attended a Roman Catholic secondary school in Southern Rhodesia.

He joined the Civil Service in 1954 as a Senior African Clerk in the Provincial Administration in Chingola, and began studying for a degree by correspondence course with Fort Hare University in South Africa, an extremely demanding course which he completed in half the usual expected time. In 1957 he married Flavia Shikopa. After rising to more senior positions in the Civil Service and obtaining his degree, there was no excuse not to select him to attend the 1961/2 Overseas Services Course in Cambridge.

Following a short period as a District Officer in Isoka, he was seconded to Britain's Consulate General in the Katanga Province of the Congo before helping to establish the new Ministry of Foreign Affairs in the lead-up to Independence in 1964.

He served the new Government as Director of Intelligence before being appointed Secretary to the Cabinet and Head of the Civil Service in 1965. Resigning at the end of 1968, he became a nominated Member of Parliament and Minister of State for Technical and Vocational Education.

From 1970 to 1972 he was Governor of the Bank of Zambia. Removed from this position by President Kaunda he joined IBM, becoming Head of IBM's operations in southern and eastern Africa before resigning in 1977.

In 1980 he was arrested on suspicion of being involved in a planned coup attempt. Together with others he was convicted of treason in 1983 and sentenced to death. Two years later he was acquitted on appeal on the grounds that the only evidence against him was a confession which had been obtained by torture.

He was exceptionally intelligent, always curious, far-seeing, a man of the highest principles and possessed of a delightful sense of humour, much loved. He died in 1994.

D'Arcy Payne

Before undertaking the Cambridge Course, D'Arcy served from 1957 to 1961 as an LDA and then as a DA in Abercorn (Mbala), Kasama, Mporokoso and Isoka. He then worked from 1962 to 1967 as a DO in Livingstone and Gwembe before becoming the Community Development Officer in Kabompo and then Warden of the Outward Bound Lake School in Abercorn (Mbala).

Returning to the UK he studied industrial management at Bath University and then joined the Co-operative Wholesale Society, holding various positions in work study and personnel management before becoming Chief Industrial Engineer. He also attended Manchester Business School during this period.

Between 1978 and 1997 he worked for Rolls-Royce plc, eventually becoming Personnel Director Aero Division and finally Director Corporate Services. He then spent several years as

Senior Consultant – China to Rolls-Royce and Adviser to the Civil Aviation Authority of China.

He has also held a number of other positions including Chairman, Council for Examination Development, University of Cambridge Local Examinations Syndicate; Council member, Loughborough University; Deputy President, Engineering Employers' Federation; Deputy Chairman, Science, Engineering and Manufacturing Technologies Alliance; Chairman, China Britain Industrial Consortium; Vice-Chairman, Great Britain China Centre; Chairman, China Education Forum, British Council. He also holds six honorary professorships at Chinese universities.

He currently spends his time walking in the Peak District in between being Chairman of the South Derbyshire Members' Centre of the National Trust, a member of the Council of the Overseas Service Pensioners' Association and a Trustee of the Overseas Service Pensioners' Benevolent Society.

D'Arcy and his wife, Sally, have two sons, a daughter and five grandchildren, all of whom live within 5 miles of them in Derbyshire.

Tony Schur

Tony studied English at Oxford before attending the Overseas Services Course in Cambridge. He then worked as a Cadet in Kabompo, returning to the UK in 1964.

Deciding to work in industry, he joined Imperial Group as a management trainee, later becoming secretary of the Tobacco Division board. He resigned after ten years and was unemployed for a while. He was then fortunate to be given an opportunity to train as a chartered accountant with Thomson McLintock, which later became part of KPMG. He left after seven years to become finance director of a fast-growing software business, and later worked as a self-employed chartered accountant with a further spell at KPMG. He was also for a time Vice-Chairman of an NHS trust and Chairman of the Immigration Advisory Service. He has also been a parliamentary candidate, a churchwarden and lay chairman of a deanery synod.

In 2010 he self-published *A View from Below: How to Improve Politics*. He is married to Sandra and has two children and two grandchildren.

David Taylor

From 1958 to 1961 David was employed as a DA in Solwezi and Mwinilunga. After attending the Cambridge Course he served as a DO (and briefly as DC) in Sesheke and then for a couple of months in Mongu.

After an unhappy experience with the Overseas Services Resettlement Bureau on his return to the UK, David worked for a time in the personnel department of Union International before resigning. He then trained as a commercial pilot at his own expense, and after a while found employment with Laker Airways, achieving rapid promotion as the airline expanded. After the company collapsed into bankruptcy he had what he describes as 'a most unpleasant job' flying a large freighter for the Rwanda Government, before being made redundant and escaping from Kigali just before the massacre.

A short and difficult time as a building labourer followed before he obtained a job with the Civil Aviation Authority, eventually becoming a flight inspector. Seconded to the European equivalent organisation in Amsterdam he worked until retirement as Deputy Director of the division which oversaw the multinational committees whose task was to write commonly agreed EC rules for the conduct of airline operations.

John Theakstone

After studying Geography at Oxford, John took a three-year short-service commission in the RAF before attending the Cambridge Course. His first posting to Mumbwa lasted for over two years and was followed by shorter spells in Broken Hill (now Kabwe) and Mkushi.

Returning to the UK in 1965 he worked as a City & Guilds administrative officer before joining the Inter-University Council for Higher Education Overseas in 1967 as Assistant Secretary/

Head of the division responsible for east, central and southern Africa. Following the merger of the IUC with the British Council in 1981 he was appointed Head of Higher Education (Africa).

Between 1993 and 1998 John was a consultant in higher education management and gender planning, working with the World Bank, the European Union, the United Nations Development Programme and other organisations. He was appointed an Honorary Professor at Mauritius University and was a recipient of a gold medal issued by the University of Khartoum in its anniversary year. He has also been an Associate Fellow at the University of London and at the University of Warwick and an Honorary Fellow of the University of Manchester.

His book *A Biographical Bibliography of Victorian and Edwardian Women Travellers* was published in the USA in 2006 with a second edition in 2010. *Ramsgreave in the Nineteenth and Twentieth Centuries: Changing Life in Rural Lancashire* appeared in 2011. Four further works titled *Convention Defied. Episodes in the Lives of Nine Victorian Women*; *The Contentious Waves. Nineteenth Century Women Face the Perils of the Sea*; *Victorian Women in War and Conflict*; and *Victorian Women Visiting the Pyramids* were released as Kindle ebooks in 2013.

Paul Wigram

Before joining the Overseas Services Course Paul did National Service with the King's African Rifles in Kenya followed by three years at Cambridge reading Geography. He served in Kasempa until October 1964, when he returned with his wife, Jinty, to Kenya, where he had been brought up.

After working for an import company for two years he took up farming and stayed with agriculture for the rest of his working life. For a time he had a small share in a wheat/beef/sheep farm which was eventually sold under the Settlement Scheme. He then spent six years working for two agricultural companies, followed by two risky years in Zaire, now the Democratic Republic of the Congo. Returning to Kenya he ran a large flower farm for Unilever at Naivasha, growing carnations and roses. He was also involved in a project to develop castor oil for export.

Since 2001 Paul has lived on 13 hectares of land in the Alentejo region of Portugal in a house which he and Jinty created from a very basic cottage. He is shortly due to move back to the UK to be nearer to his three children and three grandchildren.

INDEX